ESSAYS IN NORMATIVE ECONOMICS

ESSAYS IN NORMATIVE ECONOMICS

Abram Bergson

THE BELKNAP PRESS OF

HARVARD UNIVERSITY PRESS

CAMBRIDGE, MASSACHUSETTS

1966

CONTENTS

PREFACE

Although written over a period of nearly three decades, the essays assembled in this volume manifestly have a common theme. The claim often made for such a collection, that it represents a coherent entity, therefore, may properly be made for this one. Thus, the essays assembled in Part I all relate to the branch of economic theory which has come to be called, after Professor Pigou's great work, the "Economics of Welfare." I refer particularly to the foundations of this discipline, including the nature of the underlying concept of social welfare and the conditions for an economic optimum. Of the four essays in Part II, two, on the welfare content of national income and on the appraisal of indivisibilities, also relate to familiar themes in welfare economics. While the other two, on Frisch's *New Methods* and Staehle's "dissimilarity method," are somewhat special, the four essays together bear on the measurement of welfare. As such they are all complementary to those on the foundations of welfare economics.

As for Part III, I explore here socialist economics, but on the theoretic plane that is considered all three essays represent applications of welfare economics to socialism. The relation of the essays to welfare economics becomes self-evident and need not be labored once it is recalled that historically the theoretic analysis of socialist economic calculation has in itself been a major aspect of the development of welfare economics. I am thinking especially of the seminal work of Pareto.

All the essays, therefore, might be viewed as being in the economics of welfare, but they seemed to fall more easily under the more inclusive title that has been adopted for the volume.

Of the ten essays assembled, six were published previously, and four were written especially for this volume. In republishing previous writings I have tried to hold revisions to a minimum. Thus, in order to take into account further doctrinal developments and my own second thoughts, rather than rewrite earlier articles I have generally felt it more fitting to include new ones. This is the aim especially of the third essay, "On Social Welfare Once More," and of the very brief comment, "Socialist Calculation: A Further Word." Chiefly for the sake of clarity and coherence, however, some more or less extensive revisions in the piece on socialist wage principles seemed unavoidable, if it were to be reproduced at all. Here and there some additions and deletions had to be made also at other points, but these were almost always primarily editorial, and the one or two changes that might be of interest are noted.

I have sought to express in the different essays my indebtedness to colleagues for advice and criticism, but I must record here as well that to Professor Paul A. Samuelson. As the reader will soon become aware, my obligation to him is especially great. I must leave to another occasion the pleasant task of acknowledging my debt to former teachers, but I should explain that the earliest of the papers republished here, that on Frisch's *New Methods*, was written originally as an essay for a course I took in mathematical economics with Professor Wassily W. Leontief, a course incidentally which Professor Samuelson was also attending.

I am grateful to the *Quarterly Journal of Economics* and the Harvard University Press for permission to republish the essays which have become Chapters 1 and 2; to the *Review of Economic Studies*, for permission to republish the essay which has become Chapter 4; and to the *National Bureau of Economic Research*, for permission to republish the essay which is Chapter 5 in this volume. Chapter 6 was originally written for the RAND Corporation, and I am indebted to this organization for permission to reproduce it here. The essay should not be considered, however, as representing the views of the RAND Corporation. Chapter 8

PREFACE

is published with the consent of the Harvard University Press, for which I am grateful, and I am also indebted to Richard Irwin, Inc. for permission to reproduce the essay which has become Chapter 9.

Abram Bergson

Cambridge, Massachusetts
June 1965

PART I. SOCIAL WELFARE AND THE ECONOMIC OPTIMUM

A REFORMULATION OF CERTAIN

ASPECTS OF WELFARE ECONOMICS*

The object of this paper is to state in a precise form the value judgments required for the derivation of the conditions of maximum economic welfare which have been advanced in the studies of the Cambridge economists,[1] Pareto and Barone, and Mr. Lerner.[2] Such a formulation, I hope, will clarify certain aspects of the contribution of these writers, and at the same time provide a basis for a more precise understanding of the principles of welfare.

* Originally published in the *Quarterly Journal of Economics*, February 1938, with grateful acknowledgment to Mr. Paul Samuelson "for suggestions on many points."

[1] I use this caption to designate those economists whose names are directly attached to the Cambridge School—Marshall, Professor Pigou, Mr. Kahn—as well as others, such as Edgeworth, whose welfare analysis is in all essentials the same as that of the Cambridge group. But in the course of my discussion I shall refer mainly to the studies of the first group of economists. This will ease my task considerably, and, I believe, will involve no loss of generality.

[2] The studies referred to are Alfred Marshall, *Principles of Economics* (all references to the third—London, 1895—edition); A. C. Pigou, *Economics of Welfare* (all references to the fourth—London, 1932—edition); R. F. Kahn, "Notes on Ideal Output," *Economic Journal*, March 1935; Vilfredo Pareto, *Cours d'Economie Politique* (all references to the Lausanne—1897—edition); Enrico Barone, "The Ministry of Production in a Socialist State" (translated from the Italian article of the same title in *Giornale degli Economisti*, 1908; the translation appearing in F. A. von Hayek, ed., *Collectivist Economic Planning*, London, 1935); and A. P. Lerner, "The Concept of Monopoly and the Measurement of Monopoly Power," *Review of Economic Studies*, June 1934, and A. P. Lerner, "Economic Theory and Socialist Economy," *Review of Economic Studies*, October 1934.

I shall develop my analysis under a set of assumptions which in certain respects differ from those introduced in the welfare studies. It will be assumed throughout the discussion that the amounts of all the factors of production, other than labor, are fixed and, for convenience, nondepreciating. While a variable capital supply is included in some of the welfare studies, this is not a well-developed part of the analysis, and for present purposes it will be desirable to confine to the simpler case the discussion of the evaluations required.[3] I shall assume, also, that the variables involved in the analysis—the amounts of the various commodities consumed and services performed—are infinitesimally divisible. This assumption will be interpreted more strictly than is usually done; otherwise it is the postulate of the welfare writers, and its introduction here will involve no significant departure from their analyses. Finally, I shall assume that there are only two kinds of consumers' goods, two kinds of labor, and two factors of production other than labor in the community, and that each commodity is produced, with labor and the other factors, in a single production unit. This assumption is introduced only to simplify the notation employed. The discussion will apply, with no modification, to the many-commodity, many-factor, and many-production unit case.[4]

THE MAXIMUM CONDITIONS IN GENERAL

Among the elements affecting the welfare of the community during any given period of time are the amounts of each of the factors of production, other than labor, employed in the different production units, the amounts of the various commodities consumed, the amounts of the different kinds of work done, and the

[3] On a simple model, similar to that of Barone, the analysis may be extended to the case of a variable capital supply.

[4] The assumption that each commodity is produced in one production unit, it is true, excludes an element of "external economies" from the analysis. But in the present essay I am interested only in the maximum conditions for the community's welfare, and not in the departures from the maximum under a given institutional set-up. To the extent that in the many-production unit case there are external economies, these will require no modification in the maximum conditions I shall present, for these conditions relate only to marginal *social* value productivities.

4

production unit for which this work is performed by each individual in the community during that period of time. If we use A and B to denote the two kinds of labor; C and D to denote the two factors of production other than labor; and X and Y to denote the two consumers' goods; we may express this relationship in the form

$$W = W(x_1, y_1, a_1^x, b_1^x, a_1^y, b_1^y, \ldots,$$
$$x_n, y_n, a_n^x, b_n^x, a_n^y, b_n^y, C^x, D^x, C^y, D^y, r, s, t, \ldots). \quad (1)$$

Here C^x and D^x are the amounts of the nonlabor factors of production C and D employed in the production unit producing the consumers' good X; C^y and D^y are the amounts of these factors employed in the production unit producing the consumers' good Y; x_i and y_i are the amounts of X and Y consumed by the ith individual; and $a_i^x, b_i^x, a_i^y,$ and b_i^y are the amounts of each kind of work performed by him for each production unit during the given period of time.[5] The symbols $r, s, t, \ldots$, denote elements other than the amounts of commodities, the amounts of work of each type, and the amounts of the nonlabor factors in each of the production units, affecting the welfare of the community.

Some of the elements $r, s, t, \ldots$, may affect welfare, not only directly, but indirectly through their effect on (say) the amounts of X and Y produced with any given amount of resources—for example, the effects of a change in the weather. On the other hand, it is conceivable that variations in the amounts of commodities, the amounts of work of each type, and the amounts of nonlabor factors in each of the production units also will have a direct and indirect effect on welfare; as, for instance, a sufficient diminution of x_i and y_i may be accompanied by an overturn of the government. But for relatively small changes in these variables, other elements in welfare, I believe, will not be significantly affected. To the extent that this is so, a partial analysis is feasible.

I shall designate the function,

$$E = E(x_1, y_1, a_1^x, b_1^x, a_1^y, b_1^y, \ldots,$$
$$x_n, y_n, a_n^x, b_n^x, a_n^y, b_n^y, C^x, D^x, C^y, D^y), \quad (2)$$

---

[5] I am assuming that an individual's labor time may be divided among the different types of work in any desired proportions.

which is obtained by taking $r, s, t, \ldots,$ in (1) as given, the Economic Welfare Function.[6]

Let us write the amounts of X and Y produced respectively by the X and Y production units as functions,

$$X = X(A^x, B^x, C^x, D^x); \quad Y = Y(A^y, B^y, C^y, D^y), \qquad (3)$$

where A^x and B^x are the amounts of the two kinds of labor and C^x and D^x are the amounts of the other two factors of production employed in the X production unit; and A^y, B^y, C^y, D^y are defined similarly for the Y production unit.

If we assume that E varies continuously with $x_1, y_1, \ldots,$ we may write as a general condition for a position of maximum economic welfare that, subject to the limitations of the given technique of production and the given amounts of resources,

$$dE = 0. \qquad (4)$$

Equation (4) requires that in the neighborhood of the maximum position any small adjustment will leave the welfare of the community unchanged. By use of (3) and (4) it is possible immediately to state in general terms the conditions for a maximum welfare.[7]

One group of maximum conditions relates to the consumption and supply of services by each individual in the community. They require that the marginal economic welfare of each commodity and the marginal economic diswelfare of each type of work be the same with respect to each individual in the community.[8] If we denote the marginal economic welfare of commodity

---

[6] It should be emphasized that in (2) other factors affecting welfare are taken as given. I do *not* assume that economic welfare is an independent element which may be added to other welfare to get total welfare.

[7] The conditions I shall develop in this section are a group of necessary conditions for a maximum. They are also the conditions for any critical point, and are sufficient in number to determine the location of such a point (or points) if there is one. Below, pp. 23ff, I consider the problem of determining whether a given critical point is a maximum or not.

[8] This rather awkward terminology is adopted instead of, say, the phrase "marginal economic welfare *of* the ith individual" in order to include the possibility that an increment of X or Y given to the ith individual will affect the welfare of others.

X with respect to the ith individual, $\partial E/\partial x_i$, and of Y, $\partial E/\partial y_i$, the first group of these conditions requires that, for all i, and for some p, q, and ω,

$$\frac{\partial E}{\partial x_i} = \omega p \tag{5}$$

and

$$\frac{\partial E}{\partial y_i} = \omega q. \tag{6}$$

Similarly, if we denote the marginal economic diswelfare of the various types of work with respect to the ith individual $\partial E/\partial a_i^x$, $\partial E/\partial b_i^x$, $\partial E/\partial a_i^y$, $\partial E/\partial b_i^y$, the second group of these conditions requires that, for all i and for some g^x, h^x, g^y, h^y, and for the ω already chosen,

$$-\frac{\partial E}{\partial a_i^x} = \omega g^x, \qquad (7) \qquad -\frac{\partial E}{\partial b_i^x} = \omega h^x, \qquad (9)$$

$$-\frac{\partial E}{\partial a_i^y} = \omega g^y, \qquad (8) \qquad -\frac{\partial E}{\partial b_i^y} = \omega h^y. \qquad (10)$$

The minus signs and the multiplicative factor ω are inserted in these equations for convenience.

The remaining maximum conditions relate to production. They require that the economic welfare of the consumers' goods produced by a marginal increment of each type of work should equal the negative of the diswelfare of that increment of work, and that the increment of economic welfare due to the shift of a marginal unit of factors C and D from one production unit to another should equal the negative of the diswelfare caused by this adjustment. Using the notation $\partial X/\partial A^x$ for the marginal productivity of A^x, and a similar notation for the other marginal productivities, we may write these conditions in the form,

$$p \frac{\partial X}{\partial A^x} = g^x, \qquad (11) \qquad p \frac{\partial X}{\partial B^x} = h^x, \qquad (13)$$

$$q \frac{\partial Y}{\partial A^y} = g^y, \qquad (12) \qquad q \frac{\partial Y}{\partial B^y} = h^y, \qquad (14)$$

7

and,

$$\omega\left(p\,\frac{\partial X}{\partial C^x} - q\,\frac{\partial Y}{\partial C^y}\right) = -\left(\frac{\partial E}{\partial C^x} - \frac{\partial E}{\partial C^y}\right), \qquad (15)$$

$$\omega\left(p\,\frac{\partial X}{\partial D^x} - q\,\frac{\partial Y}{\partial D^y}\right) = -\left(\frac{\partial E}{\partial D^x} - \frac{\partial E}{\partial D^y}\right). \qquad (16)$$

In equations (11) through (14), ω, which was present in all terms, has been divided out.[9] The derivatives on the right-hand sides of (15) and (16) indicate the effect on welfare of an adjustment in C or D for which all other elements—x^i, y^i, etc.—in welfare are constant. Such an effect would arise, for example, through a positive or negative evaluation of the relative amounts and kinds of "factory smoke" emitted in the two production units for varying amounts of one or the other factors employed in each unit.

It will be convenient to designate p the *price* of X; q the *price* of Y; and g^x, g^y, h^x, h^y, the *wage* respectively of the types of work A^x, A^y, B^x, B^y. Equations (5) and (6) thus require that the marginal economic welfare per "dollar's worth" of each commodity, $\partial E/\partial x_i \cdot 1/p$ and $\partial E/\partial y_i \cdot 1/q$, be the same for each commodity and for all individuals in the community. Similarly, equations (7) through (10) require that the marginal economic diswelfare per "dollar's worth" of each kind of work be the same with respect to each kind of work and each individual in the community; equations (11) through (14) require that the wages of each type of labor should equal the marginal value productivity of that type of labor,[10] and with an analogous interpretation, equations (15) and (16) require that the marginal value productivity equal the cost due to a shift in C or D from one use to another.

MAXIMUM CONDITIONS IN DIFFERENT ANALYSES

The maximum conditions just presented are the general conditions for a position of maximum economic welfare for any Economic Welfare Function. The maximum conditions presented

---

[9] Strictly speaking, this procedure assumes a value proposition, which we shall introduce later, to the effect that ω is unequal to zero.

[10] In the present essay it will be understood that all value productivities are *social* value productivities. Compare n. 4 above.

in the welfare studies relate to a particular family of welfare functions. Their derivation thus requires the introduction of restrictions on the shape of the Economic Welfare Function presented here. Three groups of value propositions suffice for this purpose.

I shall designate the various maximum conditions derived by the names of those writers, or groups of writers, who have been especially responsible for their elucidation. For reasons which will appear I have altered somewhat the content of the conditions, and there are differences in the analyses of the various writers which must also be noted. The latter differences will be pointed out in this section and in the one following.

The Lerner Conditions. The First Group of Value Propositions: *a shift in a unit of any factor of production, other than labor, from one production unit to another would leave economic welfare unchanged, provided the amounts of all the other elements in welfare were constant.*

The First Group of Value Propositions enables us to state certain of the maximum conditions in terms of the production functions alone. From these evaluations the right-hand side of (15) and of (16) must equal zero. To refer again to the example mentioned above, the net effect on the community's welfare of the "factory smoke" arising from a shift of the nonlabor factors from one use to another is taken as zero. The two equations thus may be written,

$$p \frac{\partial X}{\partial C^x} = q \frac{\partial Y}{\partial C^y}, \tag{17}$$

$$p \frac{\partial X}{\partial D^x} = q \frac{\partial Y}{\partial D^y}, \tag{18}$$

and they now impose the condition that the marginal value productivity of factors other than labor be the same in every use.

Equations (17) and (18) still contain the variables p and q, which involve derivatives of the Economic Welfare Function. If we combine (17) and (18), however, we have two equations,

$$\frac{q}{p} = \frac{\partial X}{\partial C^x} \bigg/ \frac{\partial Y}{\partial C^y} = \frac{\partial X}{\partial D^x} \bigg/ \frac{\partial Y}{\partial D^y}, \tag{19}$$

ESSAYS IN NORMATIVE ECONOMICS

the second of which involves only the derivatives of the production functions. It requires that in the maximum position the ratio of the marginal productivity of a factor in one use to its marginal productivity in any other use be the same for all factors of production, other than labor. The first equation of (19) requires that all these ratios equal the price ratio.

The significance of (19) for the determination of maximum welfare may be expressed in the following manner: whatever the relative evaluations of commodity X and commodity Y, that is, in Barone's terminology, whatever their ratio of equivalence, (19) requires that in the maximum position, given that one factor C is so distributed that a small shift from one production unit to another would alter the amounts of X and Y in such a manner as to leave welfare unchanged—that is, given that C is so distributed that $(\partial X/\partial C^x)/(\partial Y/\partial C^y)$ equals the ratio of equivalence of the two commodities, then the other factors in order to be so distributed must have a ratio of marginal productivities equal to $(\partial X/\partial C^x)/(\partial Y/\partial C^y)$.

The condition (19) can also be interpreted in another manner, which, however, does not bring out as directly the significance of the condition for a position of maximum *welfare*. The equality of the marginal productivity ratios implies that there is no possible further adjustment for which the amount of one commodity will be increased without that of another being reduced. A shift in one factor from X to Y can at best be just compensated by a shift of another from Y to X, if (19) is satisfied.[11]

[11] Mr. Lerner, as far as I am aware, is the only economist to present (17) and (18) in the form of (19), his interpretation being the second of the two alternatives I have noted. In the studies of Pareto, Barone, and Marshall the conditions (17) and (18) are presented with the price ratios already equated to the individual marginal rates of substitution (see below). In the studies of Professor Pigou and Mr. Kahn the procedure is the same as that of Pareto, Barone, and Marshall except that Pigou and Kahn include in their analysis the possibility of departures from (17) and (18) due to aspects such as "factory smoke."

Mr. Lerner advances the conditions (19) for all factors of production, labor as well as nonlabor (*Review of Economic Studies*, October 1934, p. 57). On the face of the matter this formulation is inconsistent with Mr. Lerner's own advocacy of the supremacy of individual tastes in the sphere of consumption, and I have therefore taken the liberty to modify his conditions accordingly. The other economists also do not allow in their analysis for individual preferences as between employment in different units, as distinct from different kinds of labor.

10

A REFORMULATION

The Pareto-Barone-Cambridge Conditions. The Fundamental Value Propositions of Individual Preference: *if the amounts of the various commodities and types of work were constant for all individuals in the community except any ith individual, and if the ith individual consumed the various commodities and performed the various types of work in combinations which were indifferent to him, economic welfare would be constant.*

The First Group of Value Propositions, which were set forth previously, imply that under the assumption that the amounts of the factors of production other than labor are constant, the Economic Welfare Function may be written as

$$E = E(x_1, y_1, a_1^x, b_1^x, a_1^y, b_1^y, \ldots, x_n, y_n, a_n^x, b_n^x, a_n^y, b_n^y). \quad (20)$$

For from these propositions a shift in C or D from one production unit to another would have no effect on welfare, if all the other elements were constant. The Fundamental Value Propositions require that E be some function of the form,

$$E = E[(S^1(x_1, y_1, a_1^x, b_1^x, a_1^y, b_1^y), \ldots,$$
$$S^n(x_n, y_n, a_n^x, b_n^x, a_n^y, b_n^y)], \quad (21)$$

where the function

$$S^i = S^i(x_i, y_i, a_i^x, b_i^x, a_i^y, b_i^y) \quad (22)$$

expresses the loci of combinations of commodities consumed and work performed which are indifferent to the ith individual.

The Fundamental Value Propositions enable us to restate all the consumption and labor supply conditions in terms of the individual indifference functions, S^i. The conditions must be expressed, however, relatively to some one of them, say, (5). Thus consider the equation

$$\frac{\partial E}{\partial x_i} \Big/ \frac{\partial E}{\partial y_i} = \frac{p}{q}, \quad (23)$$

obtained from (5) and (6) by division. Using the Fundamental Value Propositions,

$$\frac{\partial E}{\partial x_i} \Big/ \frac{\partial E}{\partial y_i} = \frac{\partial E}{\partial S^i} \frac{\partial S^i}{\partial x_i} \Big/ \frac{\partial E}{\partial S^i} \frac{\partial S^i}{\partial y_i} = \frac{\partial S^i}{\partial x_i} \Big/ \frac{\partial S^i}{\partial y_i}. \quad (24)$$

11

The last ratio in (24) represents the slope of the indifference locus of the ith individual, or in the Hicks and Allen terminology, the marginal rate of substitution of commodity Y for commodity X.[12] Thus (23) requires that the marginal rate of substitution of the two commodities be the same for all individuals. By successively combining (5) with equations (7) through (10), a similar result is obtained with respect to the other elements of welfare.

All the production conditions may now be stated in terms of the indifference functions and the production functions. For equations (11) through (14), the statement that the wage of each type of work should equal its marginal value productivity may be interpreted to mean that the marginal product of a given type of work employed in producing a given commodity should equal the marginal rate of substitution of that commodity for that type of work. In the same manner, conditions (19) not only require that the ratios of marginal productivities of the various factors other than labor be equal, but that these ratios should equal the marginal rate of substitution of the two commodities.

The Fundamental Value Propositions thus require that, whatever the ratios of equivalence between the various commodities and types of work, given that the types of work performed and commodities consumed by one individual are so fixed that for any small adjustment among them economic welfare is unchanged—that is, given that the marginal rates of substitution and marginal productivities for this individual equal the respective ratios of equivalence—then for all other individuals to be similarly situated, their marginal rates of substitution must be the same as those of this individual. Under our implicit assumption of homogeneous factors, the respective marginal productivities, of course, must in any case be equal for all individuals.

Again, the Fundamental Value Propositions may be interpreted also to mean that in the maximum position it is impossible to improve the situation of any one individual without rendering another worse off.[13]

---

[12] See J. R. Hicks and R. G. D. Allen, "A Reconsideration of the Theory of Value," *Economica*, February 1934.

[13] The Pareto-Barone-Cambridge Conditions are developed by Marshall in the *Principles* (pp. 413–415, 526–527; Appendix XIV), but the derivation

A REFORMULATION

The Cambridge Conditions. Let us designate

$$m_i = px_i + qy_i - g^x a_i^x - h^x b_i^x - g^y a_i^y - h^y b_i^y, \quad (25)$$

the Share of the ith individual. In (25), p, q, etc., are taken proportional to the respective marginal rates of substitution of individuals. Thus m^i is defined, aside from a proportionality factor. The sum of m^i for the community as a whole is equal to the difference between the total wages and the total value of consumers' goods in the community.

The Propositions of Equal Shares: *If the Shares of any ith and kth individuals were equal, and if the prices and wage rates were fixed, the transfer of a small amount of the Share of i to k would leave welfare unchanged.*

The Propositions of Equal Shares enable us to state in terms of the distribution of Shares the remaining condition (5) to which we related consumption and labor supply conditions in order to reformulate them in terms of individual indifference functions (above, p. 11). According to the Propositions of Equal Shares, if the Shares of i and k are equal, then for the given price-wage situation,

$$dE = \frac{\partial E}{\partial m_i} dm_i + \frac{\partial E}{\partial m_k} dm_k = 0, \quad (26)$$

---

of the production conditions is based upon the very simple illustrative assumption of a producer-consumer expending his capital and labor in such a manner as to maximize his utility. Under more general assumptions the conditions are developed, without the utility calculus used by Marshall, by Pareto (*Cours*, I, pp. 20ff, II, pp. 90ff) and Barone; ("Ministry of Production"), and with the utility calculus, by Professor Pigou (*Economics of Welfare*, particularly pp. 131–143) and Mr. Kahn (*Economic Journal*, March 1935). All of these writers either develop the consumption conditions independently of their formulation of the production conditions (Marshall, Pareto) or assume the consumption conditions *ab initio* (Barone, Pigou, Kahn); and, as we shall indicate, the interpretations vary. Mr. Lerner in his study in the *Review of Economic Studies*, June 1934, presents all the conditions together, and interprets them most lucidly in the second of the two senses I have pointed out.

As I have noted elsewhere (n. 11), none of these writers includes in his analysis individual preferences between production units. Also, Professor Pigou and Mr. Kahn include the possibility of departures from (19), and perhaps from (11), (12), (13), (14), for the direct effects on welfare of shifts of the factors of production from one use to another.

for $dm_i = -dm_k$. Equation (26) is equivalent to the condition imposed by (5) that the marginal economic welfare per "dollar's worth" of X is the same for i and k.[14] Thus, if the Shares of all individuals are equal, the condition (5) is satisfied.[15]

[14] The proof is as follows:

$$\frac{\partial E}{\partial m_i} = \frac{\partial E}{\partial x_i}\frac{\partial x_i}{\partial m_i} + \frac{\partial E}{\partial y_i}\frac{\partial y_i}{\partial m_i} + \frac{\partial E}{\partial a_i^x}\frac{\partial a_i^x}{\partial m_i} + \frac{\partial E}{\partial b_i^x}\frac{\partial b_i^x}{\partial m_i} + \frac{\partial E}{\partial a_i^y}\frac{\partial a_i^y}{\partial m_i} + \frac{\partial E}{\partial b_i^y}\frac{\partial b_i^y}{\partial m_i}.$$

By (25),

$$1 = p\,\frac{\partial x_i}{\partial m_i} + q\,\frac{\partial y_i}{\partial m_i} - g^x\,\frac{\partial a_i^x}{\partial m_i} - h^x\,\frac{\partial b_i^x}{\partial m_i} - g^y\,\frac{\partial a_i^y}{\partial m_i} - h^y\,\frac{\partial b_i^y}{\partial m_i}.$$

Using this equation, (23), and other similar equations,

$$\frac{\partial E}{\partial m_i} = \frac{\partial E}{\partial x_i}\cdot\frac{1}{p}.$$

[15] Among the welfare studies the Cambridge Conditions are the distinctive characteristic of the writings of the members of the Cambridge School. They are advanced in the works of all the Cambridge economists, and in none of the other welfare studies we have considered. But certain qualifications must be noted.

The Cambridge economists require an equal distribution of incomes, $(px_i + qy_i)$, rather than of Shares, as the condition for equality of the marginal economic welfare per "dollar" for all individuals (with qualifications which we shall note directly, cf. Kahn, *Economic Journal*, March 1935, pp. 1–2; Pigou, *Economics of Welfare*, pp. 82ff; Marshall, *Principles*, p. 795). If it is assumed that the amounts of the various types of labor performed by each individual in the community are given, this condition is of course the same as ours. But otherwise for a requirement of equal incomes there is unlikely to be any position which satisfies all the conditions for a maximum. For it would be necessary that in the neighborhood of the maximum position the marginal productivity and marginal diswelfare of each type of work be zero.

The condition of equal incomes is not necessarily inconsistent with the other postulates. There might be some indifference functions and production functions such that all the maximum conditions are satisfied. But it may be noted here, in general, as a mimimum requirement, that the various conditions must be consistent with each other. Compare Lange, *Review of Economic Studies*, October 1936, pp. 64–65, and Lerner, *Review of Economic Studies*, October 1936, p. 73.

For convenience I have presented the Cambridge Conditions in a rather simple form. In a more elaborate exposition of the conditions advanced by the Cambridge economists I should have to introduce—and on *a priori* grounds I believe it desirable to introduce—modifications in the distribution of Shares for changes in the price-wage situation which might affect different individuals differently—some moving to a more preferable position, and others to a less preferable one—and for other special

The three groups of value propositions are not only sufficient for the derivation of the maximum conditions presented in the welfare studies; they are necessary for this procedure. For it is possible, and I shall leave the development of the argument to the reader, to deduce from the maximum conditions presented the restriction imposed upon the Economic Welfare Function by the value judgments introduced.

But it should be noted that the particular value judgments I have stated are not necessary to the welfare analysis. They are essential only for the establishment of a particular group of maximum conditions. If the production functions and individual indifference functions are known, they provide sufficient information concerning the Economic Welfare Function for the determination of the maximum position, if it exists.[16] In general, any set of value propositions which is sufficient for the evaluation of all alternatives may be introduced, and for each of these sets of propositions there corresponds a maximum position. The number of sets is infinite, and in any particular case the selection of one of them must be determined by its compatibility with the values prevailing in the community the welfare of which is being studied. For only if the welfare principles are based upon prevailing values can they be relevant to the activity of the community in question. But the determination of prevailing values for a given community, while I regard it as both a proper and necessary task for the economist, and of the same general character as the investigation of the indifference functions for individuals, is a project which I shall not undertake here. For the present I do not attempt more than the presentation of the values current in economic literature in a form for which empirical investigation is feasible.[17]

---

differences between individuals. See the reference to the distribution of *wealth* in Marshall, pp. 527, 595, and to the distribution of the *Dividend* in Pigou, p. 89; but see also the reference to the distribution of *money incomes,* in Kahn, pp. 1–2.

[16] See n. 7 above.

[17] This conception of the basis for the welfare principles should meet Lionel Robbins' requirement that the economist take the values of the community as data. But insofar as I urge that the economist also *study* these data it represents perhaps a more positive attitude than might be

DIFFERENT ANALYSES FURTHER CONSIDERED

The formulation I have used to derive the maximum conditions of economic welfare differs in several respects from that of the welfare studies. It will be desirable to review briefly the relevant points of the various expositions, and the departures of the present essay from them. I shall continue to use the set of assumptions stated on page 4.

In the Cambridge analysis,[18] the welfare of the community, stated symbolically,[19] is an aggregate of the form,[20]

$$E = \sum U^i(x_i, y_i, a_i^x, b_i^x, a_i^y, b_i^y). \tag{27}$$

In this expression U^i is some function of the indifference function, S^i, and measures the satisfactions derived by the ith individual from $x_i, y_i, a_i^x, b_i^x, a_i^y, b_i^y$. If individual temperaments are about the same—that is, if individuals are capable of equal satisfactions —the marginal utilities or derivatives of the utility functions of

---

inferred as desirable from his essays. See *The Nature and Significance of Economics* (London, 1932), particularly chap. vi. Whether the approach will prove a fruitful one remains to be seen.

It may be noted that though Professor Robbins is averse to the study of indifference curves (pp. 96ff), his own analysis requires an assumption that a movement of labor from one use to another is indifferent to the laborer and that a shift of other factors of production is indifferent to the community. Without these assumptions, for which I can see no *a priori* justification, his whole discussion of alternative *indifferent* uses, and his references to the most adequate satisfaction of demand from a given amount of means are without basis.

[18] The passages in the Cambridge studies which are particularly informative as to the Cambridge concept of welfare are Marshall, pp. 80ff, 200ff, 527, 804; Pigou, pp. 10–11, 87, 97; Kahn, pp. 1, 2, 19; and also F. Y. Edgeworth, *Papers Relating to Political Economy*, II (London, 1925), p. 102 (from the *Economic Journal*, 1897).

[19] Aside from Marshall's appendices, the exposition of Marshall, Professor Pigou, and Mr. Kahn is nonmathematical, but the few relationships we discuss here may be presented most conveniently in a mathematical form. This will also facilitate comparison with the studies of Pareto and Barone.

[20] In the analyses of Professor Pigou and Mr. Kahn some modification of (27) would be introduced to take care of the direct effects (as in the case of "factory smoke") on aggregate welfare of shifts of factors of production from one use to another.

different individuals, it is assumed, will be equal for an equal distribution of Shares.[21]

It is possible to derive all the maximum conditions, in specific terms, from the equation

$$\sum dU^i = 0. \qquad (28)$$

The technique used by the Cambridge economists is less direct and varies in certain respects. For our present purposes these procedural differences are of little special interest, but it will facilitate our discussion of the analysis of Pareto and Barone if we append the following notes.

Marshall develops the Pareto-Barone-Cambridge consumption and labor supply conditions separately from the rest of his analysis.[22] These conditions are that for some price-wage situation, p, q, g^x, h^x, g^y, h^y, and for all i,

$$w^i = \frac{U_1^i}{p} = \frac{U_2^i}{q} = \frac{-U_3^i}{g^x} = \frac{-U_4^i}{h^x} = \frac{-U_5^i}{g^y} = \frac{-U_6^i}{h^y}. \qquad (29)$$

In (29), w^i is the marginal utility of money to the ith individual and U_1^i, U_2^i, U_3^i, etc., are the marginal utilities of the various commodities and disutilities of the various types of work. In Marshall's exposition it is shown that, for any given amounts of X, Y, A^x, B^x, A^y, B^y, if the conditions (29) are not satisfied some U^i can be increased without any other being decreased. Thus for (28) to hold, (29) must be satisfied. Professor Pigou and Mr. Kahn do not develop the conditions (29), but assume them *ab initio* in their analysis.

If the conditions (29) are satisfied, (28) may be written in the form

$$\sum w^i \Delta_i = 0, \qquad (30)$$

where

$$\Delta_i = p\, dx_i + q\, dy_i - g^x\, da_i^x - h^x\, db_i^x - g^y\, da_i^y - h^y\, db_i^y. \qquad (31)$$

[21] With the qualifications of n. 15 above.
[22] See the references in n. 13 above.

The remaining conditions again may be derived from (30). However, in Mr. Kahn's reformulation of Professor Pigou's analysis,[23] it is assumed also that the Shares are distributed equally, and the remaining conditions are developed from the requirement that

$$\sum \Delta_i = 0. \qquad (32)$$

The summation in (32), with certain qualifications, is Professor Pigou's index of the National Dividend.[24] The procedures of Professor Pigou and Marshall differ from this, but the variations need not be elaborated here.[25]

Pareto and Barone also assume initially that conditions (29) are satisfied, but Pareto, like Marshall, shows in an early section of his work that, otherwise, it is possible to increase the *ophélimité* of some individuals without that of any others being decreased.[26] To develop the remaining conditions, aside from the Cambridge Conditions, Pareto expressedly avoids the use of (28) on the ground that "nous ne pouvons ni comparer ni sommer celles-ci [dU^1, dU^2, etc.], car nous ignorons le rapport des unités en lesquelles elles sont exprimées."[27] Instead Pareto proceeds directly to (32) and deduces the maximum conditions for production from it. In this, evidently for the same reason, Barone follows.[28] Neither Pareto nor Barone introduces the Cambridge Conditions into his analysis. Pareto merely assumes that the shares are distributed "suivant la règle qu'il plaira d'adopter," or in a "manière convenable,"[29] and Barone that they are distributed according to some "ethical criteria."[30]

The basis for developing production conditions directly from (32), for Pareto, is that this equation will assure that if the

[23] *Economic Journal*, March 1935.
[24] Professor Pigou's index does not include cost elements; it relates to large adjustments—whence the problem of backward and forward comparisons; and it is expressed as a percentage of the total value product at the initial position. See *Economics of Welfare*, chap. vi.
[25] But see pp. 23–26, below.
[26] *Cours*, I, pp. 20ff.
[27] *Ibid.*, II, p. 93.
[28] See Barone, p. 246.
[29] *Cours*, II, pp. 91, 93, 94.
[30] Barone, p. 265.

quantities of products "étaient convenablement distribuées, il en resulterait un maximum d'ophélimité pour chaque individu dont se compose la société."[31]

Barone adopts the requirement that the sum be zero because, in his words,

this means that every other series of equivalents different from that which accords with this definition would make that sum negative. That is to say, either it causes a decline in the welfare of all, or if some decline while others are raised, the gain of the latter is less than the loss of the former (so that even taking all their gain from those who gained in the change, reducing them to their former position, to give it completely to those who lost, the latter would always remain in a worse position than their preceding one without the situation of others being improved).[32]

Mr. Lerner, in the first of his two studies on welfare, advances as a criterion for a maximum position the condition that it should be impossible in this position to increase the welfare of one individual without decreasing that of another. From this criterion he develops graphically various maximum conditions. Like Pareto and Barone, he does not introduce the Cambridge Conditions into his analysis but, as he indicates, ignores the problem of distribution.[33] In his later paper Mr. Lerner presents our first group of maximum conditions (p. 9), on the basis of the criterion for a maximum that it should be impossible to increase the production of one commodity without decreasing that of another.[34]

In my opinion the utility calculus introduced by the Cambridge economists is not a useful tool for welfare economics. The approach does not provide an alternative to the introduction of value judgments. First of all, the comparison of the utilities of different individuals must involve an evaluation of the relative economic positions of these individuals. No extension of the methods of measuring utilities will dispense with the necessity for the introduction of value propositions to give these utilities a

[31] *Cours*, II, pp. 93, 94.
[32] Barone, p. 271.
[33] *Review of Economic Studies*, June 1934.
[34] *Review of Economic Studies*, October 1934.

common dimension. Secondly, the evaluation of the different commodities cannot be avoided, even though this evaluation may consist only in a decision to accept the evaluations of the individual members of the community. And, finally, whether the direct effects on aggregate utility of a shift of factors of production from one use to another are given a zero value, as in Marshall's analysis, or a significant one, as in the analyses of Professor Pigou and Mr. Kahn,[35] alternatives are involved, and accordingly value judgments must be introduced.

While the utility calculus does not dispense with value judgments, the manner in which these value judgments are introduced is a misleading one. Statements as to the aggregative character of total welfare, or as to the equality of marginal utilities when there is an equal distribution of Shares, provided temperaments are about the same, do have the ring of *factual* propositions, and are likely to obscure the evaluations implied. The note by Mr. Kahn, in reference to his own formulation of the maximum conditions for economic welfare, that "many will share Mr. Dobb's suspicion 'that to strive after such a maximum is very much like looking in a dark room for a black hat which may be entirely subjective after all' "[36] is not one to reassure the reader as to the nature of the welfare principles derived in this manner. To the extent that the utility calculus does conceal the role of value judgments in the derivation of welfare principles, the criticism directed against the Cambridge procedure by Professor Robbins and others[37] is not without justification.

The approach, it must also be noted, requires a group of value propositions additional to those I have presented. So far as the Cambridge economists require that the economic welfare of the community be an *aggregate* of individual welfares, value judgments must be introduced to the effect that each individual contributes independently to the total welfare. These value propositions, which imply the complete measurability of the Economic

---

[35] See p. 8, and n. 20 above.
[36] *Economic Journal*, March 1935, p. 2n.
[37] Robbins, *The Nature and Significance of Economic Science;* C. Sutton, "The relation between Economic Theory and Economic Policy," *Economic Journal*, March 1937.

Welfare Function aside from an arbitrary origin and a scalar constant, are not necessary for the derivation of the maximum conditions, and accordingly are not essential to the analysis.[38]

The derivation of conditions of maximum economic welfare without the summation of individual utilities, by Pareto, Barone, and Mr. Lerner, is a stride forward from the Cambridge formulation. Pareto's exposition of the basis for the procedure is somewhat ambiguous. Properly stated, the argument for developing production conditions directly from (32) is the same as that used in developing consumption conditions. The increment Δ_i in (31) indicates the preference direction of the ith individual.[39] If Δ_i is positive, the ith individual moves to a preferable position. The condition that $\Sigma\Delta_i$ be equal to zero does not assure that the *ophélimité* of each individual be a maximum, but that it be impossible to improve the position of one individual without making that of another worse. This, disregarding the misleading comparison of losses and gains, is the interpretation of Barone, and it is also the condition for a maximum used by Mr. Lerner.

But in avoiding the addition of utilities, Pareto, Barone, and Mr. Lerner also exclude the Cambridge Conditions from their analyses. None of the writers indicates his reasons for the exclusion, and I believe it has not proved an advantageous one. The first two groups of value propositions are introduced in the studies of Pareto and Barone by the use of, and in the argument as to the use of (32) as a basis for deriving maximum conditions, and in the analysis of Mr. Lerner by the criteria adopted for a maximum. In this respect the formulations differ little from that of the Cambridge economists. With the accompanying statements by Pareto and Barone that *the distribution of Shares* is decided on the basis of some "ethical criteria" or "rule," or with the complete exclusion of the problem by Mr. Lerner, this approach is not more conducive to an apprehension of the value content of

[38] Lange's discussion of utility determinateness (O. Lange, "On the Determinateness of the Utility Function," *Review of Economic Studies*, June 1934) errs insofar as it implies that welfare economics requires the summation of the independently measurable utilities of individuals, that is, his second utility postulate.

[39] R. G. D. Allen, "The Foundation of a Mathematical Theory of Exchange," *Economica*, May 1932.

the first two groups of maximum conditions. In the case of Mr. Lerner's study a misinterpretation does in fact appear. For in his analysis the first group of maximum conditions are advanced as objective in a sense which clearly implies that they require no value judgments for their derivation.[40]

Further, it must be emphasized, though the point is surely an obvious one, that unless the Cambridge Conditions, or a modified form of these conditions, is introduced there is no reason in general why it is more preferable to have the other conditions satisfied than otherwise. Placing $\Sigma\Delta_i$ equal to zero does not assure that there are no other positions for which welfare is greater, but only that there are no other positions for which the welfare of one individual is greater without that of another being less. In general, if conditions regarding distribution are not satisfied, it is just as likely as not that any position for which $\Sigma\Delta_i$ does not equal zero will be *more* desirable than any position for which it does equal zero.

In the Pareto-Barone analysis, though not in that of Mr. Lerner, there is reason to believe that, in a general form, maximum conditions regarding distribution are assumed to be satisfied. While the distribution of Shares is not specified, it is consistent with some "ethical criteria," or "rule." Whatever the rule is, it should follow that in the maximum position the marginal economic welfare "per dollar" with respect to all individuals is the same. Otherwise, in the light of that rule, some other distribution would be preferable. If this interpretation is correct, the special exposition used by Pareto and Barone to support their derivation of maximum conditions is inappropriate. In (32) it is true that each dollar does not express the same amount of utility in the Cambridge sense, since the value propositions of independence are not introduced. But each dollar does express the same amount of welfare. The argument used to place (32) equal to zero is thus not the Pareto-Barone one, but that if it were unequal to zero, a further adjustment increasing the summation would be possible, and this would directly increase welfare, *regardless* of whether the position of some individuals were improved and that of others worsened by the change.[41]

[40] *Review of Economic Studies*, October 1934, p. 57.
[41] This argument is more fully developed in the section following.

A REFORMULATION

EVALUATION OF A CHANGE IN WELFARE

I have noted elsewhere that the conditions for a maximum welfare which are presented on pages 4–15 are the conditions for any critical point. They are sufficient to inform us whether or not we are at the top or bottom of a hill, or at the top with respect to one variable, and the bottom with respect to another. The requirement for a *maximum* position is that it be possible to reach the position from any neighboring point by a series of positive adjustments. For the determination of such a position, it is necessary to know the sign $(+, -, 0)$ of any increment of welfare.

In the welfare studies the sign of dE is specified only for limited groups of adjustments. It will be of interest to note these conditions, and the value judgments required, though I shall not review again the formulations of the various writers.

(i) If we assume that all the conditions for a critical point are satisfied, except those relating to the distribution of the factors of production between different uses, one additional group of value judgments gives us sufficient information concerning the shape of the Economic Welfare Function to determine the sign of an increment of welfare. These value propositions are: *if all individuals except any ith individual remain in positions which are indifferent to them, and if the ith individual moves to a position which is preferable to him, economic welfare increases.* If we denote a more preferable position by a positive movement of S^i, these value propositions require that

$$\frac{\partial E}{\partial S^i} > 0, \tag{33}$$

for any i. Let us write from (21)

$$dE = \sum \frac{\partial E}{\partial x_i} dx_i + \frac{\partial E}{\partial y_i} dy_i + \frac{\partial E}{\partial a_i^x} da_i^x + \frac{\partial E}{\partial b_i^x} db_i^x$$

$$+ \frac{\partial E}{\partial a_i^y} da_i^y + \frac{\partial E}{\partial b_i^y} db_i^y. \tag{34}$$

Using equations (5) through (10), and the notation of (31),

$$dE = \omega \sum \Delta_i. \tag{35}$$

23

By (33) and the equations (5) through (10), ω must have the same sign as the price-wage rates in Δ_i. We shall take this sign as positive. Thus if the Shares are distributed equally, and if the prices and wage rates are proportionate to the marginal rates of substitution of the different kinds of commodities and types of work, economic welfare has the sign of Professor Pigou's index of the National Dividend. It will be increased by any adjustment which results in the movement of factors of production to a position of higher marginal value productivity.

(ii) If the assumption that the Cambridge Conditions are satisfied is relaxed, (35) may be written in the form

$$dE = \sum \omega^i \Delta_i \qquad (36)$$

where ω^i is the marginal economic welfare per dollar with respect to the ith individual. Using the evaluation in (33) it follows that, for any adjustment for which no Δ_i decreases and some Δ_i increases, economic welfare will increase.

(iii) Continuing to use the assumptions of (ii), let us write

$$\lambda_{ik} = \frac{\omega^i}{\omega^k}, \qquad (37)$$

and

$$dE = \omega^k \sum \lambda_{ik} \Delta_i. \qquad (38)$$

Let us introduce the value propositions: *for a given price-wage situation, and any i and k, if the Share of i is greater than that of k, a decrease in the Share of k would have to be accompanied by a larger increase in the Share of i, for economic welfare to remain unchanged.* Since it can be shown that if the Share of the ith individual increases by dm_i a concomitant decrease, $-\lambda_{ik}dm_i$, in the share of the kth will leave economic welfare unchanged,[42] these value propositions require that λ_{ik} be less than unity. It follows that, for any given adjustment, if $\Sigma \Delta_i$ is positive, and if Δ_i does not vary with λ_{ik}, or if it decreases with λ_{ik}, economic

---

[42] This relationship follows immediately from the equations:

$$dE = \frac{\partial E}{\partial m_i}\, dm_i + \frac{\partial E}{\partial m_k}\, dm_k = \omega^i dm_i + \omega^k dm_k.$$

welfare will increase. In other words, if the change in the National Dividend is not counteracted by a change in its distribution, the welfare of the community will be increased, even if some Δ_i increase and others decrease.

The adjustments in (i) are those considered by Mr. Kahn; in (ii) by Pareto, Barone, and Mr. Lerner; and in (iii) by Marshall and Professor Pigou. As Professor Pigou has pointed out,[43] the sign of an increment of welfare for some adjustments is left undetermined in his analysis. To determine the sign of dE for all adjustments, all the λ's would have to be evaluated, and a similar group of value judgments for the case where prices and wages are not proportional to the marginal rates of substitution would have to be introduced. On *a priori* grounds there is no reason why more information should not be obtained, since the comparison involved in evaluating the λ's is the same as that required for the Value Propositions of Equal Shares. For some additional and fairly rough evaluations, the range of adjustments included can be extended considerably, though an element of uncertainty is involved. Two such approximations, perhaps, are of sufficient interest to note, though they are not introduced in the welfare studies.

(iv) The assumptions of (ii) are retained. Let us suppose that with respect to some individual, say the kth,

$$\sum \lambda_{ik} = N, \tag{39}$$

the sum being taken for all i. Thus ω^k is the average ω. If we write

$$\alpha_i = \lambda_{ik} - 1; \qquad \beta_i = \Delta_i - \frac{\sum \Delta_i}{N}; \tag{40}$$

then

$$dE = \omega^k (\sum \alpha_i \beta_i + \sum \Delta_i). \tag{41}$$

The first term in the brackets may be regarded as an index of the distribution of the National Dividend. It follows immediately from (41) that: (a) if Δ_i is positively correlated with λ_{ik}, dE will be positive for an increase in the Dividend and conversely;

[43] *Economics of Welfare*, p. 645.

(b) if the coefficient of variation of the ω's is less than one hundred per cent, that is, if the standard deviation of λ_{ik} is less than unity, and if the coefficient of variation of Δ_i is also less than one hundred per cent, dE will have the sign of the index of the Dividend *regardless* of changes in its distribution.[44]

To determine precisely whether the conditions enumerated are satisfied would, of course, require a complete evaluation of the λ's. But the following rough evaluations would be sufficient to assure the likelihood of the results. For (a), it must be possible to say that "on the average" the change in distribution does not affect the "poor" more than the "rich," or vice versa. For (b) it is necessary to conceive of an individual or group of individuals who are, on the whole, in an average position from the point of view of welfare, and to determine whether, for a given position, ω^i "on the average" is likely to be somewhat less than twice the marginal economic welfare per "dollar" for the average individuals, that is, less than twice ω^k. (This should be stated in terms of the average shift in Shares for which welfare remains unchanged.) If it is determined that such a position is occupied, it would be likely that if tastes did not vary greatly—that is, if the relative variation of Δ_i were not very large—dE would increase for an increase in the Dividend. Since, however, the relative variation of Δ_i would ordinarily become excessively large as $\Sigma\Delta_i$ approached zero, it would be highly uncertain, for adjustments close to the maximum, whether or not an unfavorable change in distribution would obliterate the change in the Dividend.

---

[44] From (41),

$$dE = \omega^k(Nr_{\lambda\Delta}\sigma_\lambda\sigma_\Delta + \Sigma\Delta)$$
$$= \omega^k(Nr_{\lambda\Delta}\sigma_\lambda\sigma_\Delta/\Sigma\Delta + 1)\Sigma\Delta$$

The proposition (a) follows immediately, and (b) is based on the fact that $r_{\lambda\Delta}$ must be less than unity.

COLLECTIVE DECISION-MAKING

AND SOCIAL WELFARE*

In a recent study[1] Dr. Kenneth Arrow explores a novel approach to the problem of formulating the criterion of social welfare needed in welfare economics. The criterion must be given by some rule of collective decision-making, according to which the values of different members of the community on alternative social states are aggregated. The individual values supposedly yield a consistent ordering (that is, A over B and B over C mean A over C). If a rule of collective decision-making can be discovered which yields a consistent social ordering, this may serve as the criterion of social welfare.

The rule of collective decision-making must satisfy a number of *a priori* conditions. These are "value judgments" but are viewed as impelling.

(i) If one social state rises or remains constant in the value scale of every individual, then it rises or remains constant in the social ordering.

(ii) If for any specified alternatives the individual orderings are unchanged, so also is the social ordering. This is true even though there may be changes in the individual orderings of the remaining

* Originally entitled "On the Concept of Social Welfare," and published in the *Quarterly Journal of Economics*, May 1954, with this acknowledgment: Professor Paul A. Samuelson kindly allowed me to see some illuminating sections of an unpublished study of his on a related topic. The ethical notions referred to in the final section have been the subject of valuable discussions with Dr. John Chapman.
[1] Kenneth J. Arrow, *Social Choice and Individual Values* (New York, 1951).

alternatives. The social ordering is also unaffected by the presence or absence of some alternatives beyond those under consideration. This is the Condition of Independence of Irrelevant Alternatives.[2]

(iii) For any two alternatives, X and Y, the social ordering must not be independent of the individual orderings. This is the Condition of Citizen's Sovereignty.

(iv) The social ordering must not correspond to the ordering of some one individual no matter what the orderings of all others are. This is the Condition of Non-Dictatorship.

According to Arrow, "the most precise definition of a social state would be a complete description of the amount of each type of commodity in the hands of each individual, the amount of each productive resource invested in each type of productive activity, and the amounts of various types of collective activity . . ."[3]

Arrow's answer to the question he poses is largely negative. It is true that if the values of all individuals happen to coincide, the Condition of Non-Dictatorship loses force, and that all other conditions would be satisfied at once if the values of any one individual were taken to define the social ordering. There are also other special instances where a consistent social ordering can be established. But in the general case where there is no restriction on the ordering that is admissible for any individual, no social ordering can satisfy the specified conditions.[4] This is demonstrated by an extended application of formal logic.

[2] In explaining his logical formulation of this condition, Arrow emphasizes the fact that the social ordering of the alternatives under consideration is independent of the presence or absence of some other alternatives (*ibid.*, pp. 26, 27). But this logical formulation clearly implies that the social ordering is also independent of changes in individual orderings for alternatives other than those in question. Moreover, I believe this latter aspect is much the more interesting one for Arrow's purposes. After all, if the individual orderings are complete, then from the beginning they embrace any and all conceivable alternatives. Accordingly, the sense in which one may speak meaningfully of some alternative as bing "present" or "absent" is not at all clear. As will appear, one's view of the reasonableness of the condition might be affected by which of these two aspects is to the fore.
[3] *Social Choice and Individual Values*, p. 17.
[4] Strictly speaking it is supposed only that the ordering of any individual is unrestricted regarding some three alternatives. *Ibid.*, p. 24.

In a word, then, if the problem of the criterion is correctly envisaged it is logically insolvable! And hardly less disconcerting is the corollary that there may be no rule of collective decision-making with any *a priori* appeal. According to Mr. Little,[5] however, there is no need for the welfare economist to join Arrow in this depressing impasse: Arrow's conception of the problem of the criterion is mistaken to begin with. Questions are also in order as to the import of Arrow's theorem for political theory. On the other hand, Mr. Rothenberg[6] still considers that Arrow has formulated meaningfully the problem of the criterion. Following another approach, Mr. Hildreth[7] apparently feels that Arrow's theorem is pertinent to welfare economics, but he finds fault with the Condition of Independence of Irrelevant Alternatives.

This essay, although taking Arrow's approach as a point of departure, is not intended as a review of his book. Rather, it presents still another appraisal of the question of interpretation posed by his theorem. As between the different views cited above, I find myself in general accord with Mr. Little, but an attempt at further clarification may still be in order.

Arrow's theorem is of interest for its own sake, but his analysis might be viewed as an attempt to elaborate recent writings stressing the ethical nature of the criterion. His particular concern is with the question of how the values underlying an ethical criterion might be determined. Hence, in discussing Arrow's theorem, I shall be exploring a question that would call for inquiry in any event. Comment is the more in order here since several of the recent writings on the ethical character of the criterion are mine.[8] Also, the discussion of Arrow has tended to focus on an analytic device which I introduced in these same writings. But I take it that the Social Welfare Function is a rather secondary feature in this connection. The ultimate concern is with the nature of the problem of formulating a criterion of social welfare, however represented.

[5] I. M. D. Little, "Social Choice and Individual Values," *Journal of Political Economy*, October 1952.

[6] Jerome Rothenberg, "Conditions for a Social Welfare Function," *Journal of Political Economy*, October 1953.

[7] C. Hildreth, "Alternative Conditions for Social Orderings," *Econometrica*, January 1953.

[8] See Chapters 1 and 9.

ARROW'S THEOREM IN RELATION
TO POLITICAL THEORY

I refer first to the relation of Arrow's theorem to political theory. This question is of interest in itself, but what is said will also serve as a preliminary to the subsequent discussion of the relation of the theorem to welfare economics, which must be our main concern.

The theorem does, of course, bear on political theory. Participants in a constitutional convention, and ultimately citizens generally, are informed of the kinds of rules of collective decision-making that are open. Thus, there is no rule that satisfies Arrow's four ethical conditions while yielding consistent choices between social states. Anyone who attaches an absolute value to these requirements and who has the option presumably would be impelled in consequence to revert to a state of nature. Other more tractable individuals will now be aware that political cooperation involves the sacrifice of one or another of the conditions.

One is led to ask, then, how appealing the requirements might be from a political standpoint. This calls for more extended comment.

I cited above (p. 28) Arrow's definition of a social state. The rule of collective decision-making, of course, is itself an element in the social state properly conceived, but Arrow apparently assumes that other elements can vary without causing any important change in the rule. Hence the rule may be envisaged as aggregating values of all other elements in the social state. These consist mainly, though not exclusively, of the economic variables familiar to welfare economics. [9]

On the other hand, if the rule itself should be valued ethically, this might be done in one or the other or both of two ways. The rule might be appraised as a political process for its own sake; for example, majority rule is considered a good thing in itself. Alternatively, the rule might be appraised for its consequences, that is, in terms of the nature of the social states, exclusive of the

---

[9] If one desires to be at all realistic and to take account of such features as freedom of speech, legal security and the like, presumably these would have to be viewed as part of the rule of collective decision-making rather than as separate elements in the social state.

political process that the rule is likely to establish: the concern might be with the likely effects on the distribution of income. Arrow nowhere attempts to defend his "value judgments" on the admissible rules of collective decision-making in terms of these two approaches, so one is left in doubt which, if either, was supposed to be to the fore. I shall consider both approaches. Opinions will differ as to how much weight should be attached to each, but even on a purely ethical plane few will contend one should follow either to the complete neglect of the other.[10]

In the case of individual choices, logical consistency by its very nature is an ethical ultimate and accordingly cannot be deduced from any other value. By analogy, one is tempted to conclude that this must be true also of Arrow's collective consistency requirement. Moreover, the requirement might seem impelling in this light; at least, if one follows the first of our two approaches, that is, valuing the rule as a political process for its own sake. But a moment's reflection suffices to make clear that the analogy must be invalid. If collective consistency is of ethical value, this is only because, contrary to the supposition just stated, one follows in some measure the second approach; in other words, one values the rule in terms of its consequences. And in this light the requirement is not so appealing after all. Collective inconsistency apparently would mean that government actions might tend to go around in circles, and many will feel that this would be stultifying. But a minority fearful of majority exploitation would not be at all concerned on this account. More generally, except perhaps for aesthetic reasons, it is difficult to see why anyone should insist as Arrow does that consistency be realized throughout. An occasional inconsistency might give rise to circularity in the collective choices, but in view of ever-occurring changes in data there is no danger that the system would whirl about forever at any such point.

The Condition of Citizen's Sovereignty should be universally acceptable, no matter which approach is followed. The Condition of Non-Dictatorship obviously is appealing also, at least to those

[10] Arrow is, of course, aware of the distinction between the two approaches, but he refers to it only at the very end of his study (pp. 89ff), and in a manner suggesting that previously the rule was supposed to have no intrinsic value. I am reluctant to assume, however, that this was intended. As will become clear momentarily, if the rule has no intrinsic value, several of Arrow's conditions are entirely without force.

in the West. But it is readily seen that this appeal must be based on the first approach, where the rule is valued as a political process for its own sake. If the concern is with consequences, each of us to that extent would be a dictator. If consequences are to be evaluated, it is to our own values that we must appeal. Presumably this is what we mean when we refer to "our values."

The Condition of Independence of Irrelevant Alternatives in effect rules out any change in the "weights" to be attached to different individuals' "votes" on alternatives for which individual orderings are unchanged. This is despite any change in the individual's orderings on other alternatives.[11] One's view of this requirement will turn partly on whether he desires to allow different individuals an unequal influence on the collective choice to begin with. From a democratic standpoint, to count everyone's values equally appears ethically desirable, but again this must be in terms of the first approach. In terms of the second, dictatorship should be more impelling. Suppose one strongly favors an equalitarian income distribution in a community where most citizens think only of their own gain. On many issues, such as a minimum wage bill, for example, one might favor not equal influence for all but a more than proportional influence for the very poor.

Granting differences in influence, one must still decide on changes in relative influence which would violate Arrow's condition. I think one might very well desire such changes. An individual's values are integral to his character generally. Any change in character might be the basis for a change in relative influence, even on alternatives for which the individual's orderings are unchanged. Jones may order two alternative wine-bread diets in the same way as before, but given a new love of athletics, he may now feel much less intensely about the diet with the larger volume of wine. One would wish to take this into account in determining Jones's influence on a choice between two alternative social states, one providing more and the other less wine for Jones.

The requirement that changes in the social ordering be positively associated with changes in individual orderings is subject to much the same interpretation as the Condition of Independence

---

[11] See above, n. 2.

of Irrelevant Alternatives. To me, however, the former is some-what more appealing.

As already explained, Arrow's requirement of logical consis-tency is without force if the rule of collective decision-making is valued only for its own sake. On the other hand, several of his ethical conditions are likewise footless if the rule is valued only for its consequences. If (contrary to the procedure I have pursued above) one focuses exclusively on either of these two approaches to the complete neglect of the other, it follows that Arrow's theorem collapses altogether.

I have said that in appraising the consequences of the political process, reference must be made to "our own" values for social states, exclusive of the political process. It may be asked just who the "our" refers to. Is it suggested that each citizen will be told by, say, the political scientist to consult his own (the citizen's) values? And in any case isn't this prejudging the very problem Arrow examines or at least says he is examining, namely, the for-mulation of a criterion of social welfare? In a sense it is. But if one is to value social states, exclusive of the political process, I believe that welfare economics is of more concern than political theory. I defer further comment on this aspect, therefore, until we come to welfare economics. A question may also be raised as to whether my example concerning the two diets does not involve illegitimate interpersonal utility comparisons. I think this objection, too, will be answered by what is said later regarding welfare economics.

It is well known that if left to themselves individuals might not always choose consistently in the light of their own values, especially when complex social questions are involved. Indeed, according to the conception of welfare economics to be elaborated below, this discipline must derive its rationale in part from this fact. In appraising different rules of collective decision-making, presumably one would wish to take into account such inconsis-tencies in individual choices. One might wish to consider also that the individual values themselves may be open to criticism from one or another ethical point of view. I am not arguing here in favor of a benevolent dictatorship, but some may feel as I do that limitations of individual values are one more ground, in addition to those already mentioned, for discounting Arrow's conditions.

Thus far I have been focusing on Arrow's conditions. For a rounded view of the relation of his theorem to political theory, account must be taken also of several other aspects of the political problem as he formulates it.

For one thing, Arrow is concerned with defining a rule of collective decision-making which yields logically consistent choices for any and all alternatives and any and all individual orderings. In any actual case, however, the scope of collective decision-making generally is limited, and in part depends on the extent of the divergence in individual values, which is the source of difficulty in Arrow's analysis. Many will feel that such a limitation is itself ethically desirable. Accordingly, interest attaches not so much to the question Arrow studies but rather to that of the feasible and desirable area of collective decision-making.

For another, Arrow assumes that the individual values on social states are a datum. In the real world, of course, they are variable, at least, in the long run, and among other things are affected by the rule of collective decision-making itself. Accordingly, in addition to the two ways of appraising a political process referred to above (p. 30), there is still a third in terms of the effect of the process on individual values. In many political theories, I believe, this approach actually is the main one considered.

I must leave it to the reader to consider the practical import of other features of Arrow's analysis, particularly the omission of any element of "representativeness" in government as distinct from universal, direct decision-making.

In questioning the significance of Arrow's theorem for political theory, Little limits himself mainly to the contention that two of Arrow's ethical conditions have little intrinsic merit.[12] These are the conditions concerning the positive association of changes in the social ordering with changes in individual ones and the Condition of Independence of Irrelevant Alternatives. In my view, these conditions have more appeal if the political process is valued for its own sake than they do otherwise, but in general I follow Mr. Little in discounting them. For this and other reasons,

---

[12] Little, *Journal of Political Economy*, October 1952, pp. 430ff.

I am no less skeptical than he of the significance of Arrow's theorem in a political context.

ARROW'S THEOREM IN RELATION TO WELFARE ECONOMICS

The problem of the criterion. As implied, Arrow's theorem is in my opinion unrelated to welfare economics. This follows from my conception of the problem of the criterion as having two aspects. First, it is necessary to determine the ethical values which one would take as data in counseling one or another citizen in any particular community on decisions involving alternative social states. Reference is not to decisions of the restricted sort taken in the market, but to decisions of the large sort usually implemented by actions of government, as, for example, a tax reform. Ethical values order social states generally, but counsel is deduced from them by application of the logic of choice. This counsel, however, has a partial character because one abstracts from values attaching to political features.

The values in question presumably will be determined in the light of some position on the ethical issue as to the possibilities of meaningful value criticism. Also, depending on the position taken on this issue, the values considered as data in counseling any one citizen may be the same as those considered in counseling any other. Or they may be different. In the former case, the criterion of social welfare is given at once. It is defined simply by the values one would take as data in counseling any individual. In the latter case, however, it is necessary still to decide a second question of a methodological sort: Whom to counsel? One might still wish to counsel any and all citizens at the same time. If so, the criterion is defined only within areas on which the values of all are the same. Within this area, the criterion is given by the values held in common. Alternatively, one might wish to counsel some select group, which holds some values in common. Here the criterion is given by the values of the group in question. Still again, one might offer one's services in turn to all comers. In the case of each citizen, then, the criterion is given by the values that one would take as data in counseling the person in question. One stands ready to advise one citizen to vote against the tax reform and another for it.

Evidently Arrow's theorem can have nothing in common with questions such as these. Actually, the ethical question regarding the values to be taken as data in counseling any individual appears to be disposed of at the outset of Arrow's analysis. This results from his supposition that individuals have some definite values on social states and from his apparent decision not to go behind these values. Given this, all that remains to decide is the question of whom to counsel. Any further inquiry into the possibility of a "social ordering" as Arrow conceives it is out of place. Even if there were such an ordering, it is difficult to see what would be done with it. So far as the counseling of any individual is concerned, the pertinent criterion is given at once by the values Arrow starts with.

Possible objections. It may be objected, however, that Arrow's analysis is subject to another interpretation. While Arrow supposes each individual to have some values on social states, this does not necessarily mean that the values are beyond criticism. Moreover, his analysis might be seen to bear, though negatively, on the question of the kind of value criticism that is admissible. Thus, it is demonstrated that one could not appeal to a rule of collective decision-making to determine the values to be taken as data in the counseling of any individual on social states.

As far as I can see, this interpretation is admissible, and my contention that Arrow's theorem does not apply to welfare economics has to be qualified accordingly. However, Arrow's theorem does not bar all rules of collective decision-making but only those rules satisfying his ethical conditions and the requirement of logical consistency. For reasons already stated, this difference is important. Beyond this, just what is contributed by the theorem in this way depends on what one thinks, to begin with, of an appeal to a rule of collective decision-making as a basis for criticism of individual values. In everyday life people do very often appeal to "what most people think," to "the prevalent opinion" and the like, in support of one or another ethical position. But I believe such appeals generally are most easily construed as presupposing only that the valid values of all persons are the same. Such appeals hardly presuppose that valid values could be derived in each and every case from some definite rule of collective decision-making. As a basis for criticism of individual values, however, Arrow's theorem rests on the latter presupposition. For this some support might possibly be found in certain ethical writings, particularly those of Rousseau,[13] but such views are hardly widely credited today. As a contribution to value criticism, Arrow's theorem undermines further an already dubious ethical position.

It may be of interest, too, that in the light of this ethical position, the task of the welfare economist becomes a curious one. Suppose that some rule of collective decision-making could be discovered that satisfied Arrow's conditions or was otherwise acceptable as a source of valid values. The welfare economist, then, would have the function of informing each citizen what in the light of that rule, the collective choice would be on any public measure under consideration. The collective choice would be established initially from the uncounseled votes of individuals. The counseled votes, of course, would all be the same. If the collective choice is always right, there is no need for the welfare economist to engage in the sort of inquiry usually undertaken as to the implications of this choice. Indeed, if the ideal rule of collective decision-making is actually operative, it is difficult to see why the welfare economist should do anything at all. Whatever measures are "desirable" would be adopted without benefit of his counsel.

I have been assuming that the concern of welfare economics is to counsel individual citizens generally. If a public official is counseled, it is on the same basis as any other citizen. In every instance reference is made to some ethical values which are appropriate for the counseling of the individual in question. In all this I believe I am only expressing the intent of welfare writings generally; or, if this is not the intent, I think it should be. But some may be inclined nevertheless to a different conception, which allows still another interpretation of Arrow's theorem. According to this view the problem is to counsel not citizens

[13] See *ibid.*, pp. 426ff.

generally but public officials. Furthermore, the values to be taken as data are not those which might guide the official if he were a private citizen. The official is envisaged instead as more or less neutral ethically. His one aim in life is to implement the values of other citizens as given by some rule of collective decision-making. Arrow's theorem apparently contributes to this sort of welfare economics the negative finding that no consistent social ordering could be found to serve as a criterion of social welfare in the counseling of the official in question.

We probably have approached by now the point where methodological debate ceases to be fruitful, but the foregoing conception of welfare economics and of Arrow's contribution lends itself to diverse constructions, which I think should be made explicit. Conceivably, in counseling the official the problem might be to discover some rule of collective decision-making which would be ethically appealing to him. If anyone wishes to call this welfare economics, he is welcome to do so, but he should be clear that he is back in the realm of political theory already discussed. The problem is one of providing counsel on political institutions rather than on the economic aspects of social states. Arrow's theorem, therefore, has to be appraised in the light of the considerations set forth on pp. 30ff.

But the public official may already be attached ethically to some particular rule of collective decision-making. He is not to be dissuaded from it by Arrow's theorem. Thus, the official may believe in pure majority rule. He still holds to this belief even after Arrow informs him (as he would) that majority rule satisfies all of his (Arrow's) ethical conditions but may not lead to a consistent ordering. But in this case the official himself would still be acting quite consistently if he maintains majority rule by implementing the votes taken on each issue, or if such rule does not prevail initially, insofar as he strives to realize it. Furthermore, welfare economics is barred here not because there is no consistent ordering on social states, but because the official is ethically neutral on all economic questions. Accordingly, there is nothing for the welfare economist to counsel the official about. If he were so inclined, however, the welfare economist might still contribute to the official's decision-making by tallying votes.

Then again, the official might be attached to some rule of collective decision-making for political rather than for ethical reasons. But I think what was just said about the case where the official's attitude is ethical covers this instance as well. The reader may be allowed to appraise for himself the further case where the official has no values at all.

We have been considering the possibility that the welfare economist might counsel not citizens generally, as was assumed initially, but a public official. What of the further possibility that he counsel nobody in particular but the community as such? Is not Arrow's theorem more meaningful in this light? Writings on welfare economics might often be construed as being directed at counseling the "community as such," viewed as something above and beyond individuals. With its references to "rational behavior on the part of the community" and the like, Arrow's study is a case in point. But a moment's reflection makes clear that such a conception cannot be very meaningful. After all, even if one prefers to think of the community as an "organic entity," he must still concede that in the last analysis all decisions are made by individuals. If one does not counsel individuals, who is there to counsel?

A special case in Arrow's analysis. While Arrow considers that the formulation of a social ordering encounters no difficulties if all individual orderings are in accord, he makes an exception to this rule in one outstanding case. Suppose all agree that each individual's tastes are to "count" so far as his personal consumption is concerned. All agree, too, on the distribution of "real" income. Hence, each individual ordering for social states takes the form:

$$w^k = f^k[U^1, U^2, U^3, \ldots, U^i, \ldots U^k, \ldots U^n], \qquad (1)$$

where U^i represents the tastes of the ith individual for his personal consumption.[14]

Each individual ordering is also the operational equivalent of the utilitarian criterion of social welfare used by Marshall, Pigou,

[14] Arrow abstains throughout from the use of mathematical functions to represent orderings, but it facilitates the discussion to put his argument in these terms here. I refer to a simple model in which material consumption is the only element in the social state.

et al.,[15] and one might suppose that formula (1) would also be acceptable at once as a social ordering. Arrow holds the contrary. The individual ordering itself, he holds, violates the Condition of Independence of Irrelevant Alternatives. This has to be understood now as referring to tastes on personal consumption rather than to values on social states, but with this proviso it remains impelling. Arrow reasons as follows:

> Suppose there are present two commodities, bread and wine. A distribution, deemed equitable by all, is arranged, with the wine lovers getting more wine and less bread than the abstainers. Suppose now that all the wine is destroyed. Are the wine lovers entitled, because of that fact, to more than an equal share of bread? The answer is, of course, a value judgment. My own feeling is that tastes for unattainable alternatives should have nothing to do with the decision among the attainable ones; desires in conflict with reality are not entitled to consideration, so that [the Condition of Independence of Irrelevant Alternatives], reinterpreted in terms of tastes rather than values, is a valid value judgment, to me at least.[16]

Arrow does not restate explicitly his Condition of Independence of Irrelevant Alternatives for the case where reference is to tastes rather than values. I am not entirely sure I understand what he had in mind in this connection. But it may be conceded that formula (1) might involve giving the wine lovers more than an equal share of bread if that commodity is the only one available. As I understand it, Arrow objects to this even though every member in the community studied (except himself) might think it desirable. The prevalent values are invalid. Some may feel that at this point Arrow goes beyond the proper function of the welfare economist. If everyone agrees that such a distribution is desirable, this must be ground enough for formulating the criterion of social welfare.

From the standpoint of the present argument, however, a more serious question concerns Arrow's criticism of the prevailing values. Surely value criticism requires a more searching inquiry than Arrow has undertaken. Suppose, for example, the members of the community ultimately desire to satisfy the more basic needs

[15] See Chapters 1 and 9.
[16] Arrow, p. 73.

of all before satisfying the less basic needs of any. Suppose, too, that wine lovers are so constituted that when wine is unavailable they require more bread to live than do the bread lovers. (The example might be more appealing if reference were to young milk lovers and adult vitamin-extract lovers.) One surely would be hard put in this case to object to the allocation of a larger share of bread to the wine lovers. And Arrow's formulation of the rationale of the allocation is quite misleading, insofar as it implies that the only ground for it is consideration of the wine lovers' desire for the nonexistent wine. The ultimate criterion would be the perfectly plausible one of the comparative degree to which wants of different orders are satisfied for different individuals.

In the real world, of course, an ordering of the sort given by formula (1) might reflect many diverse considerations, and I do not suggest that I would always be in accord with the outcome. But, if it is to be especially meaningful, any value criticism undertaken, I believe, must be on a different plane from Arrow's.

But I anticipate a familiar criticism: I have introduced inadmissible comparisons between the utilities of wine lovers and bread lovers. The criticism will appear all the more in order since Arrow apparently intends his Condition of Independence of Irrelevant Alternatives to rule out this very feature. But in welfare economics objection usually is made not to interpersonal comparisons, but to the contention that these comparisons can be made without the introduction of ethical premises. No such contention has been or need be made here. The individual members of the community all are supposed to order social states on the ethical premise that distribution should be according to need.

A question may be raised, however, regarding this supposition in turn. "Need," it may be felt, is really much too vague a concept to serve as a criterion of distribution. Hence one must introduce, not one general ethical premise that distribution should be according to "need," but many more specific premises. In the extreme case, it might even be necessary to pair by separate ethical premises all the indifference curves of each household with all those of every other one. I should agree that "need" is not an especially definite concept, but I believe there is a good deal of agreement on its empirical meaning nevertheless, and with this the stated objection seems to have little weight. If this be "cardinal" rather than "ordinal" measurability of utilities, so much the worse for "ordinal" measurability.[17]

It remains to observe, however, that a redistribution of bread in favor of the wine lovers might still be favored even without resort to the concept of "need." This might be implied by the specific ethical premises pairing indifference curves. Of course, if one may not refer to any more ultimate standard, such as need, it becomes more difficult to dispute Arrow's value judgment. But similarly there is still no basis for him to discredit any alternative.[18]

[17] I believe that at the most what is involved is a comparative sort of cardinality. For some one individual taken as a standard, there is only ordinal measurability. But given some numbering system that represents the utility of this individual, the admissible numbering systems for the utilities of all other individuals are quite restricted. For any one person, the admissible systems can differ one from another only by an arbitrary constant representing the zero point.

[18] To come back to the question of the reformulation of the Condition of Independence of Irrelevant Alternatives for the case where reference is to tastes rather than to values, the following is perhaps a plausible rendition. A social state may be envisaged as comprising a set of personal consumption budgets for all individuals. Suppose now attention is directed to two social states, X and Y, and for each individual there is some personal consumption budget, x, included in X and another personal consumption budget, y, included in Y. The Condition of Independence of Irrelevant Alternatives, then, might be understood to mean that the social ordering of X and Y would be unchanged as long as all individuals' preferences between x and y are unchanged. This would be without regard to any change in the individuals' tastes regarding personal consumption budgets other than x and y, and also without regard to the presence or absence of any other alternatives.

As far as I can see, however, an individual ordering of social states might satisfy this requirement and still imply the redistribution of bread in favor of the wine lovers to which Arrow objects. On the other hand, it would rule out any redistribution of income within X and Y in the light of a change in tastes for personal consumption budgets other than x and y. But an individual with the ordering given by formula (1) might well wish to make such a redistribution, and I for one could not view this as necessarily unreasonable. Even if the preferences as between x and y are unchanged, the change in tastes might reflect a change in needs generally that one would wish to consider in distributing income in social states X and Y.

Arrow envisages that all of his conditions, and not merely that of Independence of Irrelevant Alternatives, may be reformulated to refer to

Little; Rothenberg; Hildreth. Little bars Arrow's theorem from welfare economics chiefly for two reasons. First, where an individual orders social states purely in terms of his own material consumption, the individual's "values" for social states and his "tastes" for personal consumption are one and the same. In this case, then, Arrow's *a priori* conditions impose restrictions on the relation between the Social Welfare Function obtaining before and that obtaining after a change in tastes. In conventional welfare economics no such restriction is envisaged; it is necessary only that there be a Social Welfare Function for any given set of tastes. Second, "none of the advantages claimed for theoretical welfare economics as a result of introducing . . . [a Social Welfare Function] depends in the least on the ordering of economic states being an ordering by society."[19] All welfare principles can be deduced from the ordering of any one individual.

I agree with Little in barring Arrow's theorem from welfare economics, but I have sought here to make it more explicit than he does that this follows simply from the very nature of this discipline. In welfare economics one is engaged in ethical counseling on the economics aspects of social states. Ethical counseling is only meaningful to begin with if it is directed at individuals, and accordingly takes as data the values that pertain to them. Insofar as the concern is with economic aspects, the values in question are those from which Arrow starts his analysis. A "social ordering" is not only unnecessary; there would be no place for it in the analysis even if it were available.

From this it follows, too, that Arrow's conditions concerning changes in individual orderings are actually redundant. The Social Welfare Function is *defined* by one or another individual ordering or, within limits of their agreement, by all individual orderings together. If there is a change in the individual ordering,

---

tastes for personal consumption rather than to values for social states. But, while he is no more explicit in the case of his other conditions than in that of Independence of Irrelevant Alternatives, I believe I am right in assuming that formula (1) violates only this latter condition.

In trying to appraise Arrow's special case I have had the benefit of discussions with Professor William Vickrey.

[19] Little, *Journal of Political Economy*, October 1952, p. 424.

necessarily there is a corresponding change in the Social Welfare Function.

An exception to the foregoing, however, is the special case where Arrow's conditions are reinterpreted to refer to "tastes" rather than to "values." This case, which must be distinguished from the one Little refers to (where tastes and values are one and the same), has been discussed above. In effect, Arrow is engaging here in criticism of individual values on social states, and I have argued, criticism of a dubious sort.

Apart from this special case, I have suggested that Arrow's analysis might also be viewed as negating a form of individual value criticism where appeal is made to a rule of collective decision-making to establish the valid values for any individual. If I understand Little correctly, he considers that such an appeal would be self-contradictory to begin with. If one subscribes to some values on social states, how can one entertain the conception that valid values might be given by a collective choice?[20] I agree that this form of value criticism is absurd, but I find it difficult to see how it involves a contradiction. One might subscribe to some values only provisionally and subject to verification in terms of the collective choice. For a welfare economist concerned to counsel others, rather than to appraise his own values, the question of contradiction perhaps is still less germane.

Rothenberg considers that Little's view of welfare economics is unduly narrow, so far as it bars restrictions on the change in social ordering associated with changes in individual orderings. I have already said all I have to say on this matter. I am not sure that I have fully grasped the balance of Rothenberg's provocative argument, but a central contention appears to be that the conception of the Social Welfare Function as being given by a collective decision-making process is entirely meaningful.[21] There probably is a "consensus" in any given community on the value of the prevailing collective decision-making process itself. Hence, the resultant collective choices also have ethical meaning and may properly be taken as data for the definition of social

[20] *Ibid.*, pp. 426ff.
[21] Rothenberg, *Journal of Political Economy*, October 1953, especially pp. 396ff.

welfare. It follows, too, that Arrow's conditions are to be appraised in terms of the degree to which they describe the collective decision-making process actually prevailing in any particular community.

In view of what has been said already, I think I may limit myself to one or two comments on this argument. First, suppose there is agreement on the prevailing decision-making process. Citizens may still disagree on the values of economic aspects of the social state. Accordingly, if one hopes to engage in ethical counseling on economic questions, an appeal to the collective choices must be construed as involving the dubious sort of value criticism discussed previously. An exception must be made of the situation where the collective decision-making process has an absolute value, and is vitally affected in a given choice. But, in this extraordinary case, what is called for evidently is an exercise in political theory rather than anything remotely resembling welfare economics. Second, carried to its logical extreme, Rothenberg's analysis actually leaves welfare economics devoid of both ethics and counseling. What is there for the welfare economist to do but count ballots if the collective choices are taken as data? Rothenberg struggles against this result, but I think not very successfully.

Hildreth objects to the Condition of Independence of Irrelevant Alternatives on the ground that the same individual ordering may represent preferences of very different intensity. An individual may "desperately prefer" one state to another or he may "barely prefer" it.[22] Arrow's condition bars us from considering such differences insofar as they are associated with a change in the ordering of alternatives other than those in question. In any social ordering, however, the intensity of preference should be considered. I agree, but I have felt it in order to distinguish between political theory and welfare economics. As originally formulated, the Condition of Independence of Irrelevant Alternatives pertains to political theory. As reformulated to refer to "tastes," the condition pertains to welfare economics. Hildreth's argument applies in both contexts, but in respect of political

---

[22] Hildreth, *Econometrica*, January 1953, pp. 89ff.

theory the condition has to be appraised also in the light of any intrinsic value attaching to the political process. From this point of view the condition is more appealing.

CONCLUSION

I have argued that Arrow's theorem is relevant to political theory, but only to a very special case. The theorem has little or no bearing on welfare economics.

A notable feature in welfare economics is the attempt to formulate a criterion of social welfare without recourse to controversial ethical premises. Proponents of both Utilitarian and the New Welfare Economics[23] are rarely very explicit about fundamentals, but I believe both schools are fairly considered as examples. On the one hand, ethical premises are avoided on the supposition that the utilities of different persons are empirically comparable. On the other, empirical comparability is rejected, but an ethical taint still is avoided by restricting the scope of the criterion to the area of harmonious utility changes.

In several previous essays cited earlier I argued that this goal for the criterion is an illusion. The criterion necessarily is ethical, and neither the Utilitarian nor the New Welfare Economics provides any valid alternative. As implied, I am still of this opinion, but let me now explain that in exploring Arrow's theorem I have been concerned in part to forestall the growth of a successor to this illusion, which my own previous analysis may have fostered. This is the conception that without either value criticism or value agreement one might formulate an impersonal ethical criterion of broad scope. My earlier essays are broadly relativistic in tone, in the sense that the possibility of meaningful value criticism is not considered. Also, one of my themes is the question of the scope of the criterion. But in this connection I do no more than underline that this standard must rest on "value judgments" no matter how broad or narrow the scope; and nowhere do I explain that without value criticism it might have to be either personal or restricted in range. On the same ethical basis, Arrow

[23] For references, see Chapters 1 and 9.

searches at length for a criterion which is not subject to either of these limitations. Others apparently have also considered this as a meaningful objective.

Still, if an impersonal criterion must be restricted in range, the present essay may appear from a relativistic standpoint not much more favorable to welfare economics than Arrow's theorem. This depends, however, on how narrow the scope is, and hence on the area of agreement in values. On this, the pessimistically inclined do not always seem to consider sufficiently that an individual's overt choices, especially on involved social issues, may not be optimal. Because of logical confusion, ignorance, and unthinking prejudice, the individual may not choose in accord with any con- consistent values. As seen here, welfare economics derives its rationale partly from this fact. It is still broadly meaningful, I believe, to try to impute consistent values to different individuals, but without value criticism, or at least any that is at all contro- versial, the imputed values might agree where overt choices differ. Of course, if people choose correctly they might diverge more rather than less than before. But at least the extent of the disagreement in values is a matter for inquiry and is not to be inferred in any simple fashion from the conflicting overt choices.

While welfare economics can be founded on relativism, I should record that my own ethical thinking has evolved in the course of time. Value criticism of any deep sort may be largely philosophic, at least in the present primitive state of psychology, but it still need not be devoid of meaning. Hence disagreement in values continues to be of concern, but not so much as under relativism. If one does venture beyond the area of agreement, it may be permissible to suppose that the reason need not be mere personal bias. But I cannot very well pursue this theme here. It remains only to say that the outlook for welfare economics seems improved under any likely alternative to relativism. Also, I agree with those who urge that whatever the ethical standpoint, the values taken as data should be made explicit.

In my examination of Arrow's theorem, I found it useful to be explicit on the question of purpose. This is not the place to reopen in any large way the issue as to the ethical content of the criterion, which I have just referred to, but it should be observed that the question of purpose is also important in this regard. I cannot imagine any sensible alternative to ethical counseling. Yet, given this, it follows at once that the criterion must be ethical in character. This does not by itself rule out empirical comparability, but it means that even with this supposition one still must establish why the criterion is ethically impelling.

Curiously, while the question of the rationale of the Utilitarian criterion in this deeper sense is central in ethical discussions, economic writings always focus on empirical comparability. The neglect of the former question in welfare economics is all the more curious when it is considered that it is logically prior to the latter. If one can advance the Utilitarian criterion with empirical comparability, then it should also be possible to do so without it. Thus, if I may restate in more contemporary terms a famous argument of Mill, it might be held that because of inherent psychological interrelatedness each of us would ultimately be better off as a Utilitarian. While we may behave like Economic Men, we would be happier as Social Men.[24] The elusive common dimensional unit for utilities, then, is at hand. One must bear in mind that the utilities that are in question pertain to personal consumption. Hence, just as the common dimensional unit of apples and nuts is found in utility, the common dimensional unit of utilities is found in the welfare of Social Man. Welfare is the counterpart of utility that pertains to the social state generally; that is, welfare includes the interrelatedness.[25]

[24] Mill's appeal is to ". . . the social feelings of mankind; the desire to be in unity with our fellow creatures, which is already a powerful principle in human nature, and happily one of those which tend to become stronger, even without express inculcation, from the influences of advancing civilization." J. S. Mill, *Utilitarianism*, (New York: Liberal Arts Press, 1949), p. 33.

[25] The interrelatedness in question here is rather different from that already familiar in economic theory. For one thing, the concern is with welfare in a deep sense which may or may not be reflected correctly in the individual's overt choices. For another, even supposing the overt choices do correspond to welfare, a distinction still is in order between interrelated welfares, where the individual's welfare depends not only on his own consumption but on that of others, and interrelated tastes, where the structure of the individual's preferences depends on the consumption of others. While interrelated tastes always means interrelated welfares, it is readily seen that the converse is not the case. Also, the two sorts of interrelatedness

might reflect very different psychological factors. In economic theory attention generally seems directed to interrelated tastes, but from the present standpoint interrelated welfares are the phenomena of interest.

In referring to economic theory, I have had in mind particularly positive economics, and so far as this discipline is concerned interrelated tastes are actually the only form of interrelatedness that matters. Only this kind of interrelatedness is reflected in market behavior. It remains to observe, however, that in welfare economics interrelatedness of either sort generally has been little to the fore. Nevertheless, a brief restatement of welfare economics to allow for interrelatedness has been made by G. Tintner, in "A Note on Welfare Economics," *Econometrica*, January 1946. In mathematical terms, Tintner anticipates the distinction made here between interrelated welfares and interrelated tastes. However, he focuses on the formal aspects of this problem, and from the present standpoint the import of interrelatedness is blurred as a result of the presupposition throughout that the Social Welfare Function must be of a higher order than an individual utility function that includes interrelatedness. While this presupposition is in order in the light of some ethical theories, one gains the impression that in Tintner's case this treatment may reflect the same sort of methodological confusion as is found in Arrow's analysis. The question of interrelatedness as it bears on welfare economics has also been discussed in J. S. Duesenberry, *Income, Saving and the Theory of Consumer Behavior*, Cambridge, Mass., 1949, chap. vi. But Duesenberry is chiefly concerned with the phenomenon of interrelated tastes, and as in Tintner no attempt is made to relate the phenomenon to ethical theory.

Finally, it will readily be seen that the distinction made in the text between one's utility from personal consumption and one's welfare from the social state is possible only if there are interrelated welfares but not interrelated tastes. Otherwise, utility and welfare tend to merge.

But in this case the common dimensional unit for utilities is no longer needed. Given the ethical theory that is in question here, the criterion is given by the welfare of Social Man. There is no need to compare the welfares of different people.

3

ON SOCIAL WELFARE ONCE MORE*

In welfare economics the criterion of social welfare used to appraise resource allocation became a controversial theme when this discipline was in its infancy, and so it has remained ever since. In contemplating this situation the practitioner often comforts himself with the thought that divergencies in standpoint are not apt to be of much practical import. The divergencies are perhaps sometimes rather scholastic, but on such a fundamental matter it would be surprising if they were not consequential.

What is mainly in question is the manner in which the criterion is to be determined. I have explored this problem in previous essays, but the chief of these appeared long ago.[1] In the light of the continuing discussion and further thoughts, I refer here again to the determination of the criterion.

SOURCES OF VALUES

In the essays cited, I joined with those who stressed the value content of the criterion. Indeed this feature was held to be understandable in terms of "value judgments" not only where interper-

---

* This essay was largely written in 1964 while I was a fellow at the Center for Advanced Study in the Behavioral Sciences, Stanford, California, and benefited from discussions I had with colleagues there, particularly Professors Carl G. Hempel and George H. Mahl. I am also indebted to Professor Emile Despres for helpful comments, and to Professor Paul A. Samuelson with whom I had most profitable discussions concerning the subject of the Addendum. Among other things, Professor Samuelson suggested to me use of the chart on p. 81.

[1] See Chapter 1 (referred to hereafter as "A Reformulation"); also Chapters 2 and 9.

sonal comparisons are involved, as had previously been urged, but generally. Thus, the criterion supposedly provides a basis for ranking alternative economic states, but this is achieved only through the introduction of value judgments. These determine, at least in principle, the social values realized through variation in different elements of the economic state, and in this way define social welfare. For any particular criterion that may be advanced, therefore, the corresponding value judgments may readily be perceived as restrictions on an initially abstract formula, the "social welfare function." This relates social welfare to elements in the economic state.

All of this still seems reasonable to me, as far as it goes, but admittedly it does not go far enough. In formulating the criterion, how should the economist decide what values to consider? In "A Reformulation" (above, p. 15) I referred to this question, but not very incisively:

> In general, any set of value propositions which is sufficient for the evaluation of all alternatives may be introduced, and for each of these sets of propositions there corresponds a maximum position. The number of sets is infinite, and in any particular case the selection of one of them must be determined by its compatibility with the values prevailing in the community the welfare of which is being studied. For only if the welfare principles are based on prevailing values can they be relevant to the activity of the community in question.

Subsequently, I had occasion to observe that members of a community might wish to realize very divergent values on economic states, and alluded to the possibility that for this reason the welfare economist might be impelled toward "value criticism."[2]

How decide then on the values to be considered? The question obviously admits of more than one answer, but the economist presumably will wish to refer to prevailing values. Where the values of different members of the community differ, he may also wish to consider his own values. Some will feel that this would be in order in any case.

Also, in formulating one's own values on alternative economic states a cardinal decision is that concerning the principle appli-

---

[2] Above, pp. 47ff.

cable to alternative mixes of goods consumed and labor services supplied by any household. To what extent should one be guided here by overt preferences such as the individual himself expresses in the market? And the question of "consumers' sovereignty" as so understood is, of course, not the same thing as the question of whether the consumer knows what is good for him, for even if one had misgivings on this score he might feel that as a rule no one else is apt to know better; or that, if some one else did, it would be offensive and perhaps, in a deeper sense, still contrary to the interest of the individual to overrule his overt preferences on any scale on this basis.

Yet, in the evaluation of alternative economic states, whether the consumer knows what is good for him is of interest, and, so far as it is, it should be considered that the question is not solely ethical. Rather, there is some basis for empirical inquiry. The more ultimate concern here presumably is with the individual's "satisfactions," and, however conceived, these presumably are such that overt preferences tend to correspond more or less closely with them, depending on how well-informed the individual is regarding the nature of different products and the consequences of their consumption for him.[3] Possibly the individual's satisfactions, too, will be affected as he becomes better informed, for the consumption may take place with varying degrees of apprehension of consequences (for example, for health), and satisfactions may plausibly be envisaged as varying correspondingly. But, along with overt preferences, satisfactions should thereby only become the more indicative of a still more ultimate value, as plausibly understood, the individual's "welfare."

We may meaningfully question whether the consumer knows what is good for him, therefore, when there is reason to doubt that he is well informed regarding products and their consequences. Also, such misgivings could be tested in any concrete case simply by observing how the consumer behaves when further

---

[3] Here and elsewhere I often refer to "consumption" elliptically to include performance of different kinds of labor services. Also for present purposes it may not be amiss to pass by problems posed by the fact that the household normally has many members. In effect, therefore, individual and household are identified with one another. This is a familiar, although not wholly defensible, practice in welfare economics.

information is supplied him. Once overt preferences are tested in this way, howsoever they are affected, they could no longer be suspect on grounds of consumer ignorance. But this fact would be of interest. For a community generally, it might not always be possible to test misgivings in any comprehensive way, but they might still be more or less grounded empirically.

Reference is, however, to a consumer who is thought to be rational in any deep sense. Should he be otherwise, misgivings about his overt preferences may also be in order on this account. However satisfying such preferences might seem to him, they may not appear especially favorable to his welfare if, emotionally, he is more or less pathological or unintegrated. So far as such aberrations reflect a lack of insight by the consumer into his own nature, perhaps in the last analysis they are somewhat of a piece with the consumer ignorance just considered, and hence, as a basis for discounting overt preferences, not really to be considered as fully distinct from such ignorance. In any event, appraisal of overt preferences from this standpoint surely is still not purely ethical, though admittedly if pursued far it can rapidly become highly speculative.[4]

[4] I have defined "satisfactions" and "welfare" only by implication. For purposes of welfare economics I doubt that it is very important to try to formulate explicit definitions, but as his consumption varies, the individual gratifies in varying degrees diverse needs and dispositions. To each consumption mix, therefore, there will correspond some complex mental experience. Moreover, the experiences relating to different mixes tend somehow to become ordered. Let me explain, then, that I think of the individual's "satisfactions" from consumption in terms of this ordering. That is, satisfactions from any consumption mix are greater the higher the rank of the corresponding mental state. As was implied, the individual's "welfare" is envisaged in much the same way, but to what extent this category is given by the ordering in question depends on the information at the individual's disposal, and the presence or absence of pathological and unintegrated aspects.

It may also be of value to have an illustration of the diverse cases that have been distinguished: Should the individual buy cigarettes in ignorance of injurious effects on health, and yet somehow learn of such effects while smoking, overt preferences would diverge from satisfactions, but the latter might still be indicative of welfare. Should the individual remain in ignorance of the injurious effects, overt preferences might conform to satisfactions, but these might diverge from welfare. Should the individual continue to buy cigarettes after learning of the injurious effects, one might still have misgivings about the relation of his overt preferences to welfare, though admittedly the individual might feel that they were as satisfying as any might be.

The household derives satisfactions not only from its consumption but from its experience generally. Hence, in reflecting on consumers' sovereignty it must also be considered that one household's consumption of one or another commodity might affect the satisfactions, and therefore welfare, of another.

Consumers' sovereignty presupposes in any case that each and every individual's welfare is a good. Among welfare economists this will hardly be in question, but here too there may be some basis for meaningful appraisal in terms of more ultimate standards. For example, one might be led to ponder whether to view another's welfare as other than a good would be consistent with the responsibilities of citizenship in a democracy. Under the influence of an ancient ethical current, one might also be led to inquire whether, even if the consumption of others were of no concern in and of itself, their welfare might be. Hence, one might still find his own welfare heightened by actions favorable to that of others. But the insight gained from examining one's values in this light may be limited, for, as wise men perceived long ago, attitude may be father to reason rather than reason to attitude, and the former must often be true here.

The welfare economist may wish to keep these considerations in mind in deciding on his own values on consumers' sovereignty. They may also be helpful in construing and appraising those prevailing in the community generally. No systematic inquiry on public evaluations of economic states in a Western democratic community (see below, p. 60) appears to have been made. As a general although not inviolable rule, consumers' sovereignty must be widely appealing. The principle has its critics among economists, however, and presumably to some extent among others as well. This must be so even among persons who value the welfare of others at least to some extent positively. In the population generally, such "social men" must be preponderant, but there must also be many "economic men" who value the welfare of others not at all, and some "antisocial men" who value it negatively. Naturally, to neither of the latter two types of persons could consumers' sovereignty be impelling.

Aside from consumers' sovereignty, the chief issue regarding the criterion is that concerning the distribution of the community's current output among households. So far as the different households acquire such output through the expenditure of money income, the distribution of output turns on the distribution of such income. In formulating one's values in this respect, it seems difficult to avoid turning quickly to deep-going ethical and political presuppositions such as those bearing on whether the welfare of another is viewed as a good. Yet one does naturally reason again in terms of individual satisfactions and welfare in the sense already understood, although it seems difficult, even so, to reduce one's values for income distribution to any simple principle.

Thus, it is a common feeling that, other things being equal, as one's income increases the corresponding gains in satisfactions will tend to decline. In evaluating income distribution, this feeling of diminishing satisfactions no doubt is to be reckoned with. The satisfactions of one individual, however, may also depend on the incomes of others. Such a dependence is related to but not the same thing as that of its satisfaction from others' consumption of one or another good, and may also be apart from any more basic dependence of its satisfactions on the satisfactions of others. The individual may be more or less satisfied with his consumption depending on the consumption of others, but without his necessarily being concerned whether the consumption of others is satisfying or dissatisfying to them. And if the consumption of others matters to the individual, volume as well as structure may be of concern. The dependence of the individual's satisfactions on the volume of consumption of others presumably tends to be inverse, and must be relatively marked when reference is to others in the same social group, to whose way of life the individual is continually exposed and among whom his status may very often be measured by his consumption level. To repeat, the individual's satisfactions may depend in these ways on the level of consumption of others without his really being concerned in any way about their welfare.

These different forms of interdependence admittedly may be difficult to distinguish in practice. This is especially true of dissatisfactions from the level of another's consumption relative to one's own, on the one hand, and dissatisfactions from another's satisfactions, on the other. But even apart from any concern with the structure of another's consumption, interdependence evidently can go much beyond that where another's welfare is of itself a source of dissatisfaction. As a result, the interdependence may be felt to be much more impelling ethically than it would otherwise be. In any event, interdependence has to be considered in the decision on income distribution as well as in that on consumers' sovereignty.[5]

If one subscribes to consumer's sovereignty, however, he is also committed on this account regarding income distribution. At any rate, in evaluating income distribution, one must consider not only satisfactions from consumption but dissatisfactions from effort, responsibility, and the like, and given consumer's sovereignty these must be evaluated according to the household's own preferences, though the precise implications for income distribution probably are more complex than has been supposed.[6]

The welfare economist may wish to consider these aspects in deciding on his own values regarding income distribution, and in weighing those of different members of the community. The values of these different members must be especially in conflict regarding income distribution. Here social, economic, and antisocial men necessarily differ from each other. In addition, social men differ among themselves, reflecting in part variations in feelings of interdependence such as were just referred to.

FORMULAS FOR THE CRITERION

Each welfare economist, then, must finally decide for himself how to represent the criterion. But there hardly will be any serious dissent if it is held to be given initially by a familiar sort of formula:

$$W = W(U^1, U^2, \ldots, U^i, \ldots, U^n). \tag{1}$$

[5] I said that the different forms of interdependence are difficult to distinguish in practice. In that case in which an individual's satisfactions depend on another's real income, the distinction is also not very clear conceptually, for the comparative levels of real income of different households must vary among the households depending on their tastes. But, while relative real income is thus an ambiguous notion, the kind of interdependence in question, I believe, is still broadly meaningful and also important.

[6] See the Addendum to this chapter.

Here W is social welfare and U^i, the utility of the ith household, represents its welfare from the goods consumed and labor services performed not only by it but by all other households. It may suffice here to refer to a simple community in which these elements alone constitute the economic state. If satisfactions indicate welfare, those derived by a household from the economic state also indicate its utility. At this stage, further satisfactions and dissatisfactions accruing to one household from the *utilities* of others are deemed to have been sufficiently taken into account in the decision to consider W as varying positively with U^i. In effect, then, dissatisfactions from the utilities of others are disregarded.

Formula (1) is very general. Let us abstract provisionally, however, from satisfactions derived by one household from another's consumption. Suppose also that consumers' sovereignty is to prevail. In this case, the criterion takes the more specific form:

$$W = W(I^1, I^2, \ldots, I^i, \ldots, I^n). \qquad (2)$$

Here I^i represents the overt preferences of the ith household among different goods it consumes and labor services it supplies. I^i increases, remains unchanged, or decreases, depending on whether the household moves to a preferable position, to one indifferent to it, or to a less preferable one. W varies positively with I^i.

If consumers' sovereignty prevails, it still may not be considered inviolate. Formula (2), therefore, may have to be modified. If divergencies from the principle are not very numerous, however, the modification might not be material except in special contexts. But should consumers' sovereignty be rejected generally, formula (2) would no longer be applicable. The criterion would have to be given instead by whatever alternative principle or principles were favored.

Formula (2) provides a basis for ranking alternative economic states where, in terms of the goods they consume and services they render, some households "gain" and none "lose," or where some lose and none gain. In situations where some gain and others lose, formula (2) has to be supplemented by an appropriate evaluation of these divergent shifts. So far as the gains and losses result from variation in goods consumed, they represent in effect a change in income distribution, and this must be evaluated together with any changes in work done. For reasons suggested, the welfare economist may feel it inappropriate to subscribe at this point to any simple principle, and one welfare economist may differ from another on the evaluation appropriate to any particular case. But some evaluation is needed if the alternatives in question are to be ranked.

While these evaluations are needed to determine the criterion, they may be introduced in various ways, depending on the information at hand. Thus, if, as is often done, reference is made to "real" national income data as an index of social welfare, a commitment is already presupposed to formula (2). Such data alone could be indicative of social welfare, however, only if there were no change in the distribution of "real" income. To determine the comparative desirability of the alternative states, therefore, it remains to evaluate any change in "real" income distribution together with that in aggregate "real" income. Any changes in the volume of work of different sorts performed by different households must also be considered.[7]

If one household experiences satisfactions or dissatisfactions from the consumption of a good by another, further exceptions to consumers' sovereignty may be in order. Imaginably, the intensity of such effects in the case of one good or another might be measured in the first instance by the amount the second household would pay to induce the first either to consume or not consume it. Even if only one or another commodity is the source of the interdependence, however, its appraisal becomes intertwined with that concerning income redistribution, for, in principle, determination of the "marginal social welfare of money" to different households must also be involved in any final evaluation of the

---

[7] Just how to appraise changes in the community's welfare from "real" national income data is a familiar but perhaps still not sufficiently explored theme. The concern of this essay, however, is with the definition of the criterion of social welfare rather than with the use of national income data as an indicator of such welfare. In any event, I review the latter problem in Chapter 6. There is no need, therefore, to pursue it further here.

interdependence. The involvement with income redistribution becomes the greater when one household experiences satisfactions or dissatisfactions from changes in the levels of aggregate consumption of others. Supposedly, in evaluating income redistributions one must take account of such interrelatedness, although it might be difficult to appraise its import.

In writings on welfare economics, the purpose of this discipline is not always made clear. As seen here, the concern is counseling. Different members of a community may be called on to form an opinion on some measure affecting the economic state. Reference is usually to an action by government, or at least to one that is likely to affect many households. The counseling takes as a point of departure some appropriate criterion by which different economic states may be ranked, and determines in this light whether the action is desirable or undesirable.

Whether involving a governmental measure or otherwise, the action taken may have some value, positive or negative, in its own right, and quite apart from the consequences regarding the prevailing economic state: the same income redistribution might be regarded differently depending on whether it results from a simple transfer from rich to poor or from a measure to increase educational opportunities. Moreover, a change in economic state may in any case have important consequences which are not readily considered in the initial ranking of such states: a change in income distribution may markedly affect the distribution of political power. In a complete appraisal all such "extra-economic" aspects would have to be considered, although they are not usually the subject of any formal analysis.

Counsel might be offered in any community, but attention in this essay is focused, as is most often done in welfare economics, on a Western democratic one.

Formulas adopted for the criterion must be seen in this light. Thus formulas (1) and (2) provide a basis for counseling on measures affecting economic states in a Western democratic community. For such a community, guidance is offered especially to "social men" who might accept consumers' sovereignty in essentials. The formulas are consistent with diverse principles of income distribution, but when the redistribution occurring in any particular case is evaluated the welfare economist's clientele must narrow further: to those who find the evaluation appealing.

As a social scientist, however, the welfare economist will wish to make his values explicit. This requires that he set forth the underlying facts on the redistribution, so far as they are known: the facts on who gains and who loses how much. On this basis, even persons who find his evaluation of income distribution unappealing may benefit from his counsel. They are then free to reformulate it in the light of their own evaluations. To the welfare economist this might be distressing, but he can reflect that without his counsel decision-making might tend to be still worse from his standpoint. Sometimes, the changes in distribution may be too complex to allow for any deep conviction as to their evaluation anyhow, and he may then hesitate to advance one to begin with.

Should formulas other than (1) and (2) be favored for the criterion, persons who might find the counsel appealing would differ accordingly.

In a Western democratic community practically any citizen may be called on to form an opinion on a measure affecting the economic state. He may have to do so either as a public official, or simply as a private citizen who elects such an official. As given by formulas such as (1) and (2), the criterion should be useful in counseling either sort of person, but of more interest is the public official. Yet, for the latter, extra-economic aspects not evaluated in the criterion must be particularly important. Because of his concern for these consequences, especially those relating to his own political status, the public official nevertheless might sometimes find more appealing than he would otherwise the welfare economist's evaluation of income distribution. As a public official, he may be more of a social man than he would be otherwise. But the temptation is great for the welfare economist to try to extend the analysis to embrace extra-economic aspects, particularly political constraints. The public official, however, will probably hesitate to delegate the task of gauging their import, and even if he should do so he may not wish to delegate it to the welfare economist.

While its concern is counseling, welfare economics may be broadly either one or another of two sorts: pure and applied.

In pure welfare economics, the aim is not so much to appraise a particular measure in the real world as to elaborate theoretically a conceptual framework for such an appraisal. This is what is usually attempted in textbooks. In applied welfare economics, the aim is to appraise a particular measure in the real world. As far as possible one seeks to determine the actual gains and losses that result, and appraises the measure accordingly. The approach to the criterion that has been set forth seems appropriate to either of these two branches, but in pure welfare economics no particular evaluation of income redistribution is called for to begin with. As it turns out, the conceptual framework essentially rests on formulas such as (1) and (2). Thus, all the conditions for the famous Paretian optimum may be derived on this basis. This is why, in applied welfare economics, one's counsel can so readily be reformulated in terms of alternative evaluations of income redistribution. An evaluation by someone, however, is always needed for a complete appraisal in applied welfare economics.

This essay and discussions by others of the criterion, to which I shall turn below, belong, strictly speaking, neither to pure nor applied, but to meta-welfare economics. Practitioners of the latter are foolhardy enough to seek to counsel, not different members of the community about measures affecting economic states, but the welfare economist about the criterion. In practice, meta-welfare economics is likely to be merged with welfare economics, pure or applied as the case may be. But the problem of formulating the criterion is conceptually somewhat different from that of applying it. On the one hand, one engages in an exercise in methodology and applied ethics. While this is not entirely extra-scientific it is substantially so. On the other, one draws on the principles of positive economics and adds to them purely deductive precepts. This is no more and no less scientific, therefore, than positive economics. The recurring question of verifiability must be viewed accordingly. Thus, in regard to their verifiability, principles employed in formulating the criterion are not entirely different from those employed in applying it, but they are largely so. The welfare economist, therefore, has reason enough to observe the rule referred to earlier: to make explicit the values in terms of which he defines the criterion.[8]

CAMBRIDGE AND THE NEW WELFARE ECONOMICS

While stressing the value content of the criterion, in "A Reformulation" and elsewhere, I also criticized various analyses which seemed to obscure this aspect. Among these the chief was the justly famous utilitarian one elaborated mainly by Professor Pigou. In the present essay I am nearer the "Cambridge" formulation[9] than I was before, but there are still divergencies. Thus, a feature of the Cambridge formulation is the supposition that what is good for the household regarding consumption is not necessarily the same thing as what it chooses. Nevertheless, it is in some degree still an empirical matter. Evidently I now follow the Cambridge analysis at this point. I am not sure that in this sphere I was previously quite as vulnerable as some other writers to the late Sir Denis Robertson's criticism that "mental juices" were in the process of being "squeezed out" of welfare economics,[10] but I agree that, in formulating the criterion, reference is usefully made to some standard more ultimate than overt preferences.

---

[8] In applying formulas (1) and (2) for the criterion it was said that one derives counsel directed primarily to social men. Yet so far as gains and losses to different households might be specified, the counsel might be of interest to persons with diverse views on income distribution. Does it not follow also, therefore, that it might also be of interest to economic men or even antisocial men? Thus, might not a measure recommended by the welfare economist be appealing to either sort of man depending on just who gained and who lost? Obviously the answer is yes, but the conceptual framework elaborated in pure welfare economics would still be appropriate primarily for social men, and to such persons concrete recommendations made in applied welfare economics might often be appealing even though the precise households which might gain or lose thereby could not be readily delineated.

[9] I used this description formerly, and it may not be amiss to use it again, although scholars outside Cambridge have contributed to and applied the formulation in question. Among different proponents of the Cambridge view of the criterion, there are also doctrinal differences, but these are of only limited interest here. See E. J. Mishan, "A Survey of Welfare Economics," *Economic Journal*, June 1960, p. 205 n. 2 and p. 265 n.

[10] *Utility and All That* (London 1952), pp. 17ff.

The treatment accorded the household's welfare here, however, is still different from that in the Cambridge analysis. Thus, in the *Economics of Welfare*, overt preferences in principle might diverge from satisfactions, although just why is not entirely clear. But in practice they tend generally to conform to satisfactions.[11] However, satisfactions may well diverge from welfare and hence also from "the ethical value of the world" because of the "reflex effects" of different forms of consumption, such as "municipal baths" or a "public bar," on the "quality of people"; and for other reasons.[12] But the concern of welfare economics is only with "economic welfare," or those satisfactions which generally can be "brought into relation with a money measure." Changes in economic welfare presumably tend to be indicative of those in welfare. In any case, the burden of proof lies with those who would hold otherwise.

Distinctions such as Professor Pigou makes between overt preferences and satisfactions and between satisfactions and welfare I believe can be useful, and I have sought to retain them, but I would stress rather more than he seems to do the empirical as distinct from ethical component of judgments as to the relation of satisfactions to welfare. Moreover, to take either category as an

[11] Pigou is explicit about one notable case where this is not so, that of choices between present and future. Such choices lie outside the scope of this essay, but it should be observed that for Pigou the "defective telescopic faculty" leads to an undervaluation of both one's own future satisfactions and those of one's heirs. How the undervaluation might be verified in the former case Pigou did not pause to consider. Presumably it might be illuminating if late in life an individual expressed regret at his previous choices, though he might simply be living longer than he could reasonably have expected, and this possibility must be considered. As for undervaluation of satisfactions of heirs, from the standpoint that will be taken here on "interpersonal comparability" this must be construed as reflecting the application by Pigou of a rule of equity other than that which the individual himself accepts.

On the relation of overt preferences, satisfactions and welfare, I refer to A. C. Pigou, *Economics of Welfare*, 4th ed. (London 1948), pp. 23ff. In "Some Aspects of Welfare Economics," *American Economic Review*, June 1951, Pigou might seem to conceive of these categories differently. Particularly, welfare is identified with satisfactions, and may differ from "goodness." Professor Pigou apparently refers here, however, to economic welfare. His usage, therefore, is really the same as in the *Economics of Welfare*.

[12] *Economics of Welfare*, pp. 12ff.

argument in the criterion is properly seen as representing, not a convention as to the subject matter of welfare economics, but a value premise. The scope of welfare economics is conventional, but the relevant convention concerns the nature of the causes of social welfare rather than the nature of the states of mind to be considered. Thus, reference is to welfare as this is affected by economic causes, and to economic welfare only in this sense rather than as a category that is necessarily psychologically distinct from noneconomic welfare. And rather than presume that economic causes are not offset by noneconomic causes, it would seem reasonable to consider this as a matter to be evaluated in each case.

Finally, in appraising welfare in practice one almost inevitably takes as a point of departure overt preferences such as find expression in money terms, but misgivings about such preferences cannot be suppressed simply because the misgivings relate to aspects more or less beyond the reach of the market. Granting this, one may as well consider misgivings originating in divergencies in overt preferences not only from satisfactions but from welfare.

The famous Cambridge conception of the criterion as being given, in respect of income redistributions, by purely empirical comparisons of satisfactions of different individuals has been under attack ever since Pareto, but is still vigorously defended.[13] As before, I find myself among the critically inclined.

I do not deny that there are minds other than mine; or that one often engages in a mental exercise which is commonly understood to involve comparisons of satisfactions of different people. But the exercise necessarily involves some convention by which the satisfactions of different people are scaled against each other, and for the convention itself there can be no proof. Hence, should any particular comparison be disputed, there is really no final way to corroborate it. Thus, the convention might be simply that people generally would enjoy similar satisfactions in similar circumstances, and given this one may be led to speculate how their satisfactions might compare in dissimilar circumstances. But the

---

[13] See A. C. Pigou, *The American Economic Review*, June 1951; Robertson, *Utility and All That*, pp. 30ff; Sir Roy Harrod, "Themes in Dynamic Theory," *Economic Journal*, September 1963, pp. 416ff.

convention itself is beyond proof. One might seek to classify people also according to different qualities, but the same difficulty arises as before. If we agree that Jones and Smith enjoy equal satisfactions when both appear happy, we may speculate that Jones's satisfactions are less than Smith's when Jones is sad. But how can we know that their satisfactions are equal when both appear happy? Shall we say this only if they have a similar "capacity for enjoyment"? How settle when different persons are similar in this regard? Questions such as these have been raised before but have not yet been answered satisfactorily, nor, I think, can they be.

That a convention can have no proof is, of course, no bar to its introduction, but that one is required does not yet seem generally understood. Also, for purposes of formulating the criterion, any convention introduced should be ethically impelling. It is thus difficult to avoid the conclusion that satisfactions are commensurated, just as apples and nuts ultimately are, by a value premise. And the commensurating convention in effect comes to the same thing as a rule of equity that is to be guiding. Reference, however, has been to satisfactions. These may or may not be reliably indicative of welfare, which is ultimately of concern. In any event, the optimum income distribution is most meaningfully considered as one where among different households there is an equation, not of marginal satisfactions per dollar, or even of marginal individual welfare per dollar, but of marginal *social* welfare per dollar. Also, the income distribution for which this is so is not determined by an empirical comparison of marginal social welfare per dollar among different households. Rather it is determined by the rule of equity, which itself defines social welfare in the sphere of income distribution.[14]

Although in discussions of interpersonal comparability, reference often is made to the comparison of total satisfactions, what matters, of course, is the comparison of increments of satisfactions. What has been said, however, applies to the latter as well as to the former.

As was implied, I do not bar cardinal measurability of satisfactions. To speak of such measurability seems rather pretentious so far as reference is to the ability of the households by intro-

[14] See below, n. 15.

spection to describe qualitatively the possible variation in successive increments of satisfactions that might result from successive increments of income. Apparently, the relation can be scaled more definitely only by observation of overt choices where risk is a factor. Interpretation of resulting measurements in this case appears to be difficult.

But even admitting cardinal measurability, and indeed even supposing the cardinal magnitudes are at hand, these would define the relation of satisfactions to income only in terms of two dimensional constants. Thus, according to familiar reasoning, if $S(M)$ represents any admissible set of magnitudes for the total satisfactions derived from money income, M, so too would all other sets given by the formula,

$$AS(M) + B. \tag{3}$$

Here A and B are the dimensional constants. In the comparison of increments of satisfactions, A alone matters, but this must still be settled by convention. If one specifies levels of income for which $AS'(M)$ for one household equals that for another, the relation of corresponding magnitudes for other income levels is determined. But the initial condition follows from the convention rather than from cardinal measurability. Furthermore, satisfactions as before may not always be indicative of welfare, and whether for this or for some other reason cardinal measurements may not be ethically impelling in any event.

Although something like cardinality has its place, we are concerned in this essay only with the formulation of the criterion. In applying the criterion, ordinality apparently is quite sufficient.

As the Cambridge welfare economists are aware but do not always consider, the utilitarian calculus must in any case be elaborated in a complex way so far as there is interdependence of satisfactions. Under consumers' sovereignty, allowance must also be made for satisfactions and dissatisfactions from such aspects as more onerous or more responsible work.[15]

---

[15] In discussing interpersonal comparability, I have avoided referring to "utility" since in this essay this means for any household welfare derived from an economic state. In the Cambridge analysis, utility is equated with satisfactions. If we suppose, however, that satisfactions do represent welfare from the economic state, utility corresponds to both categories,

Love is, as Sir Denis Robertson said, a "scarce resource."[16] As latter-day utilitarians, Cambridge welfare economists may sometimes overestimate its scarcity, but if men are not always economic no doubt they are often not especially social either. For the welfare economist, the resulting conflicts in values of different individuals concerning economic states must be frustrating, and it must be especially so to one who is himself intensely social, as the Cambridge welfare economists obviously often are.[17] The desire to found welfare economics on a criterion which is at once objective and impersonal and yet ethically appealing to social men is therefore understandable. But even one who would wish to be similarly oriented may properly feel that this endeavor has also been a needless source of doctrinal confusion. It is not useful, either, to conceive of welfare economics, as apparently is done in the Cambridge analysis, as not "a normative science of what ought to be," but "a positive science of what is and tends to be";

and we may consider in this light a further distinctive feature of the Cambridge analysis, the conception of social welfare as the sum of the utilities of different households. Thus the criterion is given by the formula $W = U^1 + U^2 + \ldots U^i \ldots U^n$.

Reasons to prefer the more general formula (1) used here are several: (i) In formula (1), the marginal social welfare per dollar for any household might vary with the utility of any other. The reader may judge how appealing a rule of equity allowing for such deep-going interdependence might be, but nothing is gained analytically by excluding it as is done by the formula given above. (ii) In the formula given above, U^i is often taken essentially to depend on the ith household's own consumption. In (1), however, I have taken U^i to depend also on the consumption of other households, but if it is conceived as not doing so, use of a formula such as (1) might still serve as an indirect, although awkward way of allowing for the interdependence in question. In effect, the interdependence would be among the aspects to be considered in formulating the rule of equity. (iii) Even if we pass by both the foregoing kinds of interdependence, W is properly represented not by the formula above but by this one:

$$W = A^1 U^1 + A^2 U^2 + \ldots A^i U^i \ldots + A^n U^n + B.$$

Thus the relation between W and U^i is understood to be determined only after the corresponding dimensional constant has been fixed, and hence only in the light of the equity rule adopted.

[16] *Economic Commentaries* (London, 1956), p. 154.
[17] See, for example, the preface to the third edition of the *Economics of Welfare* (this is reprinted in the fourth, cited above); also Robertson, *Utility and All That*, p. 39; Harrod, *Economic Journal*, September 1963, pp. 416ff.

as—in other words—a discipline concerned only to inquire into "certain important causes that affect economic welfare," and not with prescription, although the former can provide the basis for the latter.[18]

The kind of treatment of the criterion which has its beginnings in Pareto, and becomes relatively developed in Hicks and Kaldor, no longer seems as widely appealing as it once did, although it is still influential. Concerning this "New Welfare Economics," I shall say only that, as before,[19] I am in accord with the rejection of empirical interpersonal comparisons. But the attempt to make welfare economics "scientific" and "immune from positivist criticism" by omitting from it evaluations of income redistributions is surely misplaced. Value premises are not really avoided, although admittedly those introduced are relatively uncontroversial; and as others, most notably Scitovsky and Samuelson, have shown, nothing of practical interest can be deduced without evaluation of income redistributions in any case. Still, in this essay the evaluation of income redistribution by the welfare economist, as distinct from his clientele, is not quite so important as it might have seemed from my previous discussion. In this respect, therefore, perhaps I am closer to the New Welfare Economics than I was before.

For Pareto, *ophélimité* differed from utility in a way broadly suggestive of that in which overt preferences differ from welfare in this essay. But *ophélimité* alone is considered in Pareto's famous derivation of normative precepts for the socialist state.[20] Similarly, Hicks takes overt preferences as a point of departure, and one gathers that Kaldor, too, would proceed in this way although he is less explicit.[21] The question of whether, if at all,

[18] Pigou, *Economics of Welfare*, pp. 5ff.

[19] In "A Reformulation," which was published in February 1938, and hence preceded the pertinent essays of Hicks and Kaldor, I referred only to the analysis of Pareto, together with the related one of Barone. The standpoint that was called for regarding Hicks and Kaldor was fairly evident, however, and subsequently (see Chapter 9 below) I referred briefly to the former.

[20] *Cours d'Économie Politique*, I (Lausanne, 1896), pp. 3ff; II (Lausanne, 1897), pp. 90ff, 364ff.

[21] See J. R. Hicks, "The Foundations of Welfare Economics," *Economic Journal*, December 1939; N. Kaldor, "Welfare Propositions of Economics and Interpersonal Comparisons of Utility," *Economic Journal*, September 1939.

consumers' sovereignty should be violated and if so on what basis is thus not explored. None of these writers attempts to deal systematically with interdependence.

I turn finally to some more recent analyses of the criterion, which were not considered previously. Although I shall also refer briefly to one formulation that I have discussed before, I must still be very selective.

With a very kind acknowledgment to me, Professor Samuelson in his *Foundations of Economic Analysis* analyzes the determination of the criterion in a manner similar to that in which I analyzed it in "A Reformulation." The values defining the criterion, however, are assumed to be those of some "ethical observer," or are given by "some ethical belief—that of a benevolent despot, or a complete egotist, or 'all men of good will,' a misanthrope, the state, race, or group mind, God, etc."[22] For the welfare economist who is in doubt how to formulate the criterion I fear this has been no more helpful than my affirmation that reference be made to "prevailing values."

Mr. Little's discussion of the determination of the criterion is complex and subtle.[23] Perhaps I am not unfair to put the bare essentials in these terms. The satisfactions an individual derives from consumption are conceptually an empirical matter, and variations in such satisfactions may be inferred with some assurance, although by no means with certainty, from the individual's overt choices. Comparisons may also be made empirically of satisfactions, or increments thereof, of different persons. People make such comparisons every day, and to deny that they could be made would be to deny that there are minds other than one's own. It follows that variations in satisfactions for the community generally are in principle also empirical in nature, and such satisfactions necessarily serve in welfare economics as the criterion of the community's welfare, as this is affected by economic causes.

[22] *Foundations of Economic Analysis* (Cambridge, Mass., 1947), chap. viii, pp. 221, 228.
[23] I. M. D. Little, *A Critique of Welfare Economics*, 2nd ed. (Oxford, 1957).

Nevertheless, value premises are presupposed because it is difficult to carry out "a controlled experiment for a whole community" to see whether satisfactions have increased or not; even if such experiments could be carried out, "there would be considerable disagreement" as to whether satisfactions increased or not; satisfactions of the community are taken to represent the criterion in any case only because they are felt to be a good thing; variations in satisfactions tend to be identified with variations in welfare generally and not merely economic welfare, and this is essentially a subjective matter; and last but not least the language of welfare economics generally is of an emotive or persuasive sort, characteristic of value propositions.

Mr. Little has rightly criticized "A Reformulation" for failing to make clear that, while the criterion presupposes value premises, such premises may have some empirical basis. At least they may do so if what is good for an individual is construed in anything like a conventional Western sense, and as so construed is taken as an argument in the criterion—and no welfare economist will dispute that it should be so construed and so treated in the criterion when reference is to a Western democratic community.

If the satisfactions of the community as a whole were empirically observable, however, I should think that the difficulty in arranging a controlled experiment to observe them would have to be considered as a source of uncertainty about them, but not as a reason why propositions about such satisfactions should be considered as value judgments. After all, the inability to conduct controlled experiments is not peculiar to welfare economics; it is characteristic of positive economics as well. Also, the inability of people to reach agreement even with controlled experiments already strongly suggests that at some point or other the satisfactions of the community generally are even in principle not empirically observable.

In any case, in this essay as in Mr. Little's analysis the premises to be introduced as to what is good for an individual are seen as partly open to empirical inquiry, but I have sought to be somewhat more explicit than he is as to the basis on which such an inquiry might be conducted.[24] Also, for Mr. Little what is

[24] We also differ to some extent in vocabulary. Mr. Little very often refers to the "happiness of an individual," apparently on the understanding that

good for the individual is an argument in the criterion apparently from the very nature of social welfare as it is affected by economic causes. I think the decision to treat it as such is more correctly viewed as following from a value premise. This determines the specific character of the criterion and in a manner which is not the only one imaginable. Also any determination of the criterion, in the last analysis, rests on a value premise not because of the persuasive language employed, but because the very purpose of welfare economics is counseling. The persuasive language is itself employed because this is the purpose. For reasons already indicated, I do not find convincing Mr. Little's arguments for the empirical nature of interpersonal comparisons. Hence, the determination of the criterion here again presupposes value premises.

In "A Reformulation" I did not leave to "superman" the decision as to just what values are to be considered in defining the criterion, but Mr. Little is no doubt right to question the analysis at this point also. Here too I may now have achieved some further clarification.[25]

---

this is the same thing as "economic welfare." See *ibid.*, p. 76. In outlining his reasoning on the determination of the criterion, I have taken the liberty to refer instead to satisfactions, which Mr. Little, I believe, also considers as "economic welfare."

[25] In his *Critique*, chap. vii, Mr. Little also is critical of "A Reformulation" on the ground that I focus on optimum conditions and neglect the problem of delineating an improvement. In this way welfare economics tends to be transformed into "the theory of socialist economics." Since the main concern of "A Reformulation" avowedly was to clarify the value premises of alternative formulations, Mr. Little is in effect finding fault here with my choice of subject matter. But, as he is aware, I did refer briefly to the problem of delineating an improvement, and perhaps not unfruitfully. In any event, partly due to Mr. Little, this matter has been substantially clarified in the course of time. It is still somewhat controversial, however, and while I am now inclined to favor a treatment of it, broadly similar to that advocated by Mr. Little, further clarification is attempted in Chapter 6 below.

In criticizing the "social welfare function" approach to the criterion, Mr. Little refers to Professor Samuelson's analysis in his *Foundations* as well as to "A Reformulation." Professor Samuelson is well able to defend himself, but, as Mr. Little would be the first to acknowledge, anyone who seeks to formulate criteria for an improvement must be in debt to Professor Samuelson, particularly to his famous essay "The Evaluation of Real National Income," *Oxford Economic Papers*, 1950, No. 1.

In formulating the criterion, the welfare economist, I have assumed, will wish to consider the values on alternative economic states held by different members of the community. Where these diverge, he may also wish to consider his own values. But should not the criterion be required fairly to reflect at one and the same time even the divergent values of different members of the community? Particularly, should it not be given by some rule of collective decision-making, for example, "majority rule," which aggregates in an acceptable way the preferences of one and all?

In his celebrated monograph,[26] Professor Arrow answers in the affirmative, but then proceeds to demonstrate that if conceived in the proposed manner the criterion cannot be formulated. Generally, no consistent formula can be derived which also conforms to conditions on the collective decision-making process that are held to be ethically impelling. Yet Little has concluded that Arrow's "impossibility theorem" is more germane to political theory than welfare economics, and elsewhere I have argued similarly, although on rather different grounds.[27] This I still feel is the correct view, but the limited applicability of Arrow's analysis to welfare economics perhaps can now be seen more clearly.

Thus I argued previously that Arrow's analysis might apply to welfare economics if one were prepared to accept a particular view of the purpose of this discipline:[28]

According to this view, the problem is to counsel not citizens generally but public officials. Furthermore, the values to be taken as data are not those which might guide the official if he were a private citizen. The official is envisaged instead as more or less neutral ethically. His one aim in life is to implement the values of other citizens as given by some rule of collective decision-making. Arrow's theorem apparently contributes to this sort of welfare economics the negative finding that no

[26] Kenneth J. Arrow, *Social Choice and Individual Values*, 2nd ed. (New York, 1963).

[27] See I. M. D. Little, "Social Choice and Individual Value," *Journal of Political Economy*, October 1952, and my essay, Chapter 2 above. The literature on the impossibility theorem is now voluminous, although very often attention is focused on aspects not of immediate interest here. For references, see the new chap. viii that Arrow has added to his study in its new edition.

[28] Above, p. 37.

consistent social ordering could be found to serve as a criterion of social welfare in the counselling of the official in question.

I also considered other imaginable applications of the impossibility theorem to welfare economics, but the foregoing I believe is the most interesting one, and Arrow has now explained that his "interpretation of the social choice problem agrees fully with that given by Bergson. . . ."[29] The import of the impossibility theorem for welfare economics, therefore, hinges on how one regards such a conception of the purpose of this discipline. With this there can be no quarrel on formal grounds, but in the paragraph quoted above I sought only to formulate the purpose appropriate to the impossibility theorem. The purpose of welfare economics as I would have it is quite different. In counseling a public official I assume that the welfare economist might take as data the same values he employs in counseling generally. At least, no attempt need be made in behalf of the official to aggregate values of individuals in accord with an ethically impelling rule of collective decision-making. At this point I believe I have only expressed the conventional presupposition in welfare economics. Arrow's analysis, therefore, represents a break with this discipline as traditionally conceived.

But, granting this, may not Arrow's conception of how to counsel a public official on measures affecting economic states still be the more appropriate one? In trying to answer, the reader will wish to consider that with the criterion formulated as I have proposed the official might not always find the resultant counsel appealing. He might have to adapt it to his own values on economic states, particularly regarding income distribution. Because of political constraints, the counsel might have to be adapted the more, although at this point the criterion as formulated might also turn out to be appealing after all. Rather than make any definite recommendation even on economic aspects, the welfare economist may prefer simply to leave it to the public official finally to evaluate the new measure in the light of his own values on income distribution and his appraisal of political constraints.

[29] Arrow, p. 107.

Arrow assumes that the official has no values of his own on economic states. Still, Arrow would go beyond the welfare economist as I conceive the latter by trying on behalf of the public official to analyze the political process. But even should the official have no values on economic states, he presumably would wish to retain office. He hardly would be especially interested, therefore, in an exercise concerning whether a consistent criterion of social welfare can be extracted from a rule of collective decision-making that conforms to some ethically impelling conditions; conditions, that is, which apparently would preclude consideration of such aspects as the political loyalties and influence of different groups, and the manner in which choice of one alternative rather than another might alter such loyalties and influence.

But is this not to say that the actual political process is less than ideal? And if one is to counsel the public official at all, should not the counsel conform to the ideal? Without urging conformity to such a political ideal, the welfare economist might still hope that the world would be a better place to live in with his counsel than without it. Moreover, he may not feel that Arrow's conditions properly define the ideal political process to begin with. At least, opinions may differ on how impelling they are ethically. At this point, however, we surely have left welfare economics for political theory.[30]

[30] By implication, Arrow considers that he not only has analyzed correctly the problem of formulating the criterion, but has also provided a basis for value criticism. Thus, one of his chief conditions is that of the Independence of Irrelevant Alternatives: The social ordering of any specified alternatives is independent of the presence or absence of some alternatives other than those under consideration. This condition is seen as impelling in respect not only of collective decision-making but of the formulation of an individual's own values on economic states. Particularly it bars formula (2) from the latter standpoint.

How impelling the Condition of Independence of Irrelevant Alternatives is at this point the reader must judge for himself, but I have already stated reasons for not considering it so (above, pp. 39ff.). Perhaps my reasoning was open to criticism so far as my reference to "need" may have been construed as implying empirical interpersonal utility comparisons, but I do not think this is at all essential. To paraphrase an example Arrow uses, one may decide on a distribution of orange juice and vitamin tablets that is equitable to all, and feel impelled, when the supply of orange juice dries up, to supply more of the vitamin tablets to the sick than to the healthy. In doing so one apparently would violate the Condi-

The impossibility theorem has been construed as pointing to a flaw, possibly a fatal flaw, in welfare economics. There is, I think, no need for concern on this score.

In his notably lucid exposition of the principles of welfare economics, Mr. Graaff is explicit that the inclusion of individual welfare as an argument in the criterion, and one with which the criterion varies positively, rests on a value premise.[31] With this

---

tion of Irrelevant Alternatives, but might still feel it in order to assure the sick the requirements for recovery at the expense of denial of abundance to the healthy. This might be deemed ethically impelling even though one admittedly could not compare empirically the satisfactions of the sick to those of the healthy.

I alluded earlier to the possibility that in deciding one's own values for economic states one might take as a point of departure "deep-going ethical and political presuppositions." This raises a question as to whether Arrow's conditions might not be a basis for value criticism in another sense: more or less like the public official to whom Arrow addresses himself, one feels that ultimately the most desirable values on economic states are these obtained by aggregation of everyone's values, through a collective decision-making process conforming to Arrow's conditions. On this, and on the ethical value of Arrow's condition *qua* conditions on collective decision-making, see above, pp. 30ff.

On p. 31 I argue that intransitivity in collective choices would mean that "government actions might tend to go around in circles." Just what would happen in the case of collective intransitivity presumably would depend on the specific institutional arrangements. Thus, government actions would indeed tend to go around in circles if, say, the community considered in any time period only one alternative to the pre-existing situation, and any collective choice between the alternative and the pre-existing situation were implemented. Suppose, however, that in behalf of the community some executive should seek in any period to realize an optimum among a series of alternatives that were open. Here, the intransitivity would mean rather that the executive's actions would be indeterminate, at least until he received further instructions. But, granting such complexities, I still believe I was correct on the more basic point that I made previously: that collective transitivity is to be valued not for its own sake, but for its consequences, and that, depending on the individual's own values, the consequences of collective intransitivity might not always be undesirable.

I also argued previously (p. 31) that in respect of individual choices, "logical consistency by its very nature is an ethical ultimate and accordingly cannot be deduced from any other value." Strictly speaking, this is true regarding consistency of individual values which are themselves of an ultimate sort. For individual values of a lower order, however, consistency presumably should be deducible as a desideratum from more ultimate values, provided these are consistent.

[31] J. de V. Graaff, *Theoretical Welfare Economics* (Cambridge, 1957), pp. 4ff, 33–34.

there can be no quarrel here. Welfare from consumption, however, is identified with overt preferences, for "it is very hard to think of a way of defining welfare *ex post*," and any attempt to distinguish for people other than ourselves between such welfare and "welfare *ex ante* . . . leads very rapidly to a paternalistic approach." One may dislike paternalism and still hold that appraisal of the overt preferences of others can in some degree be meaningful. Mr. Graaff apparently considers, as I do, that interpersonal comparisons involve a value judgment. However, he does not explore on what basis this might be made, though as a rule theoretic analysis is felt to be worthwhile only where there is likely to be wide agreement on ethical premises. For this reason, attention is focused chiefly on implications of the single premise that social welfare varies positively with the welfare of any individual. Graaff's essay, therefore, falls under the heading of what has been called here pure, as distinct from applied, welfare economics.

Among the foregoing writers, interdependence is necessarily of only limited interest to Arrow. This phenomenon may affect the values of any one individual for economic states, and so far as it does it receives due consideration when the values of different individuals for economic states are aggregated. For the rest, the writers referred to all consider interdependence, and Little and Graaff dwell on it in some detail. Where individual welfare is taken as a good, however, they apparently would have the criterion reflect all forms of interdependence. In this essay, use of formula (1) as the criterion implies that in principle one discounts dissatisfactions from other people's satisfactions, although admittedly it might be difficult in practice to distinguish such dissatisfactions from others.

Addendum

CONSUMERS' SOVEREIGNTY
AND "REAL" INCOME DISTRIBUTION

On p. 57 I refer to the relation of consumers' sovereignty and the evaluation of "real" income distribution. I shall try here to be more explicit on this question, on which I suspect there are often misapprehensions. Indeed, I myself have been prey to them.

It suffices to consider a simple community in which there are only two households. For the moment, let us assume that the only variable elements in the economic state are the amounts of two different consumers' goods, X and Y, consumed by each household.[32] If, as is advisable, we abstract here from interrelatedness, formula (1) takes the specific form:

$$W = W[U^1(x_1, y_1), U^2(x_2, y_2)]. \tag{1a}$$

We may as well assume also that the utility realized by each household from its consumption conforms fully with its overt preferences, and that consumers' sovereignty is accepted on this basis. The variant of formula (2) that applies to the case of two households, thus, comes in effect to the same thing as formula (1a). Either formula may be taken to represent social welfare.

For some given supplies of X and Y, suppose that a distribution of the two goods between households has been established which is considered optimal. According to familiar reasoning, these conditions must then obtain:

$$W_1 U_1^1 = W_2 U_1^2; \tag{4}$$

$$W_1 U_2^1 = W_2 U_2^2. \tag{5}$$

The subscripts are employed in the usual way to denote partial derivatives. Taken together, (4) and (5) imply that the two households are on their mutual "contract curve," that is, no further redistribution of X and Y between them is possible such that one household might gain without the other losing. Analytically, this requirement may be formulated in this way:

$$\frac{U_1^1}{U_2^1} = \frac{U_1^2}{U_2^2}. \tag{6}$$

---

[32] Reference to only two consumers' goods simplifies the analysis without, I believe, any consequential loss of generality.

ADDENDUM: CONSUMERS' SOVEREIGNTY

Conditions (4) and (5) also mean, however, that for either commodity the marginal social welfare realized per unit consumed by one household is the same as that realized per unit consumed by the other. In other words, in terms of the values defining the criterion, no redistribution of either commodity alone is possible which would increase the community's welfare. Any redistribution of either commodity alone, of course, must benefit one household and injure the other, but from the standpoint of the values defining the criterion, the benefit to the one might outweigh the injury to the other. Given (4) and (5), opportunities for such redistributions must already have been exploited.

Conditions (4) and (5) may also be interpreted in another way. Suppose that the consumption of X and Y by each household is valued at some prices, p and q, such that for, say the first household,

$$\frac{U_1^1}{U_2^1} = \frac{p}{q}.$$ (7)

By implication, we must also have

$$\frac{U_1^2}{U_2^2} = \frac{p}{q}.$$ (8)

Furthermore, in terms of these prices, the marginal social welfare per dollar must be the same for the two households. Taken together with (7) and (8), this requirement is formally equivalent to (4) and (5). Thus, the marginal social welfare per dollar is the same for the two households if either

$$\frac{W_1 U_1^1}{p} = \frac{W_2 U_1^2}{p},$$ (9)

or

$$\frac{W_1 U_2^1}{q} = \frac{W_2 U_2^2}{q}.$$ (10)

Both these conditions must follow from (4) and (5) for any p and q, but we may also deduce (4) and (5) from either (9) or (10) if we know (7) and (8).

In Figure 1, $0'$ and $0''$ represent the consumption of X and Y by the two households that corresponds to an optimum allocation. Hence, the slope at $0'$ of the indifference curve of the first household that goes through $0'$ is the same as the slope at $0''$ of the indifference curve of the

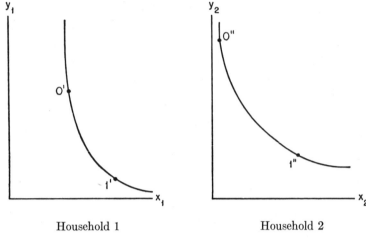

Household 1   Household 2

FIGURE 1

second household that goes through $0''$. With this, the households are on their contract curve. In Figure 2, I show the "point" utility-possibility schedule, 00, that corresponds to the total supplies of goods available to the two households together, X^0, Y^0. Also shown is a curve of constant W. At α this is tangent to the utility possibility schedule (i.e., $W_1/W_2 = F_1/F_2$, where $F(U^1, U^2) = 0$ is the utility possibility schedule). This again means that the marginal social welfare per unit of either commodity or (in terms of appropriately determined prices) per dollar is the same for the two households, for as is readily seen $(F_1/F_2) = (U_1^2/U_1^1) = (U_2^2/U_2^1)$.

Suppose now that total supplies of X and Y vary in such a way that it is feasible for each household to remain on the same indifference curve as before. Also, at the new consumption levels, which are thus experienced ($1'$ and $1''$ in Figure 1), the households are on the contract curve corresponding to the new supply position, X^1, Y^1. To come to the relation of consumers' sovereignty and "real" income distribution, what is in question from this standpoint, I believe, is this: Given consumers' sovereignty and given that $0'$ and $0''$ represent an optimum use of X^0 and Y^0, what commitment, if any, is implied as to whether $1'$ and $1''$ represent an optimum use of X^1 and Y^1?

The answer is that a commitment is indeed implied. Moreover, it may seem odd. Once we have decided that welfare is given by expres-

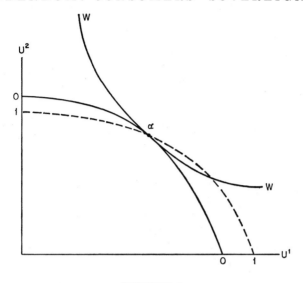

FIGURE 2

sion (1a), and that $0'$ and $0''$ represent an optimum use of X^0 and Y^0, we are no longer free to decide, by introducing further value judgments, whether or not $1'$ and $1''$ represent an optimum use of X^1 and Y^1. Since W depends only on U^1 and U^2, and U^1 and U^2 are constant for the variations in consumption in question, W_1 and W_2 are unchanged. Hence, whether or not conditions (4) and (5) continue to be satisfied in the new supply position depends entirely on the nature of the household utility functions, U^1 and U^2. These are understood here to be only ordinal indicators, but W must be related to any pair of ordinal indicators considered in such a way that the resultant ranking of economic states conforms to the values taken as guiding. Hence, for any given pair of ordinal indicators, there is a corresponding W, and, to repeat, W_1 and W_2 are unchanged by the shift in supplies. Thus, whether or not $1'$ and $1''$ will represent an optimum use of X^1 and Y^1 depends only on the comparative tastes of the two households. With supplies of X^1 and Y^1 available, depending on the comparative tastes of the two households, a redistribution of "real" income favoring one household or the other may well be called for.

Let us try to be more precise regarding the circumstances in which a redistribution is in order and the nature of such a redistribution.

81

Consider the ratio

$$D = \frac{W_1 U_1^1}{W_2 U_1^2}. \tag{11}$$

This represents the ratio of the marginal social welfare derived from the consumption of X by the first household to the marginal social welfare derived from the consumption of X by the second household. Initially, with supplies X^0 and Y^0 allocated in an optimal way, D is unity. We wish to know whether and how D would vary if supplies should change so that each of the two households would enjoy the same utility as it did initially. Also, the households are supposed to continue on a contract curve. If D remains constant at unity, no redistribution of "real" income is called for. If D increases, however, "real" income must be redistributed favorably to the first household, in order to bring D back down to the optimal level of unity; and if D decreases, "real" income must be redistributed favorably to the second.

Although reference has been made to large changes in supplies, it suffices to consider the behavior of D in the neighborhood of the initial optimum. Differentiating with respect to, say, x_1, we have

$$\left(\frac{dD}{dx_1}\right)_{U^1,U^2} =$$

$$\frac{W_2 U_1^2 W_1 (dU_1^1/dx_1)_{U^1} - W_1 U_1^1 W_2 (dU_1^2/dx_2)_{U^2}(dx_2/dx_1)_{U^1,U^2}}{(W_2 U_1^2)^2} \tag{12}$$

As is appropriate here, variations are considered along a path for which U^1 and U^2 are constant. W_1 and W_2 are also constant along this path, and are so treated in the differentiation. Also, all derivatives are to be evaluated at an initial position which is optimal, and hence one at which (4) and (5) hold. We may reformulate (12), therefore, as

$$\left(\frac{dD}{dx_1}\right)_{U^1,U^2} = \left(\frac{d\log U_1^1}{dx_1}\right)_{U^1} - \left(\frac{d\log U_1^2}{dx_2}\right)_{U^2}\left(\frac{dx_2}{dx_1}\right)_{U^1,U^2} \tag{13}$$

While variations are along a path for which U^1 and U^2 are constant, they must also be such that the two households remain on their contract curve. From this we have

$$\left(\frac{dx_2}{dx_1}\right)_{U^1,U^2} = \left(\frac{d(U_1^1/U_2^1)}{dx_1}\right)_{U^1} \Big/ \left(\frac{d(U_1^2/U_2^2)}{dx_2}\right)_{U^2} \tag{14}$$

ADDENDUM: CONSUMERS' SOVEREIGNTY

In (13) and (14) the variation of D with respect to x_1 is expressed in terms of marginal utilities. For present purposes, such a formulation has its point, but the variation of D may also be expressed in terms of marginal rates of substitution, and this formulation, too, is of value. Let

$$G^1(x_1, y_1) = \frac{U^1_1}{U^1_2}, \tag{15}$$

and

$$G^2(x_2, y_2) = \frac{U^2_1}{U^2_2}. \tag{16}$$

These, of course, are the marginal rates of substitution of interest. It follows at once that

$$\left(\frac{dx_2}{dx_1}\right)_{U^1,U^2} = \frac{(dG^1/dx_1)_{U^1}}{(dG^2/dx_2)_{U^2}}. \tag{17}$$

Also, as may readily be proven,

$$\left(\frac{d \log U^1_1}{dx_1}\right)_{U^1} = \frac{G^1_1}{G^1}, \tag{18}$$

and

$$\left(\frac{d \log U^2_1}{dx_2}\right)_{U^2} = \frac{G^2_1}{G^2}. \tag{19}$$

Taken together with equations (13) and (14), these additional relations represent the alternative formulation that is desired.

Whether considered with or without (17), (18), and (19), equations (13) and (14) tell us whether and how D varies in the neighborhood of the optimum. Evidently, as was indicated, the change depends only on the tastes of the two households. Thus, that the shape of W does not matter is seen at once, since none of the terms on the right of (13) and (14) turns on this aspect. From (17), (18), and (19), the variation in D is also seen to be independent of the ordinal indicators used for the utilities of the two households.

To proceed further we must consider that a term such as those on the right of (14) represents for a household the rate of change, with respect to its consumption of X, of the ratio of its marginal utilities from X and Y, or of its marginal rate of substitution between the two commodities.

The consumption of Y is understood to vary with that of X so that total utility is constant. If, as is usually assumed in theory, the household's indifference curves are convex from below, a rate of change such as is in question must be negative. Moreover, its magnitude depends on the degree to which the two commodities are substitutable one for the other. The rate of change is greater the less the substitutability.

By implication, for variations considered, the consumption of X by the second household must increase along with that of the first, and $(dx_2/dx_1)_{U^1 U^2}$ is positive. It also exceeds, equals, or falls short of unity depending on whether substitutability is greater for the second household than the first, is the same for the two households, or is less for the second household than for the first.

A term like those on the right of (14) also represents the reciprocal of the gradient of the so-called compensated demand schedule for X, that is, the schedule representing the relation of the consumption of X to its price, with money income varying concomitantly so that the household's utility is unchanged. The price of Y, however, must be taken as unity.

As for the other terms on the right of (13), $(d \log U_1^1/dx_1)_{U^1}$ represents the relative rate of change in the marginal utility of X with respect to the consumption of X by the first household. As before, reference is to a change in consumption of X such that the household's utility is unchanged. The expression $(d \log U_1^2/dx_2)_{U^2}$ represents the corresponding variation for the second household. The two terms might seem to be such as to reflect the Law of Diminishing Marginal Utility, and in fact the change in marginal utility of concern should usually be negative, as is that considered in the Law of Diminishing Marginal Utility, but, as will appear, this need not always be so. More basically, the Law of Diminishing Marginal Utility depends on the ordinal indicator considered for utility, while as was implied the terms now of interest relate only to the indifference map. Particularly, a term such as is in question relates to the spacing between indifference curves, or rather to the variation in such spacing. Thus, assuming $(d \log U_1^1/dx_1)_{U^1}$ is negative, the greater it is absolutely, the more the increase in the increment in X needed for the first household to reach a neighboring and higher indifference curve as consumption varies along any one such curve. The variation in increment of X is understood relatively to the increment yielding some shift in indifference level that is taken as a standard. Alternatively, as may be seen from (18), reference is to the relative rate of change in the marginal rate of substitution, and hence in the gradient of the indifference curve, as the first household increases

84

its consumption of X, that of Y being constant. The expression $(d \log U_1^2/dx^2)_{U^2}$ is to be construed similarly in respect to the second household's preferences and consumption.

A term such as is considered also determines the direction of change in consumption in respect of a change in the household's income, though curiously immediate reference is to the consumption of Y rather than that of X. Thus, if the consumption of Y increases with income, $(d \log U_1^1/dx_1)_{U^1}$ and $(d \log U_1^2/dx_2)_{U^2}$ must be negative. Given the degree of substitutability between X and Y, however, the smaller these terms are absolutely, the smaller is the degree to which the consumption of Y increases with income, and hence the greater the degree to which the consumption of X increases with income. At least, this is so as between households confronted with the same commodity prices.[33]

What follows as to the change in D? Along the path in question, this represents the difference between two terms, one being the relative change in the marginal utility of X to the first household and the other the product of the corresponding aspect for the second household and the change in the consumption of X by the second household that is associated with any given change in consumption of X by the first. The latter product, therefore, represents the relative change in the marginal utility of X to the second household that is associated with the given change in consumption of X by the first.

In response to the change in supplies in question, then D would continue to be unity, as it was initially, whenever the relative change in the marginal utility of X for the second household that is associated with a given change in consumption of X by the first is the same as the relative change in the marginal utility of X for the first household that results from the change in its consumption. Also, such a relation obviously would obtain whenever the tastes of the two households are the same, for in this case $(dx_2/dx_1)_{U^1,U^2}$ is unity, and $(d \log U_1^1/dx_1)_{U^1}$ equals $(d \log U_1^2/dx_2)_{U^2}$. Or, rather, those results follow if tastes are the same, and, as is likely in this case, formula (1a) is symmetric, so that the initial optimum is one where the two households consume equal amounts of X and Y.

Of more interest, however, is the case where tastes differ. Here, except in special circumstances, D could hardly be expected to be unchanged as supplies vary. Depending on the tastes of the two households, however, it might increase or decrease. Suppose, for example,

---

[33] These relations follow from the familiar formulas for income-demand schedules.

that Y is not for the first household and is for the second readily substitutable for X. In this case $(dx_2/dx_1)_{U^1,U^2}$ must exceed unity. Suppose, too, that relative to its initial level the marginal utility of X declines little for the first household as the household's consumption of X increases, that of Y decreasing to assure that utility is unchanged, and that the corresponding variation in the marginal utility of X is very pronounced for the second household. In this case D would increase, and markedly. Circumstances in which it would decrease are also readily perceived.

Reference has been made to the relation of different terms in (13) and (14) to demand schedules. It should be observed that the variation of D with respect to x, may be expressed entirely in terms of such schedules. Particularly, as may be demonstrated,

$$\left(\frac{dD}{dx_1}\right)_{U^1,U^2} = \frac{q}{p(dx_1/dp)_{U^1}}\left[\left(\frac{dy_1}{dM_1}\right)_{p,q} - \left(\frac{dy_2}{dM_2}\right)_{p,q}\right]. \quad (20)$$

Here $(dx_1/dp)_{U^1}$ is the gradient of the schedule of the first household's compensated demand for X in respect of its price, $(dy_1/dM_1)_{p,q}$ is the gradient of the first household's demand for Y in respect of money income, and $(dy_2/dM_2)_{p,q}$ is the corresponding feature for the second household. I shall leave it to the reader to interpret the variation of D in respect of X in terms of (20).

I have tacitly assumed that the change in supplies is such that the amount of X available increases. With this, the amount of Y available presumably must decrease. Restatement of the argument for the case where the amount of Y increases and that of X decreases is left to the reader.

It may be useful to relate the foregoing to Figure 2. The utility possibility schedule 00 shown there corresponds to supplies of X^0 and Y^0. With supplies of X^1 and Y^1, there normally would be another such curve. Since, with the new supplies, we have imposed the condition that the two households could enjoy the same utility as before while being on their new contract curve, the new utility possibility schedule, 11, must have one point, α, in common with the old one. Essentially what has been said is that, with tastes of the two households the same, the slope of 11 must be the same as that of 00 at α. Hence α remains the optimum. With tastes of the two households different, the slope of 11 at α will differ from that of 00. Hence α can no longer be the optimum.

ADDENDUM: CONSUMERS' SOVEREIGNTY

In Figure 2, the latter alternative is the one illustrated.[34] The case shown is also one where D increases and a redistribution favorable to the first household is indicated.

I said that the commitment regarding "real" income distribution when supplies vary from X^0 to Y^0 to X^1 and Y^1 might seem odd. Since, with supplies of X^1 and Y^1, each household enjoys the same utility as it did with supplies of X^0 and Y^0, some may feel that if the marginal social welfare per dollar were the same for two households initially, it should still be the same with supplies changed. Hence α should still be the optimum after the change. This should be so whether tastes are the same or differ. At least, this was my own presupposition when I began to think again about this matter, and it came as quite a surprise to me that, depending on whether tastes are the same or different, one might actually be committed to redistribute "real" income so as to favor one or another of the two households.

Yet one might be, and the commitment perhaps becomes more palatable when one considers that in his decision as to what is optimal initially, one in effect commensurates, from the standpoint of social welfare, small changes in the consumption of the two households in the neighborhood of the optimum. The same small changes in consumption, however, may mean very different things to the household, depending on the household's initial budget position. This is so even among alternative initial budget positions yielding the same utility. Also, the difference in significance persists even though, as here, utilities are only ordinally measurable. Moreover, if such gains may vary for any one household, they may also vary differently for different households. In effect, we find that there must be a redistribution in favor of the household which, in response to a change in supplies such as has been considered, experiences the more limited relative decline in such gains from a small increment in the consumption of the product that increases, and which is relatively reluctant to substitute an alternative product for this one.

In his monograph on welfare economics,[35] Mr. Graaf distinguishes two related frontiers. To refer, as before, to a community with only two

---

[34] Although with tastes the same the two utility possibility schedules have the same slope at α (in this case, for suitably chosen ordinal indicators, U^1 and U^2 would also be equal at α and the slope there would be -1), I believe the two schedules would as a rule diverge elsewhere. As before, I assume that when tastes are the same, formula (1a) is symmetric.

[35] *Theoretical Welfare Economics*, pp. 45ff.

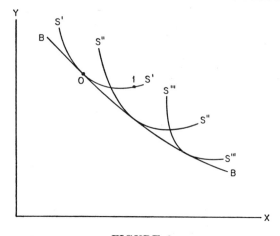

FIGURE 3

commodities, X and Y, and only two households: The first frontier is the Scitovsky, more usually known as the Scitovsky community indifference curve. For any given level of consumption of one commodity by the two households together, the Scitovsky frontier indicates the minimum amount of the other commodity which is required for the two households to experience any given levels of utilities. The second frontier, which Mr. Graaf kindly designates as the Bergson, relates to any given level of consumption of one commodity by the two households the amount of the other which is required if the community's welfare, as given by formula (1a), is to be constant.

In Figure 3 are shown a series of Scitovsky frontiers, each corresponding to some given levels of utilities for the two households. The collection of utilities considered in delineating any one of the Scitovsky frontiers depicted is understood to yield the same welfare for the community generally as the collection considered in delineating any other. Hence, corresponding to all the Scitovsky frontiers depicted, there is only one Bergson frontier. This is also shown.

As Mr. Graaf explains, the Bergson frontier must be an envelope, or at least inner limit, of the Scitovsky frontiers to which it corresponds, but, as is not made entirely clear, while a Scitovsky frontier presupposes that the households are on a contract curve, i.e., that (6) obtains, the Bergson frontier has the property that for any point on it a full optimum is realized in respect of "real" income distribution; thus, both (4) and (5) obtain. That this is so is seen at once when it is consid-

ADDENDUM: CONSUMERS' SOVEREIGNTY

ered that if either (4) or (5) did not obtain, it would always be possible to realize the same social welfare with less of either commodity, or both. This could always be done by redistributing some of one commodity or the other in favor of the household for which the marginal social welfare per unit is higher.

If we bear these facts in mind, the foregoing analysis may be restated in another interesting way. Thus, the allocation of X_0 and Y_0 from which we began is necessarily a position on a Bergson frontier. In the figure, this is designated as 0. The same position must also lie on some Scitovsky frontier, shown as $S'S'$. If, now, supplies change to X_1 and Y_1, and the two households experience the same levels of utility as before, and yet remain on a contract curve, evidently the community must have shifted to another position, say 1, on $S'S'$. What has been argued here essentially is that, while 1 is on the same Scitovsky frontier as 0, normally it will not be on a Bergson frontier. Either (4) or (5) is violated, or both relations are. A redistribution of "real" income is required, therefore, if the Bergson frontier is to be reattained.

Though reference has been to choices between consumers' goods, I was first led to speculate about the relation of consumers' sovereignty to "real" income distribution where labor is a variable. But, to turn to the latter case, it may suffice to refer to circumstances in which choices concerning labor relate only to the length of the working day. Also, what is to be concluded here becomes evident when we consider that, if we view as leisure one of the two commodities just treated, all that has been said still applies.

"Real" income must now be understood, however, to include leisure as well as consumption. Also, so far as a redistribution is in order, the effect might sometimes be to favor and sometimes to penalize a household which in changing circumstances is led to work relatively long hours and in effect "earn" more money. Thus, suppose leisure should become more abundant, but supplies of the single consumer's good remaining in question contract so that each household enjoys the same utility as before. Initially, the allocation of leisure and the consumers' good between households was optimal; subsequently the two households are still on a contract curve. Should the first household be relatively reluctant to substitute leisure for consumption, the change in circumstances would mean that it would tend to reduce its work-day less than the second. Should the first household also experience only a relatively limited decline in the marginal utility of leisure, as leisure and consumption vary as supposed, D would increase and a redistribution favorable to the first household would be in order. Imaginably, however, the decline in the marginal utility of leisure might be so great that D would decrease. If so, a redistribution favorable to the second household would be called for.

The relation of consumers' sovereignty to "real" income distribution is a subject to which I have already referred in earlier essays that are reproduced in this volume. As will be evident, my earlier treatment of this matter left something to be desired. This is especially true of the discussion on p. 202.

While I have felt impelled to try here to treat systematically the relation of consumers' sovereignty and "real" income distribution, the practical consequences may not be very great. For one thing, under consumers' sovereignty one is committed, even in principle, with respect to the evaluation of "real" income distribution only for variations from some initial position. In judging whether the initial position itself is optimal, one is still free to refer to any standpoint on equity that is appealing. For another, one may be led not so much to redistribute "real" income in the manner suggested as to feel even more uncertain than he might have felt otherwise just what "real" income distribution is ever to be considered optimal. The knowledge that a redistribution is called for in the circumstances envisaged might serve only to weaken conviction that any particular distribution is really optimal.

PART II. PROBLEMS OF MEASUREMENT

4

REAL INCOME, EXPENDITURE

PROPORTIONALITY, AND FRISCH'S

NEW METHODS*

An essential and at the same time dubious element in the technique of measuring marginal utility developed by Frisch is the substitution of one variable, the price of living, for the prices of individual commodities in the utility function. Despite the importance of this procedure to his analysis, Frisch neither in his *Sur un problème d'économie pure*[1] nor in his later and more exhaustive *New Methods of Measuring Marginal Utility*[2] advances a satisfactory explanation.

The substitution is the first step in Frisch's analysis. Using it as basis, he achieves by an ingenious transformation the simplification of expressing the *real* money utility—the marginal utility of real income—as a function of real income alone. And with the additional assumption that one commodity, sugar, has an

* Originally published in *The Review of Economic Studies*, October 1936, with an acknowledgment of my great indebtedness and gratitude to Professor Wassily Leontief for his encouragement and criticism and to Professor Paul Samuelson. The latter suggested the likelihood of the expenditure proportionality condition stated on p. 107. Since the essay appeared, Professor Samuelson has pointed out to me that in solving the differential equations (44) and (45), the case where $n = 0$ should have been treated as a special one, with the solutions taking a familiar logarithmic form.

[1] *Norsk Matematisk Forenings Skrifter*, Serie 1, Nr. 16, 1926.
[2] *Beiträge zur Ökonomischen Theorie* (Tübingen, 1932). Hereafter referred to as *New Methods*.

independent utility,[3] he expresses marginal utility, more precisely *real* money utility, in a form which lends itself readily to statistical measurement.

Given the first step, the logic of the subsequent development cannot be challenged. But the first step is open to two criticisms: First, the concepts of price of living and real income, if they are to be used in theoretical work, require exact formulation.[4] While Frisch devotes some attention to the subject of index numbers in his *New Methods*,[5] his discussion is confined to the problem of making distance comparisons of real income and of the price of living; he does not give these variables the precise definition which their insertion in a utility function demands.[6] Second, the substitution of the single variable, price of living, for several variables in the utility function cannot be treated as it is by Frisch—as a plausible first approximation.[7] As Allen has pointed out, an assumption, rather than an approximation, is involved.[8] And the nature of this assumption must remain in doubt so long as Frisch's concepts are not strictly defined.

Fortunately, Frisch has not allowed this state of affairs to continue. In a recent and important paper, "Annual Survey of General Economic Theory: The Problem of Index Numbers,"[9] he reformulates the discussion of index numbers which appeared in *New Methods*.[10] As a by-product of this revision, the develop-

---

[3] The utility of that commodity thus depends only on the quantity of it consumed.

[4] It is interesting to note in this connection that Keynes, in his latest work on monetary theory, forsakes such concepts as general price level, stock of real capital, and national dividend because of their lack of precision. See *The General Theory of Employment, Interest, and Money*, (New York, 1936) chap. iv.

[5] Section 9.

[6] R. G. D. Allen, in the course of a general consideration of Frisch's analysis, makes a similar criticism: "On the Marginal Utility of Money and Its Application," *Economica*, May 1933, p. 192.

[7] *New Methods*, p. 5.

[8] *Economica*, May 1933, p. 193.

[9] *Econometrica*, January 1936. Hereafter referred to as *Annual Survey*.

[10] Frisch's contribution to index number theory in his *New Methods* is based on the methods of measuring marginal utility developed in the same work. The reformulation in *Annual Survey* is chiefly a response to criticisms by Allen (*Economica*, May 1933), of both the marginal utility technique and the index number discussion.

ment of his technique of measuring marginal utility is clarified.

In the *Annual Survey*, Frisch carefully defines real income[11] and the two related concepts, price level and price index. He alters his derivation of a statistically feasible expression for the *real* money utility. He introduces a very useful concept, expenditure proportionality, and shows that his earlier expression for the *real* money utility assumed this condition. At the same time he generalizes the earlier formula.

It is now clear that Frisch's technique of measuring marginal utility, as developed in *New Methods*, rests on two assumptions, independence and expenditure proportionality. Both of these assumptions must impose restrictions upon the shape of the functions which are involved in his analysis. Consequently, both limit the application of his technique. The generalization in *Annual Survey* obviates the second condition. But, for reasons to appear later, however important it may be for the theory of index numbers, the generalized expression cannot be used to measure marginal utility. In order to evaluate Frisch's new methods, therefore, it is important to determine the restrictions imposed by *both* assumptions. Herein lies the chief task of this paper.

The theoretic basis of Frisch's methods of measuring marginal utility is developed from a consideration of the activities of one individual. In our discussion we shall follow Frisch in this respect. As is customary, we shall assume that the individual upon whom we focus seeks to maximize the satisfaction, or utility, he derives from the consumption of goods, subject to the condition that his total expenditure is fixed and, under a previous assumption,[12] equal to his money income. We shall also assume that the individual takes the prices in the market as given so far as his purchases are concerned, and that the prices are so in fact.[13]

---

[11] Frisch, in *Econometrica*, adopts the expression, "real expenditure," thereby avoiding an extra assumption. I shall retain his earlier and more familiar term, "real income," and will assume, therefore, that income equals expenditure.

[12] See n. 11.

[13] Frisch implicitly makes this assumption in *New Methods*. In the course of his index number discussion in *Annual Survey* (p. 14) he also considers the case where an individual is confronted with prices which depend on the amounts of his own purchases.

If we denote the amounts of the various commodities consumed as $y^1, y^2, \ldots y^n$, the individual's utility may be expressed as a function, $U(y^1, y^2, \ldots y^n)$, of these quantities.[14] We assume that the individual desires to maximize this function subject to the budgetary condition

$$p^1 y^1 + p^2 y^2 + \ldots p^n y^n = I. \tag{1}$$

Here $p^1, p^2, \ldots p^n$, the respective prices of $y^1, y^2, \ldots y^n$, and I, the individual's income, are given and in the maximizing process are regarded as constants.

FRISCH'S ANALYSIS

The fundamental equation which Frisch uses to measure *real* money utility is

$$\frac{w(r)}{P} = \frac{u'(x)}{h}. \tag{2}$$

Here r stands for real income; $w(r)$, the *real* money utility; P, the price of real income, or price of living; x, the amount consumed of one commodity, sugar (we use the letter x, rather than, say, y^1, to distinguish this commodity from the others); $u'(x)$,[15] the marginal utility of sugar; and h, the price of sugar (again, this corresponds to, say, p^1).

In *New Methods* Frisch derives (2) through an assumption and an "approximation."[16] The assumption is that sugar is an independent commodity. Thus the marginal utility of sugar may be written as a function of x alone. The "approximation" is

---

[14] While ordinarily it might be desirable to avoid the word utility and the expression, utility function, and use instead (say) tastes and indifference function, nothing is to be gained by such a procedure here. Frisch's assumption of independence implies that the utility function is determinate, or measurable, in the Lange sense. The arbitrariness of the function is limited to two constants, one fixing the scale of measurement and the other, the origin. See Oscar Lange, "The Determinateness of the Utility Function," *Review of Economic Studies*, June 1934.

[15] To facilitate our later discussion I have changed slightly the form of the expression used by Frisch. Sometimes I also use elsewhere symbols which differ from those of Frisch.

[16] *New Methods*, Sections 1 and 2.

involved in writing, the *nominal* money utility—the marginal utility of money income—as a function of I and P; thus,

$$\omega = \omega(I, P). \tag{3}$$

instead of expressing it as a function of I and the prices of the individual commodities, $h, p^2, \ldots p^n$; that is,

$$\omega = \omega(I, h, p^2, \ldots p^n). \tag{4}$$

The two concepts *real* money utility and *nominal* money utility derive their meaning, in Frisch's analysis, from an analogy with the marginal utility of the single commodity, sugar, measured per pound and per dollar's worth.[17] By an intuitive extension of this analogy, Frisch relates the two concepts by the equation

$$w = P\omega(I, P). \tag{5}$$

If it is assumed that ω is affected proportionately by a change in the monetary unit, w can be written in the form[18]

$$w = w(I/P) = w(r). \tag{6}$$

Since in equilibrium

$$\omega = \frac{u'(x)}{h}, \tag{7}$$

equation (2) follows.

In *Annual Survey*[19] Frisch uses another approach. He first defines the concepts of price index, expenditure proportionality, real income, and price level.

Price index. For any price situation $h_t, p_t^2, \ldots p_t^n$, the amounts $x_t, y_t^2, \ldots y_t^n$ of the commodities consumed will vary with income, I_t. The resulting *locus* of points, $x_t, y_t^2, \ldots y_t^n$, may be called an

---

[17] *Ibid.*, pp. 12, 13.

[18] For any λ, $\omega(I, P) = \lambda\omega(\lambda I, \lambda P)$. Thus $w(I, P) = w(\lambda I, \lambda P)$. If we take $\lambda = 1/P$ we have $w(I, P) = w[(I/P), 1]$, and since 1 is a constant, we may write this $w(I, P) = w(I/P)$. Frisch also gets the same result by a second method. *New Methods*, p. 14.

[19] Sections 3, 4, and 7.

expansion path.[20] For each point on the t expansion path there will be associated a value of U—the utility function—and a value of I_t. Assume that along every expansion path $(t = 0, 1, 2, \ldots)$, I_t and U are monotonically related. The function

$$I = I_t(U) \tag{8}$$

accordingly is single-valued. Consider the ratio

$$P_{0t} = \frac{I_t(U)}{I_0(U)} . \tag{9}$$

This ratio expresses the relationship between the money expenditures necessary to secure equal amounts of utility in the price situations $t = t$ and $t = 0$. P_{0t} is the index of the change in prices between 0 and t.

Expenditure proportionality. Ordinarily P_{0t} will vary with U. It will be different for different levels of utility, even though individual prices are constant. If for any t, however, P_{0t} does not depend on U, we have the condition of expenditure proportionality.

Real income and price level. Consider the expansion path, $t = 0$. Real income along this path, the base path, may be expressed by the function $r_0(U)$, and price level by the function $P_0(U)$. These two functions must satisfy the relation

$$r_0(U) = \frac{I_0(U)}{P_0(U)} . \tag{10}$$

In addition, I gather from Frisch's discussion[21] that $r_0(U)$ is subject to the restriction $r'_0(U) > 0$. Otherwise, in the general case,[22] the functions $r_0(U)$ and $P_0(U)$ are entirely arbitrary.

[20] This does not contradict our statement that in the maximizing process I is regarded as given. Frisch's analysis implies simply that, given the price situation, the equilibrium position $x_t, y_t^2, \ldots y_t^n$, will depend on the level at which income is fixed. The expansion path is the *locus* of equilibrium points which correspond to different income levels.

[21] *Annual Survey*, pp. 31, 32.

[22] General case is used here in contrast with the case of expenditure proportionality. In the latter case, as we shall see, a greater restriction on the indicated functions is justifiable.

Along any other expansion path, $t = t$, price level is defined by the relation

$$P_t(U) = P_0(U) \cdot P_{0t}(U), \tag{11}$$

and the real income, by the relation

$$r_t(U) = \frac{I_t(U)}{P_t(U)}. \tag{12}$$

By substitution this equals $r_0(U)$, so we may drop the subscript and write

$$r(U) = \frac{I_t(U)}{P_t(U)} = \frac{I_0(U)}{P_0(U)}. \tag{13}$$

Using these concepts, Frisch derives a new expression for the relationship between the *real* money utility and the *nominal* money utility. He precisely defines *nominal* money utility as

$$\omega_t = \frac{dU}{dI_t}, \tag{14}$$

and *real* money utility as

$$w = \frac{dU}{dr} = w(r). \tag{15}$$

In (15) U is regarded as a function of r.[23] Thus

$$\omega_t = w(r) \Big/ \frac{dI_t}{dr}. \tag{16}$$

Evaluating the derivative dI_t/dr by differentiating (13), we have[24]

$$\omega_t = w(r) \Big/ P_t(r)\left(1 + \frac{d \log P_t(r)}{d \log r}\right). \tag{17}$$

---

[23] We restrict $r_0(U)$ so that $r'_0(U) > 0$. Since $r(U) = r_0(U)$, $r'(U) > 0$. Hence the function $U(r)$ will be single-valued.

[24] I_t and P_t now may be regarded as functions of r, for we are so regarding U, and these variables depend upon U.

It follows that equation (2) must also be modified. If x is assumed independent again, (7) still holds,[25] and we may write

$$w(r) \Bigg/ P_t(r) \left(1 + \frac{d \log P_t(r)}{d \log r} \right) = \frac{u'(x)}{h}. \tag{18}$$

Equation (18) follows, I have said, "if x is assumed independent again." As a matter of fact, in *Annual Survey*, Frisch derives an expression for *real* money utility on the assumption that a subset of commodities, rather than one commodity, is independent.[26] This expression reduces to (18) when the assumption of *New Methods* is used, so without danger of misinterpretation we may regard (18) as the modification—for reasons which will appear immediately, the generalization—of (2) developed in *Annual Survey* for the case where one commodity is assumed independent. In our discussion we shall continue to work with the latter assumption. While use of the assumption of *Annual Survey* would

[25] If we write the equilibrium relation

$$K = \frac{u'(x)}{h} = \frac{U_{y^2}}{p^2} = \frac{U_{y^3}}{p^3} = \ldots = \frac{U_{y^n}}{p^n},$$

where $U_{y^2}, U_{y^3}, \ldots U_{y^n}$, are the marginal utilities of the commodities $y^2, y^3, \ldots y^n$, it may be shown that

$$\omega_t = \frac{dU}{dI_t} = K.$$

For,

$$\frac{dU}{dI_t} = u'(x) \frac{dx}{dI_t} + U_{y^2} \frac{dy^2}{dI_t} + \ldots + U_{y^n} \frac{dy^n}{dI_t}$$

$$= K \left(h \frac{dx}{dI_t} + p^2 \frac{dy^2}{dI_t} + \ldots + p^n \frac{dy^n}{dI_t} \right)$$

$$= K$$

This proof is taken from Allen, *Economica*, May 1933, p. 190. We use total, rather than partial, derivatives because the subscript t already implies that prices are held constant.

[26] The expression (with slight changes in symbols) is

$$w(r) \Bigg/ P_t(r) \left(1 + \frac{d \log P_t(r)}{d \log r} \right) = m(\overline{x}) \Bigg/ H_t(\overline{x}) \left(1 + \frac{d \log H_t(\overline{x})}{d \log \overline{x}} \right)$$

Assuming an independent subset, $x^1, x^2, \ldots x^m$, the terms $\overline{x}$, $H_t(\overline{x})$, and $m(\overline{x})$ may be defined for this subset in the same way as r, $P_t(r)$, and $w(r)$ are defined for all commodities.

necessitate little change in our argument, the assumption of *New Methods* has the advantage of simplicity and also of being the one which Frisch himself has used to measure marginal utility.

The difference between Frisch's analysis in *New Methods* and in his more recent paper crystalizes in equations (5) and (17). The reason for the divergence, Frisch states in *Annual Survey*, is that equation (5) assumes expenditure proportionality. In his words: "my original formula [(5)] does hold under expenditure proportionality, which was assumed in the statistical work in *New Methods*" And in reference to a more applicable form which he derives from (18): "This is a generalization of the isoquant method [in the *New Methods*] to the case where expenditure proportionality is not assumed."[27]

While Frisch does not elaborate these statements, the reasoning upon which they are based may readily be inferred from his analysis. If we adopt the convention,

$$P_0(U) \equiv 1, \tag{19}$$

it follows that

$$P_t = P_{0t}. \tag{20}$$

Thus, in the case of expenditure proportionality

$$\frac{d \log P_t}{d \log r} = \frac{d \log P_{0t}}{d \log r} = \frac{r}{P_{0t}} \cdot \frac{dP_{0t}}{dU} \cdot \frac{dU}{dr} = 0 \tag{21}$$

and (17) reduces to (5).

I turn to our main concern. Apparently (2) requires two assumptions, independence and expenditure proportionality. It is also apparent that equation (18) obviates the second assumption. The problems which we wish to consider, and to which we have already directed the reader's attention, are: (i) can the generalized equation (18) be used to measure real money utility, and, if not, (ii) what restrictions do Frisch's assumptions involve? Since the importance of problem (ii) depends upon the answer to problem (i), it will be desirable to consider the first problem first.

[27] *Annual Survey*, p. 34, n., p. 36.

THE POSSIBILITY OF GENERALIZATION

On the face of it, though the statistical task might be over-whelming, measurement of *real* money utility by use of (18) would seem quite feasible theoretically. The terms on the right-hand side of (18) involve no new problem. And, as Frisch indicates, if some convention is adopted for $P_0(U)$, the terms on the left, other than $w(r)$, are subject to approximation.[28] Formally, one must agree, a series of values could be determined for the term $w(r)$ by this procedure and I should prefer to interpret Frisch's statement cited on p. 101 in this sense only.[29] For while values can be determined for $w(r)$, they can in no sense be called *measurements* of *real* money utility. The difficulty centers in the clause "if some convention is adopted for $P_0(U)$."

For the terms on the left-hand side of (18) to be statistically determinable, two decisions must be made, one as to what path shall be chosen as the zero-path, or base, and the other as to what function should be accepted for the price level along this path. These two decisions represent *two* elements of arbitrariness in the real income function.[30] The only restriction imposed on them by the definition of real income is that they be such that $r'(U) = r'_0(U) > 0$.

If no further limitation were imposed on the conventions adopted for the real income function, this function would be quite arbitrary in both the general case and the expenditure propor-tionality case. In *Annual Survey* Frisch does present an additional criterion which he believes restricts the real income function in the case of expenditure proportionality. But he grants that in the general case the function is still arbitrary. While I agree with this conclusion, I do not believe Frisch's argument is impelling. Since the point is important to our discussion, I shall seek further support for it.

---

[28] *Annual Survey*, p. 36.
[29] This interpretation is quite plausible. For Frisch's index number purposes a determination of the values of $w(r)$ in a purely formal sense is sufficient. It does not matter whether these values may be regarded as measure-ments of marginal utility.
[30] Only the second causes arbitrariness in the case of expenditure propor-tionality. See below, p. 104.

The problem may be approached by considering the units in which real income is measured. As Frisch defines this concept the only restriction on the unit of real income for one value of U and on the relation between this unit and the unit chosen for another value of U is that the value of real income when measured in these units should increase with an increase of U. While this is the only limitation imposed by definition, it is self-evident that if it were possible to choose the units in such a way that along the path chosen as base the unit used to measure real income is the same— in kind and magnitude—for one value of U as for another, this convention ought to be adopted. This condition is both crucial and, when coupled with the implications of the real income concept as used in Frisch's analysis, restrictive. On the one hand, if the units *cannot* be the same for every value of U, there is no possible limitation on their relationship. The shape of the real income function, since it is dependent upon this relationship, must be entirely arbitrary. On the other, as real income is used in Frisch's analysis, this condition leaves little freedom of choice as to the real income convention along the base path. While, ordinarily, identity of units could be achieved by using as the unit of real income, the unit of utility, this is precluded in Frisch's analysis. If the concepts, utility of real income and marginal utility of real income, are to have any meaning, it is essential that the unit in which real income is measured be independent of the unit of utility.[31] I believe I am correct in saying that the only meaningful possibility in this case is that the unit used be a composite commodity made up of the individual commodities in constant proportions along the base path.[32] If this convention can be adopted, it leads immediately to the base path real income function

$$r_0(U) = \frac{I_0(U)}{c}. \tag{22}$$

[31] Cf. W. Leontief, "Composite Commodities and the Problem of Index Numbers," *Econometrica*, January 1936, p. 53.

[32] There are alternatives, such as using as the unit of real income (say) a pound, irrespective of its content. But it would be impossible to derive any consistent relationship between real income and utility with such a unit. Utility does not depend on the number of pounds of goods *per se*.

For, since the prices of the individual commodities are constant, and since the unit of real income for every value of U along the base path contains these commodities in constant proportions, the price level—the price of a unit of real income—is constant.[33] For convenience the magnitude of the real income unit may be chosen such that the constant c equals unity.

In the case of expenditure proportionality the convention (22) *can* indeed be adopted. Not only is it possible to select as base *one* path along which the commodities are consumed in constant proportions, but, as we shall see, a necessary and sufficient condition for expenditure proportionality is that every expansion path should have this property. Thus, one of the two elements of arbitrariness in the real income function—the choice of a price-level function—is not present. Further, in the case of expenditure proportionality, the other element of arbitrariness is not operative, aside from a scalar constant, no matter what price-level convention is adopted. For consider the ratio

$$\frac{\bar{r}(U)}{r(U)} = \frac{r_1(U)}{r_0(U)}, \tag{23}$$

Here $\bar{r}(U)$ and $r(U)$ are the real income functions having respectively the expansion paths $t = 1$ and $t = 0$ as base. For a given price-level convention—any function of U, though the same function for the two base paths—(23) equals the ratio of the income functions, which ratio is constant by definition in the case of expenditure proportionality.[34]

---

[33] Since the product of the price level and real income must equal money income for every value of U, it is proper to regard the price level as the price of a unit of real income.

[34] Frisch believes constancy of (23) in itself leads immediately to the convention (22). He states (replacing his symbols by those of this paper): "If it is possible to formulate the convention in such a way that (23) becomes independent of U, and further r, respectively $\bar{r}$, a plausible expression for real expenditure, *that* particular convention ought to be adopted. In the case of income [expenditure] proportionality this leads to (22). Otherwise (22) is more or less arbitrary." See *Annual Survey*, p. 32. It is true that if the convention (22) is adopted in the case of expenditure proportionality (23) is constant. But the converse is not at all inevitable. There are an infinity of other conventions—say, $r_0(U) = I_0(U)^2$, $r_0(U) = I_0(U)$. U—which lead to the same result in the case of expenditure proportionality.

In the general case there is no reason to expect that there is even one expansion path along which the commodities are consumed in constant proportions. And even if, in particular instances, there is one or more of such paths, the real income function is still arbitrary. For the path (or paths) of constant proportions taken as base, convention (22) is appropriate, but if the base is shifted the real income function will be altered. This *must* be so in the general case.

The conclusion is clear that, while in the case of expenditure proportionality the real income function is determined to the extent of an arbitrary scalar constant, in the general case no restriction on the real income function, in addition to the *a priori* one that $r'(U)$ is greater than zero, is justifiable. The implications of this for the measurement of *real* money utility are immediate. If in the general case no further restriction can be imposed on the real income function, efforts to measure this concept on the basis of (18) must prove futile.

Frisch's measurements of *real* money utility in *New Methods* are based on an assumption that the only arbitrary element in this function is a proportionality factor.[35] While the absolute values of the *real* money utility function have no significance, Frisch is able to advance values for its rate of change and its *relative* rate of change (relative to a change of real income) which do possess an absolute significance.

In the general case this is no longer possible. If the real income function is restricted only as to the sign of its first derivative, any transformation $R[r(U)]$, $R'(r) > 0$ may serve as this function as well as r. Since such a transformation may alter everything but the rank or order of the real income function, the numbering system used for it is *only* restricted as to rank or order. The *real* money utility function is a first derivative involving r. A transformation $R[r(U)]$, $R'(r) > 0$ may alter everything but the sign of this function.[36] Accordingly, the numbering system used for it is

---

[35] In Frisch's analysis, the admissibility of all linear transformations of the utility function accounts for the arbitrary factor. But it should be noted that even if the utility function were completely determinate, Frisch's technique of measuring *real* money utility would result in the values of that function containing an unknown, though not arbitrary, proportionality factor. See *New Methods*, Sections 3 and 4.

[36] Using the transformation $R[r(U)]$, $w(R) = w(r)/R'(r)$.

not even restricted as to rank. It need only be added that the rate of change and the relative rate of change—since the former involves a differential and the latter a derivative of the *real* money utility function—are entirely unrestricted. Under the circumstances there is no basis to advance any series of values as measurements of these concepts. With an appropriate transformation any other series has an equal claim to this status.

IMPLICATIONS FOR THE UTILITY FUNCTION

To simplify our discussion of the restriction imposed by the assumptions of expenditure proportionality and independence, we shall develop our argument first on the basis of a two-commodity analysis and then shall extend it, briefly, to the many-commodity case. This course, though laborious, will enable the reader to follow the argument without being distracted by the mathematical manipulations necessary in the many-commodity analysis. The conclusions of the two-commodity analysis, as will appear, are modified in only two respects by the generalization.

Expenditure proportionality. The condition of expenditure proportionality, as Frisch's analysis in *Annual Survey* demonstrates, is of considerable importance not only to his technique of measuring marginal utility, but for general index number theory.[37] We turn first to the restriction imposed upon the utility function by the assumption of this condition.

Consider the slope function,[38]

$$F = F(x, y) = -\left(\frac{dy}{dx}\right)_U = \frac{U_x}{U_y}. \qquad (24)$$

[37] In the case of expenditure proportionality the much discussed upper and lower limits for index numbers—the Laspeyre and Paasche formulae—are truly limiting. They relate to one number. In the general case this is not so. Here the Laspeyre formula is the upper limit for one index number and the Paasche formula the lower limit for another. See Frisch's discussion of the Haberler Limits, *Annual Survey*, p. 25.

[38] Since we are dealing with only two commodities we shall drop the superscripts from y and p.

This function is called by Hicks and Allen[39] the marginal rate of substitution of commodity y for commodity x. When the individual has attained a maximum, or equilibrium position, F equals the price ratio h/p.

We shall prove the following theorem: *a necessary and sufficient condition that P_{0t} be independent of U for any t* (the condition of expenditure proportionality) *is that F be homogeneous to the zero degree.*

First, let us prove necessity: given that P_{0t} is independent of U, to prove that F is homogeneous to the zero degree. From the hypothesis, differentiating (9) with respect to U,

$$\frac{dP_{0t}}{dU} = \frac{I_0 \dfrac{dI_t}{dU} - I_t \dfrac{dI_0}{dU}}{I_0^2} = 0. \tag{25}$$

Thus

$$I_0 \frac{dU}{dI_0} = I_t \frac{dU}{dI_t}. \tag{26}$$

Consider the two points: x_0, y_0, on the zero path; and x_t, y_t, on the t-path. Suppose they are so related that

$$U(x_0, y_0) = U(x_t, y_t). \tag{27}$$

Then we can evaluate the derivatives in (26) at these points.[40] If we do this, and substitute for I_0 and I_t their budgetary equivalents, we have

$$(h_0 x_0 + p_0 y_0) \frac{U_x(x_0, y_0)}{h_0} = (h_t x_t + p_t y_t) \frac{U_x(x_t, y_t)}{h_t}. \tag{28}$$

Since in equilibrium $h/p = U_x/U_y$, (28) may be stated as

$$U_x(x_0, y_0)x_0 + U_y(x_0, y_0)y_0 = U_x(x_t, y_t)x_t + U_y(x_t, y_t)y_t. \tag{29}$$

---

[39] J. R. Hicks and R. G. D. Allen, "A Reconsideration of the Theory of Value," Part I, *Economica*, February 1934, Part II, *Economica*, May 1934. If we designate the family of curves in the x, y-plane described by taking $U(x, y)$ constant at different values, the indifference *loci*, $F(x, y)$ is the slope at the point x, y of the particular indifference *locus* passing through the point x, y.

[40] For the method of evaluation, see above, n. 25.

Equation (29) must hold for every $x_0, y_0; x_t, y_t$, for which (27) is valid. If we hold x_0, y_0 fixed, and vary t, and thus, also x_t, y_t, (27) describes an indifference curve—a *locus* of constant utility. Accordingly, if we take x_0, y_0 constant, (29) must hold as long as x_t, y_t remains on the indifference curve defined by (27). Let us therefore hold x_0, y_0 constant and differentiate (29) with respect to x_t, so varying y_t, that (27) holds. Since the left-hand side of (29) drops out, we now deal with the point x_t, y_t alone. For convenience we will omit the subscript t. Thus we have

$$0 = \left[U_{xx} + U_{xy} \left(\frac{dy}{dx} \right)_U \right] x + U_x$$
$$+ \left[U_{xy} + U_{yy} \left(\frac{dy}{dx} \right)_U \right] y + U_y \left(\frac{dy}{dx} \right)_U. \qquad (30)$$

Substituting for $(dy/dx)_U$ its equivalent, $-(U_x/U_y)$,

$$\left(U_{xx} - U_{xy} \frac{U_x}{U_y} \right) x + \left(U_{xy} - U_{yy} \frac{U_x}{U_y} \right) y = 0. \qquad (31)$$

If we multiply through by U_y, and then divide through by U_y^2, (31) may be written

$$\left(\frac{\partial(U_x/U_y)}{\partial x} \right)_y x + \left(\frac{\partial(U_x/U_y)}{\partial y} \right)_x y = 0 \qquad (32)$$

or

$$F_x x + F_y y = 0. \qquad (33)$$

From (33) it follows by Euler's theorem that $F(x, y)$ is homogeneous to the zero degree. Q.E.D.

Now as to sufficiency: given that F is homogeneous to the zero degree, to prove that P_{0t} is independent of U for any t. From the hypothesis we may retrace our steps from (33) to (30). Now consider the function

$$M(x, y) = U_x x + U_y y. \qquad (34)$$

By (30)

$$\left(\frac{dM}{dx} \right)_U = M_x - M_y \frac{U_x}{U_y} = 0. \qquad (35)$$

108

Thus,

$$dM = \frac{M_x}{U_x} dU. \qquad (36)$$

From (36), when $dU = 0$, $dM = 0$: so when U is constant, M is constant. Hence, for two points x_0, y_0 and x_y, y_t for which (27) holds, (29) must be true. If we evaluate the terms in (25) we have

$$I_0^2 \cdot \frac{dP_{0t}}{dU} = \frac{h_t h_0}{U_x(x_t, y_t) \cdot U_x(x_0, y_0)}$$

$$\times [U_x(x_0, y_0)x_0 + U_y(x_0, y_0)y_0 - U_x(x_t, y_t)x_t - U_y(x_t, y_t)y_t]$$
$$(37)$$

And by (29) the right-hand side of (37) equals zero. Q.E.D.

The condition that F be homogeneous to the zero degree is equivalent to the condition that all the expansion paths be straight lines through the origin. For given the homogeneity to the zero order, the slope function can be written in the form[41]

$$F = F(y/x) \qquad (38)$$

If we take a given price situation, h_t, p_t and vary I_t, the *locus* of points x_t, y_t described will be a path of constant F.[42] Accordingly, if F is constant, by (38) y/x must be constant.[43] Thus the expansion path t is given by the equation

$$y = c_t x. \qquad (39)$$

[41] By definition, if $F(x, y)$ is homogeneous to the zero degree $F(x, y) = F(\lambda x, \lambda y)$ for any λ. If we take $\lambda = 1/x$ we obtain (38).

[42] Taking a given price situation h_t, p_t means that the price ratio h_t/p_t is constant, and since in equilibrium F is equal to h_t/p, F must be constant. It may be noted here that the expansion path could be defined by constancy of the price ratio instead of constancy of the price situation (see *Annual Survey*, p. 16). The advantage of—and, I presume, Frisch's reason for—using constancy of the price situation is this: while the *locus* of points x, y in the indifference plane is unaltered by taking ah_t, ap_t, instead of h_t, p_t the third-dimensional relation between I_t and U is altered, proportionately, by this procedure.

[43] If, in a particular region of the indifference plane, it is assumed that the individual can attain only one equilibrium position, y/x must be single valued for that region.

Conversely, if we are given (39) as the equation of the expansion path, F must be homogeneous to the zero degree. For, if F is constant for all x, y along the path (39),

$$F(x, y) = F(\lambda x, \lambda y) \tag{40}$$

Stated in another way the homogeneity of F to the zero order is equivalent to the condition that straight lines through the origin intercept the indifference *loci* at points of constant slope.[44]

Independence. The condition of expenditure proportionality limits the shape of the indifference curves alone. Homogeneity of the slope function leaves the third dimension—utility—unrestricted. If to expenditure proportionality is added the assumption of independence, this is no longer true.

Frisch assumes in *New Methods* that one commodity, sugar, is independent of all others. In the two-commodity case this means that both commodities are independent. To avoid possible misunderstanding on this account, we shall indicate in our discussion of the two-commodity case what difference in results will appear when the analysis is extended to several commodities.

If the two commodities, x and y, are independent, we can write the utility function in the form

$$U(x, y) = u(x) + v(y) \tag{41}$$

[44] There is another interesting interpretation of the condition of expenditure proportionality. Consider the family of functions $J[U(x, y)]$. All of these functions define the same indifference *loci*; they only differ in the third dimension. Now it may be shown—I shall leave the proof to the reader—that a necessary and sufficient condition that one member, $H(x, y)$, of the family $J[U(x, y)]$ be homogeneous to the first degree is that $F(x, y)$ be homogeneous to the zero degree. This condition is thus identical with the restriction imposed on the isoquants by the marginal productivity theorem. In the third dimension, of course, the marginal productivity theorem assumes that $H(x, y)$ is the production function, whereas here we assume only that another member $U(x, y)$ of the family $J[U(x, y)]$ *is* the utility function. But considering only the two dimensional relations defined by the indifference curves and the isoquants, the restriction is the same.

Any linear transformation of this function is also admissible, but no other.[45] From (41) the slope function becomes

$$F = \frac{u'(x)}{v'(y)}. \tag{42}$$

By (33)

$$\frac{u''(x)}{u'(x)} x = \frac{v''(y)}{v'(y)} y. \tag{43}$$

Since x and y are independent, and since (43) must hold for every x and y, each side of this equation must equal a constant. For convenience, let us write the constant as $n - 1$. We have two differential equations:

$$\frac{d \log u'(x)}{d \log x} = n - 1, \tag{44}$$

$$\frac{d \log v'(y)}{d \log y} = n - 1. \tag{45}$$

The solutions of these differential equations are

$$u(x) = Ax^n + k_1, \tag{46}$$

$$v(y) = By^n + k_2, \tag{47}$$

where A, B, k_1, and k_2 are constants. Thus the utility function may be written

$$U(x, y) = Ax^n + By^n. \tag{48}$$

For convenience we omit the k_1 and k_2, since in any case, any linear transformation of (48) is admissible.[46]

---

[45] See above, n. 14.

[46] If the utility functions satisfies certain *a priori* conditions, the range of possible values for the parameter n in (48) is considerably restricted. If, for values of x and $y > 0$, the utility derived from x increases when x increases and the utility derived from y increases when y increases, A, B, and n must have the same sign. If, in addition, the individual can attain a relative maximum position at any point x, y in a region of positive values of x and y, n must be <1. Finally, if U is not constant for all values of x and y, and if for a finite linear transformation, $G(U)$, of U, $G[U0, 0] = 0$, n must be >0.

The logarithmic derivatives in (44) and (45) are utility elasticities, or, as Frisch would designate them, utility flexibilities. Evidently Frisch's assumptions require that both be constant. As will appear, in the many-commodity case the restriction is less—only the utility flexibility for x must be constant. The many-commodity analysis also involves less restriction of the function $U(x, y)$. In place of y^n in (48) there appears a function of all the other commodities, which function must be homogeneous to the order n. But these two qualifications are the *only* modifications in the conclusions of the two-commodity analysis necessitated by extension of the discussion to the many-commodity case.

The restriction imposed upon the utility function by Frisch's assumptions is now apparent. On this basis alone there is reason to believe that the methods of measuring marginal utility developed by Frisch have a narrow range of application. But reference thus far has been to restrictions imposed on the utility function, and we have yet to consider those imposed on the *real* money utility function. We turn now to this aspect.

IMPLICATIONS FOR THE REAL MONEY UTILITY FUNCTION

In determining the restriction imposed upon the *real* money utility function we shall consider together Frisch's two assumptions, expenditure proportionality and independence. Since the real money utility function involves the third dimension, utility, it is fairly obvious that the condition of expenditure proportionality leaves this function unrestricted. A separate treatment of the effects of the assumption of this condition, therefore, would yield only negative results.[47]

Let us adopt the convention $P_0(U) \equiv 1$ for the price level along a base path. Thus, expressing r_0 and I_0 in terms of x_0 and y_0,

$$r_0[U(x_0, y_0)] = I_0[U(x_0, y_0)] = h_0x_0 + p_0y_0. \qquad (49)$$

[47] It is possible, with the aid of the theorem which is stated above, n. 44, to determine the shape of the real income function from the condition of expenditure proportionality alone. But to proceed further, it is necessary to assume independence.

From (39),

$$r_0[U(x_0, y_0)] = (h_0 + c_0p_0)x_0. \tag{50}$$

Along the base path, then, real income, aside from a proportionality factor, is measured by the amount consumed of one commodity.

For another point, x_t, y_t on the expansion path $t = t$,

$$r[U(x_t, y_t)] = r_0[U(x_0, y_0)], \tag{51}$$

provided (27) is realized. From (48) and (39),

$$U(x_t, y_t) = (A + Bc_t^n)x_t^n, \tag{52}$$

$$U(x_0, y_0) = (A + Bc_0^n)x_0^n. \tag{53}$$

Thus condition (27) requires that

$$x_0 = \frac{(A + Bc_t^n)^{1/n}}{(A + Bc_0^n)^{1/n}} x_t. \tag{54}$$

By (50), (51), and (54),

$$r[U(x_t, y_t)] = \frac{(h_0 + c_0p_0)}{(A + Bc_0^n)^{1/n}} \cdot (A + Bc_t^n)^{1/n} x_t, \tag{55}$$

or, replacing the quotient on the right-hand side by R_0,

$$r[U(x_t, y_t)] = R_0(A + Bc_t^n)^{1/n} x_t. \tag{56}$$

Accordingly, real income along any path $t = t$ is measured by the amount consumed of one commodity.

While in equation (56) we have written r as a function of x_t and y_t, it is possible from (56) and (39) to regard x_t, and y_t, as depending upon r. Using (56) and (52), then, we can express utility as a function of r,

$$U(r) = \frac{r^n}{R_0^n}. \tag{57}$$

Here R_0 is the only constant involved. It depends on the base path constants and on the constants A and B. On *a priori* grounds it may be limited to positive values,[48] but otherwise it is unrestricted.

It is possible, finally, to determine the *real* money utility function:

$$w(r) = \frac{dU}{dr} = \frac{nr^{n-1}}{R_0^n}.$$ (58)

While in (57) any linear function of r^n/R_0^n is admissible as an expression for $U(r)$, the only arbitrary element in (58) is a scalar constant.

In his *Sur un problème d'économie pure*, Frisch lists five conditions which he believes the real money utility function ought to satisfy *a priori*. From a consideration of these conditions he concludes that: "La forme la plus simple que l'on puisse employer comme formule d'interpolation pour l'utilité marginale de la monnai est donc la formule:"[49]

$$w(r) = \frac{\text{constant}}{\log r - \log a}$$ (59)

Here "a" is a constant indicating the minimum of existence. In his *New Methods* Frisch again indicates a preference for (59) as an analytic expression for *real* money utility.[50]

The difference between (59) and (58) is evidently great. If we turn to the conditions on the basis of which Frisch deduces (59) the discrepancy is understandable. The first three conditions are:

(i) Il existe un nombre positif "a" (le minimum d'existence au niveau des prix donné P_0) tel que $w(r) > 0$ et possède des derivées de premier et second ordre pour $a < r < \infty$.

(iiA) $\lim_{r \to a} w(r) = \infty$ (iiB) $\lim_{r \to \infty} w(r) = 0$

(iii) $\dfrac{dw(r)}{dr} = w'(r) < 0$ dans l'intervalle $a < r < \infty$.[51]

The relation of (58) to these conditions is obvious. Condition (iiB) will be satisfied if $n < 1$. But as to the other conditions, all

[48] See n. 46.
[49] Page 22. I have inserted the symbols used in the present paper.
[50] Page 31.
[51] *Sur un problème d'économie pure*, p. 19.

involve the constant "*a*." In (58) there is no *positive* number which could be given the properties of a minimum of existence, no *positive* critical value for *r*. For $n < 1$, the only critical value of *r* in (58) is *zero*.[52] If this is interpreted as a minimum of existence, the other conditions will be satisfied for $n > 0$.

The last two of Frisch's five conditions relate to the logarithmic derivative of $w(r)$—the money flexibility. We have encountered this function before, though not by name. Because of the fact that the *real* money utility function is affected by an arbitrary proportionality factor, Frisch in *New Methods* turns to the rate of change and the *relative* rate of change of *real* money utility. The relative rate of change is the money flexibility. Though Frisch advances a series of values for the rate of change of real money utility,[53] his main interest in *New Methods* is to measure the *relative* rate of change—the money flexibility—for different values of income.[54]

Frisch's last two conditions are:

(iv) La proportion de decroissance $-\overline{w}(r) = -\dfrac{d \log w(r)}{d \log r}$ est plus grande que l'unité pour des valeurs de $r (> a)$ assez petites.

(v) $\lim\limits_{r \to \infty} \overline{w}(r) = 0$[55]

From (58) the money flexibility is[56]

$$\overline{w}(r) = \frac{r}{\dfrac{nr^{n-1}}{R_0^n}} \cdot \frac{n(n-1)r^{n-2}}{R_0^n} = n - 1. \tag{60}$$

Since *n* is a constant, conditions (iv) and (v) cannot both be satisfied. If either be valid none of the first three conditions will be satisfied.

---

[52] If $n \geq 1$ there is no critical value for *r*.

[53] *New Methods*, p. 30.

[54] For a discussion of the money flexibility, see *ibid*, Sections 1, 2, and 3, and Allen, *Economica*, May 1933, pp. 186, 191.

[55] *Sur un problème d'économie pure*, p. 19.

[56] The value of the flexibility, it will be recalled, is the same as that for the commodity *x*.

In the light of Frisch's five conditions, all of which on *a priori* grounds seem quite reasonable, (58) certainly appears to be *rara avis*. But to the evidence of these conditions must be added a further point. By (60) it is apparent that, *under the assumption of independence and expenditure proportionality, the money flexibility which is the variable Frisch is mainly interested in measuring is equal to a constant.*[57] While a question of fact is involved, constancy of the flexibility surely casts doubt upon the range of applicability of Frisch's procedure. When to this is added the evidence of his five conditions, the usefulness of his technique is seriously open to question. Interestingly, under Frisch's assumptions, measurement of the money flexibility would be a very simple process. It would be sufficient to determine its magnitude for but one value of real income.

THE MANY-COMMODITY CASE

To develop our analysis in the many-commodity case we shall consider only three commmodities. This number will be sufficient to assure the generality of our argument.

The theorem on expenditure proportionality. Consider the two slope functions,[58]

$$F = F(x, y, z) = - \left(\frac{\partial y}{\partial x}\right)_{U,z} = \frac{U_x}{U_y}, \qquad (61)$$

$$G = G(x, y, z) = - \left(\frac{\partial z}{\partial x}\right)_{U,y} = \frac{U_x}{U_z}. \qquad (62)$$

In equilibrium, F equals h/p and G equals h/q.

For the expenditure proportionality theorem we have: *a necessary and sufficient condition that P_{0t} be independent of U for any t is that F and G be homogeneous to the zero degree.*

---

[57] This has an interesting implication. Frisch, in his contribution to index number theory (*Annual Survey*, sec. 7), regards the money flexibility as an indifference function. An obvious exception is the case where the logarithms of real money utility and real income are linearly related.

[58] To avoid the use of superscripts I have decided to use as symbols for the quantities of the three commodities x, y, z rather than x, y^2, y^3, and as symbols for prices h, p, q rather than h, p^2, p^3. This is inconsistent with our earlier notation but is much less laborious.

First, as to necessity: given that P_{0t} is independent of U, to prove that F and G are homogeneous to the zero degree. From the hypothesis we again have (26). Consider the two points: x_0, y_0, z_0 on the zero path and x_t, y_t, z_t on the t path. Suppose they are so related that

$$U(x_0, y_0, z_0) = U(x_t, y_t, z_t). \tag{63}$$

Evaluating the derivatives and the terms I_0 and I_t in (26) at these points, we have

$$(h_0 x_0 + p_0 y_0 + q_0 z_0) \cdot \frac{U_x(x_0, y_0, z_0)}{h_0}$$

$$= (h_t x_t + p_t y_t + q_t z_t) \cdot \frac{U_x(x_t, y_t, z_t)}{h_t}. \tag{64}$$

Using the equilibrium values for (61) and (62),

$$U_x(x_0, y_0, z_0) x_0 + U_y(x_0, y_0, z_0) y_0 + U_z(x_0, y_0, z_0)$$

$$= U_x(x_t, y_t, z_t) x_t + U_y(x_t, y_t, z_t) y_t + U_z(x_t, y_t, z_t) z_t \tag{65}$$

Equation (65) is valid for all points for which (63) holds. Let us hold x_0, y_0, z_0, and thus U, constant. Further, let us vary t in such a way that z_t is constant. Then differentiating (65) with respect to x_t and for convenience dropping the subscript t,

$$0 = \left[U_{xx} + U_{xy} \left(\frac{\partial y}{\partial x} \right)_{U,z} \right] x + U_x + \left[U_{xy} + U_{yy} \left(\frac{\partial y}{\partial x} \right)_{U,z} \right] y$$

$$+ U_y \left(\frac{\partial y}{\partial x} \right)_{U,z} + \left[U_{xz} + U_{yz} \left(\frac{\partial y}{\partial x} \right)_{U,z} \right] z. \tag{66}$$

Using (61),

$$\left(U_{xx} - U_{xy} \frac{U_x}{U_y} \right) x + \left(U_{xy} - U_{yy} \frac{U_x}{U_y} \right) y$$

$$+ \left(U_{xz} - U_{yz} \frac{U_x}{U_y} \right) z = 0. \tag{67}$$

117

If we multiply through by U_y and then divide through by U_y^2, (67) may be written

$$\left[\frac{\partial\left(\dfrac{U_x}{U_y}\right)}{\partial x}\right]_{y,z} x + \left[\frac{\partial\left(\dfrac{U_x}{U_y}\right)}{\partial y}\right]_{x,z} y + \left[\frac{\partial\left(\dfrac{U_x}{U_y}\right)}{\partial z}\right]_{x,y} z = 0, \quad (68)$$

or

$$F_x x + F_y y + F_z z = 0. \quad (69)$$

In the same manner, if in (65) t is varied in such a way that y_t is constant, it may be shown that

$$G_x x + G_y y + G_z z = 0. \quad (70)$$

Equations (69) and (70) are sufficient conditions that F and G be homogeneous to the zero degree. Q.E.D.

As to sufficiency: given that F and G are homogeneous to the zero degree, to prove that P_{0t} is independent of U. Consider the function

$$M(x, y, x) = U_x x + U_y y + U_z z. \quad (71)$$

From the hypothesis

$$\left(\frac{\partial M}{\partial x}\right)_{U,z} = M_x - M_y \frac{U_x}{U_y} = 0, \quad (72)$$

$$\left(\frac{\partial M}{\partial x}\right)_{U,y} = M_x - M_z \frac{U_x}{U_z} = 0. \quad (73)$$

For, given the homogeneity of F, we can proceed immediately to equation (66). Similarly, from the homogeneity of G we can proceed to a corresponding equation. From (72) and (73),

$$dM = \frac{M_x}{U_x} dU. \quad (74)$$

For dU equal to zero, dM must equal zero: hence, for U constant, M must be constant. Consider again two points x_0, y_0, z_0 and x_t, y_t, z_t for which (63) holds. Then (65) must be true. The constancy of P_{0t} with respect to U follows in the same way as in the two-commodity analysis. Q.E.D.

The homogeneity of F and G to the zero degree is equivalent again to the condition that all expansion paths are straight lines through the origin. For given the homogeneity we can write

$$F = F\left(\frac{y}{x}, \frac{z}{x}\right), \tag{75}$$

$$G = G\left(\frac{y}{x}, \frac{z}{x}\right). \tag{76}$$

For a given price situation h_t, p_t, q_t, and varying income, I_t, the *locus* of points x_t, y_t, z_t will be determined by the intersection of the two surfaces F constant and G constant. The expansion path is given by

$$y = c_t x, \tag{77}$$

$$z = d_t x, \tag{78}$$

which is the solution of the equations F and G constant.[59] The converse—that F and G are homogeneous to the zero degree if (77) and (78) define the t expansion path—follows in the same manner as in the two commodity case.

Independence and the utility function. In the three commodity case Frisch's assumption of independence implies that the utility function may be written in the form

$$U(x, y, z) = u(x) + v(y, z) \tag{79}$$

Any linear function of this is also admissible. From (79)

$$F = \frac{u'(x)}{v_y(y, z)}, \tag{80}$$

$$G = \frac{u'(x)}{v_z(y, z)}, \tag{81}$$

[59] If, in a particular region of the indifference manifold, it is assumed that the individual can attain only one equilibrium position, the solution must be unique for that region.

and from (80) and (69), (81) and (70),

$$\frac{u''(x)}{u'(x)} x = \frac{v_{yy}(y, z)}{v_y(y, z)} y + \frac{v_{yz}(y, z)}{v_y(y, z)} z, \tag{82}$$

$$\frac{u''(x)}{u'(x)} x = \frac{v_{yz}(y, z)}{v_z(y, z)} y + \frac{v_{zz}(y, z)}{v_z(y, z)} z. \tag{83}$$

Since x, y, and z are independent, and since (82) and (83) must hold for every value of x, y, and z, the two sides of (82) and (83) must equal a constant. For convenience, let this constant be $n - 1$. Equations (44) and (46) follow immediately for the function $u(x)$. As to $v(y, z)$, from the right-hand side of (82) and (83) we have

$$v_{yy}(y, z)y + v_{yz}(y, z)z = (n - 1)v_y(y, z), \tag{84}$$

$$v_{yz}(y, z)y + v_{zz}(y, z)z = (n - 1)v_z(y, z). \tag{85}$$

Equation (84), by Euler's theorem, is a sufficient condition that $v_y(y, z)$ be homogeneous to the order $(n - 1)$. Similarly for (85) and $v_z(y, z)$.

From the homogeneity of $v_y(y, z)$ and $v_z(y, z)$ to the order $n - 1$ it may be shown that there is a function $\bar{v}(y, z)$, differing from $v(y, z)$ by a constant, which is homogeneous to the order n. Consider the identities,

$$v(y, z) - v(a, b) = \int_a^y v_1(\bar{y}, z) \, d\bar{y} + \int_b^z v_2(a, \bar{z}) \, d\bar{z}, \tag{86}$$

$$v(\lambda y, \lambda z) - v(\lambda a, \lambda b) = \int_{\lambda a}^{\lambda y} v_1(\bar{y}, \lambda z) \, d\bar{y} + \int_{\lambda b}^{\lambda z} v_2(\lambda a, \bar{z}) \, d\bar{z}. \tag{87}$$

In (87) let us change our variables to $\bar{y} = \lambda w$; $\bar{z} = \lambda m$. Then

$$v(\lambda y, \lambda z) - v(\lambda a, \lambda b) = \lambda \int_a^y v_1(\lambda w, \lambda z) \, dw$$

$$+ \lambda \int_b^z v_2(\lambda a, \lambda m) \, dm. \tag{88}$$

Using (86), (88), and the homogeneity of $v_y(y, z)$ and $v_z(y, z)$,

$$v(\lambda y, \lambda z) - v(\lambda a, \lambda b) = \lambda^n[v(y, z) - v(a, b)]. \qquad (89)$$

This must hold for every λ, y and z, a and b. Differentiating with respect to λ, and then putting $\lambda = 1$:

$$v_y(y, z)y + v_z(y, z)z - nv(y, z)$$
$$= v_1(a, b)a + v_2(a, b)b - nv(a, b). \qquad (90)$$

Since y and z, a and b are independent, we may place both sides of (90) equal to a constant for convenience nk_2. If we take

$$\bar{v}(y, z) = v(y, z) + k_2 \qquad (91)$$

we have from (90),

$$n\bar{v}(y, z) = \bar{v}_y(y, z)y + \bar{v}_z(y, z)z. \qquad (92)$$

By Euler's theorem this is a sufficient condition that $\bar{v}(y, z)$ is homogeneous to the order n.

In the three commodity case, from (92) and (46) we can write

$$U(x, y, z) = Ax^n + \bar{v}(y, z). \qquad (93)$$

For convenience we omit again the constants k_1 and k_2.[60]

The real money utility function. Adopting the convention $P_0(U) \equiv 1$, and considering the point x_0, y_0, z_0 on the expansion path $t = 0$, we have

$$r_0[U(x_0, y_0, z_0)] = I_0[U(x_0, y_0, z_0)] = h_0 x_0 + p_0 y_0 + q_0 z_0. \qquad (94)$$

From (77) and (78),

$$r_0[U(x_0, y_0, z_0)] = (h_0 + c_0 p_0 + d_0 q_0)x_0. \qquad (95)$$

---

[60] With slight modifications in method of statement, the argument of n. 46 concerning the range of values for the parameter n still holds.

For another point, x_t, y_t, z_t, on the expansion path $t = t$,

$$r[U(x_t, y_t, z_t)] = r_0[U(x_0, y_0, z_0)], \tag{96}$$

provided (63) is true. By (77), (78), and (93),[61]

$$U(x_t, y_t, z_t) = (A + Q_t)x_t^n, \tag{97}$$

$$U(x_0, y_0, z_0) = (A + Q_0)x_0^n. \tag{98}$$

Condition (63) requires that

$$x_0 = \frac{(A + Q_t)^{1/n}}{(A + Q_0)^{1/n}} x_t. \tag{99}$$

By (95), (96), and (99)

$$r[U(x_t, y_t, z_t)] = \frac{(h_0 + c_0 p_0 + d_0 q_0)}{(A + Q_0)^{1/n}} (A + Q_t)^{1/n} x_t, \tag{100}$$

or, for simplicity,

$$r[U(x_t, y_t, z_t)] = R_0(A + Q_t)^{1/n} x_t. \tag{101}$$

From equations (77), (78), and (101) we may regard x_t, y_t, and z_t as functions of r. By (101) and (97) we may write

$$U(r) = \frac{r^n}{R_0^n}. \tag{102}$$

The *real* money utility and the money flexibility may be derived in the same way as in the two commodity case.

[61] Equations (97) and (98) may be proved readily. On the expansion path $t = t$,

$$U(x_t, y_t, z_t) = Ax_t^n + \bar{v}(c_t x_t, d_t x_t).$$

Since $\bar{v}$ is homogeneous to the order n

$$\lambda^n \bar{v}(c_t x_t, d_t x_t) = \bar{v}(\lambda c_t x_t, \lambda d_t x_t)$$

This must hold for any λ. Taking $\lambda = 1/x_t$

$$\bar{v}(c_t x_t, d_t x_t) = \bar{v}(c_t, d_t)x_t^n = Q_t x_t^n$$

Similarly for the expansion path $t = 0$.

5

INDEX NUMBER THEORY AND THE

DISSIMILARITY METHOD*

The "dissimilarity method" that Dr. Staehle has devised for purposes of calculating indexes of the cost of living, particularly the comparative level of costs in different countries, is quite novel. Inevitably, therefore, it also poses questions. In order to assess the method briefly, I propose to comment on these related aspects: the conceptual question that is raised for comparisons of living costs by differences in tastes; the applicability of the "conventional method" of calculating cost of living indexes when tastes are different, and the conditions under which this method yields accurate results; the general applicability of the dissimilarity method, and the conditions under which this method yields accurate results.

With regard to the first question, I wish only to make the following suggestion. I wonder whether it would not be advisable here simply to acknowledge that in *theory* there are as many valid measures of the change in the cost of living as there are taste patterns. Or rather, we should say there are as many *sets* of valid measures, since for each given taste pattern (that is, indifference map) there is a set of valid measures of the change in the cost of living, one measure for each level of real income. To acknowledge that the measure of the change in living costs depends upon tastes simply represents a further elaboration of the theory of

* Originally published as a comment on Hans Staehle, "The International Comparison of Real National Income," in National Bureau of Economic Research, Conference on Research in Income and Wealth, *Studies in Income and Wealth*, vol. XI (New York, 1949).

index numbers, entirely analogous to the one that already took place when the dependence of the measure of the change in living costs on the level of real income was recognized.

Logically, the dependence of the measure of the cost of living on tastes is the corollary of our acceptance of individual preferences as the standard of value. Only if some other standard is used can we obtain a valid measure of the change in the cost of living that does not depend upon individual tastes.

At the risk of being set down as a heretic in these matters, I wish to urge that the foregoing formulation of the problem be adopted as an alternative to the one currently in vogue, according to which comparisons of the cost of living when tastes differ are said to be meaningless "in strict logic." This, I gather, is Dr. Staehle's view, though happily he does not allow it to interfere with his practical work in the field. My own view is that once one has acknowledged that in theory the measure depends upon tastes, that there are many valid measures when tastes differ, one has said all one can say; to go further and say that the comparisons are meaningless is not only not particularly illuminating but likely to be misleading. One might as well say that comparisons are meaningless when tastes are identical and real incomes different. If the measure could be determined for each set of tastes dealt with and each level of real income, obviously this would be a very considerable accomplishment. Very interesting and meaningful propositions could be constructed if such indexes were at hand.

Granting this, I find it difficult to agree with Dr. Staehle that the conventional method of calculating the change in the cost of living is inapplicable when tastes differ. I am referring to the method whereby A's collection of goods is valued at the prices confronting B, and vice versa, to establish how much each would have to pay for his collection if he had to pay the other's prices. The difference in the cost of living in the two price situations is measured by comparing what each consumer would have to pay in the other's price situation with what he actually pays in his own. If tastes differ, this method inevitably leads to two measures of the difference in living costs, one from the viewpoint of A's tastes, the other from the viewpoint of B's tastes. This plurality of measures, however, in no way discredits the conventional method.

To repeat, if tastes differ, the plurality of measures is logically appropriate.

Even if tastes are the same, as has been noted, one is ordinarily confronted with an analogous situation, that is, with two measures of the change in the cost of living. This is because of differences in the real income of A and B. No one suggests that the conventional method is inapplicable merely because real incomes differ.

The conventional method, moreover, has the virtue that the conditions under which it yields 100 percent accurate results can be stated. This is a virtue Staehle does not claim for his dissimilarity method, though my impression is that analogous conditions can be established for it too.

The conventional method has a very long history, but as far as I am aware, no one has yet troubled to state precisely the conditions under which its results are completely accurate. It may be profitable to dwell for a moment on this question.

Suppose A's money income were increased (decreased) just sufficiently to enable him to buy his old collection of goods at B's prices. It is a familiar proposition of index number theory that in actuality A would be better off than before, since when faced with B's prices he might economize on goods that were relatively more expensive than they were in his own price situation and buy more goods that were relatively cheaper than in his own price situation. To the extent that A would be better off, the conventional method overstates the increase (understates the decrease) in the cost of living to A. But, evidently, this situation is excluded in the following case: when the commodities A consumes are completely complementary, that is, when A consumes goods in proportions that are fixed with respect to *relative price changes*. In this case, if A is fully compensated for any change in the total cost of his old collection of goods due to price changes, he will consume the different commodities in exactly the same quantities (as well as proportions) as formerly.[1]

---

[1] The case of complete complementarity is analyzed in many mathematical studies of consumers' behavior. It need only be observed here that each indifference curve is represented geometrically by two straight lines at right angles, that the consumers' equilibrium position must be at the focus

In other words, as Staehle explains, the problem of measurement is solved if one can determine for A the collection of goods that would yield him the same real income as his old collection and that he would wish to consume if confronted with B's prices. In the case of complete complementarity, obviously the new collection of goods is the same as the old. The change in the cost of living is thus accurately measured by the conventional method.

If both A's consumption and B's are characterized by complementarity, the conventional method yields two measures of the change in the cost of living, each of which is entirely accurate: one represents the change in the cost of living from the viewpoint of A's tastes and real income, the other from the viewpoint of B's tastes and real income. I think this is worth stressing. The usual practice of referring to the two results obtained by the conventional method as constituting limits for the change in the cost of living is misleading so far as it implies that there is some unique, intermediate, "true" measure that is more accurate than either limit. In the case studied here, each measure obtained by the conventional method is entirely valid in its own right.[2]

If consumption is characterized by complementarity and, in addition, tastes are the same, A's and B's budget positions will both lie on the same expenditure line (expansion path).[3] However, the conventional method will still yield two measures of the cost of living: one from the viewpoint of A's real income, the other from the viewpoint of B's real income. Both are completely accurate.

Only if A consumes goods in the same proportion (not necessarily the same absolute quantities) as B do the two measures

---

of one or another of the right-angle indifference curves (regardless of the price situation), and that there is only one expenditure line or expansion path (the line connecting the different foci) representing the change in the budget position due to changes in money income. This last contrasts with the situation in which consumers' goods are more or less competitive with one another, in which case there is a different expenditure line for each price situation.

[2] Without referring to the conditions under which the conventional method yields accurate results, W. W. Leontief, in "Composite Commodities and the Problem of Index Numbers," *Econometrica*, January 1936, has called attention to the plurality of correct measures of the price level.

[3] See n. 1 above.

merge and yield a unique measure of the change in the cost of living. This is the so-called case of expenditure proportionality.

Complete *complementarity* and *expenditure proportionality* are, of course, not one and the same thing. With *complementarity*, the structure of consumption is not affected by *relative price* changes, but may be affected by changes in *real income*. With *expenditure proportionality* the structure of consumption is not affected by changes in *real income*, but may be affected by changes in *relative prices*. If both conditions obtain, the structure of consumption is not affected by changes in either.[4]

I have commented on the conventional method in some detail mainly in order to clarify its logical foundations, about which it seems to me there are many misconceptions. The foregoing discussion suggests also the need for further empirical work in this field, in particular on the question concerning the degree to which consumers' behavior in the real world approximates the case of complete complementarity. Budget studies could probably shed some light on this question. I suspect that the approximation, *in terms of broad categories* of consumption, may not be bad; that consumers, in determining the total amount of food they buy, housing space they rent, and so on, may not be as sensitive to relative price changes as we are often inclined to assume. There is already abundant evidence, however, that as a rule the case of expenditure proportionality does not hold.

To acknowledge that the change in the cost of living depends upon tastes is not in any sense to question the usefulness of the method devised by Staehle, which yields only one measure even though tastes differ. One must simply interpret Staehle's index as being at one and the same time an approximation to the change in the cost of living from the viewpoint of both A and B. How good an approximation it might be would depend on, among other things, how different tastes are.

With respect to Staehle's interesting method, I wish to raise a question about one central feature. As I understand it, the relative similarity in the proportions in which commodities are consumed is taken as the test of whether real incomes of different households

---

[4] In this case there is only one expenditure line (expansion path) for all price situations, a straight line through the origin.

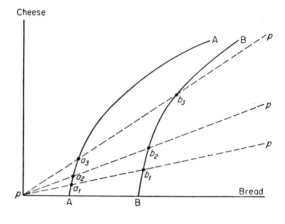

FIGURE 1

AA: expenditure line (expansion path) of A households, facing price
situation 0.

BB: expenditure line (expenditure path) of B households, facing price
situation 1.

a_1, a_2, a_3: budget positions of households A_1, A_2, A_3.

b_1, b_2, b_3: budget positions of households B_1, B_2, B_3.

Lines pp: loci of budget positions for which the structure of consumption is identical and Staehle's D is 0.

facing different price situations are equivalent. This test evidently
leaves open the awkward possibility that A will be said to be as
well off as B, even though B is consuming more of everything, or
of practically everything, than A, provided only that their consumption is in more or less similar proportions.

Figure 1 provides an extreme example of the sort of case I have
in mind. The value of Mr. Staehle's D would be a minimum and
in fact zero in the following cases:

(i) For the pair of households, $a_1 b_1$ among comparisons of a_1
with b_1, b_2, and b_3;

(ii) For the pair of households $a_2 b_2$, among comparisons of a_2
with b_1, b_2 and b_3;

(iii) For the pair of households $a_3 b_3$, among comparisons of a_3
with b_1, b_2, and b_3.

Evidently, these minimum values would represent a "valley" of the type to which Staehle refers. In this situation, *one would be compelled to conclude from Staehle's method that the real income of the households paired in each case was the same, even though the B households were all consuming much more of everything than the A households.*

It is of course not necessary to suppose that as between the A and B households there are pairs of the sort just considered for which the structure of consumption is identical. Staehle's method encounters the same difficulties if this situation is only approximated.

What is the probability that any such situation as the one envisaged will ever confront us? Under two assumptions this sort of situation could be excluded.

(i) If the tastes of the households facing one price situation are similar to those facing the other;

(ii) If consumption is characterized by complete complementarity in the sense referred to a moment ago.

In this case, evidently, all the observed budget positions would tend to cluster about a single expenditure line, rather than about two expenditure lines as seen in Figure 1. In this case Staehle's D test would work without fail—the pairs of households for which D is a relative minimum and very small would be consuming goods in the same quantities as well as in similar proportions.

This is subject, however, to one qualification. The dissimilarity test would still break down in the case of expenditure proportionality. Here D would be zero for any pair of households, even though their real incomes are, in fact, very different.

The conditions I have stated are sufficient conditions; if they hold, the dissimilarity method works. Are they also necessary? I believe they are, in the sense that the more nearly each is satisfied, the more nearly accurate Staehle's method is likely to be. Clearly, if tastes differ radically, anything can happen: a situation comparable to that in Figure 1 is quite conceivable. If tastes are the same but the various goods consumed are highly competitive, a difference in the price situation may give rise to two situations, in neither of which Staehle's method would work satisfactorily. On the one hand, the structure of consumption might be very different for households having the same real income (with the different budget positions being situated on the same indifference curve). Here D would be large, even though real income is the same. On the other hand, the structure of consumption might be similar even though real incomes are very different (as in Figure 1). Here D would be very small, even though real income is different.

If the foregoing is correct, a serious question must arise whether the dissimilarity method is at all superior to or indeed can even be considered on a par with the conventional method. As indicated above, the conventional method supplies us with a satisfactory approximation if the assumption of fixed proportions holds approximately. It is *not* necessary to assume also that tastes are similar. Whether tastes are similar or not would determine whether one gets one or two answers concerning the change in the cost of living for a given level of real income. So far as tastes differ, however, the dissimilarity method might yield very odd results. This might be so even if there is complementarity.

With respect to the method of Frisch to which Staehle refers, perhaps it is permissible for me to call attention to an essay of mine published some years ago.[5] According to my analysis, the measure Frisch takes as an index of the level of real income turns out under his own assumptions to be constant for all levels of real income. For this reason, Frisch's measure cannot very well be used for the purpose Staehle's D is intended to serve; that is, to select households with equivalent real incomes.

[5] See Chapter 4.

6

NATIONAL INCOME AND WELFARE*

In order to appraise from the standpoint of a community's welfare a government measure with wide impact, the economist may proceed variously, but almost inevitably he refers to national income data. How such data are to be construed in the appraisal, however, is now the subject of a sizable and often controversial literature. This essay reviews briefly this important theme.

The national income data considered, of course, properly comprise measurements not only of volume but of distribution. But even on this basis one can only hope to appraise the effect on the community's welfare of but a few of the consequences of the new governmental measure. From such data one seeks to gauge the impact on welfare of variations in the volume and disposition of the current output of different commodities. Even if this is accomplished, any further changes induced in, say, the community's political institutions or cultural life must still remain to be evaluated. The new measure may also affect economic aspects, other than the volume and disposition of current output, that are valued in some degree for their own sake. For example, the volume and disposition of wealth, working hours, and unemployment are all likely to be of this nature. National income data necessarily are unrevealing regarding the immediate impact of changes in these features on welfare.

Yet to appraise a public measure from the standpoint of the community's welfare is a formidable task. If through national

* This essay was written initially for the RAND Corporation, and circulated privately as RAND P-3004, October 1964. I am indebted to Professor Robert Dorfman for helpful comments.

income calculations one can summarize meaningfully the impact on welfare of changes in the production of different commodities and their disposition, this surely would represent a valuable simplification. It is with this restricted application of national income data that the literature referred to has been chiefly concerned. This will also be the concern here.

THE ANALYSIS FOR A CONSUMERS' GOODS ECONOMY

The problem of so applying national income data varies somewhat in character depending on the sorts of goods considered, and their uses. Of particular interest conceptually are consumers' goods which are made available to households individually at money prices. In pertinent writings attention is often focused on such goods. Let us begin, therefore, by referring to a simple community where only such goods are produced.

In discussions of the import of national income for social welfare, the nature of social welfare is not always explained. As seen here, this concept is defined by value judgments supplied by some source. For present purposes, it may be just as well to think of the economist himself as being this source, though presumably the appraisal would be appealing only to persons who shared his values. But while it is advisable to be clear on these fundamentals, I need not insist especially on the particular standpoint taken. Should the reader prefer another one, he should not find it difficult to restate the analysis correspondingly.[1]

Whatever the standpoint on fundamentals, one must still decide on the nature of the dependence of social welfare on factors of concern, particularly the volume and disposition of current output. In the community in question, this output consists of consumers' goods and, for such a community, welfare very often is taken to be such as may be represented by the formula:

$$W = F(U^1, U^2, \ldots, U^i, \ldots, U^n). \qquad (1)$$

---

[1] In saying that social welfare is defined by value judgments, I do not mean to imply that the values in question are of the nature of ultimates and beyond the reach of empirical inquiry. On the contrary, they are often far from ultimates, and therefore significantly open to such inquiry. See Chapter 3.

Here U^i represents the "satisfactions" or "utility" of the ith household from its consumption, while W, the community's welfare, varies positively with U^i. Supposedly, U^i is observed in overt preferences such as the household expresses in an open market. Provisionally, and subject to review, I too take welfare as given by formula (1).

The formula in principle provides a partial basis for ranking, from the standpoint of welfare, economic states that vary in respect of the volume and disposition of consumers' goods output. Thus, such economic states may be ranked whenever some households move to a preferred position and none suffer, or some households move to a less preferred position and none gain, or no one either benefits or suffers. The formula is not incisive, however, where some households benefit and others suffer. There is no need to agree here on any specific principle of evaluation for such cases. In accord with the view taken of the basis for defining social welfare, however, use of formula (1) is understood to rest on a value judgment, in this case one in favor of "consumers' sovereignty." The variation of welfare when there are conflicting changes in utilities, therefore, is understood correspondingly to reflect such further value judgments on "income" distribution as seem appropriate in the circumstances.

While in the community under consideration current output consists only of consumers' goods, welfare must still depend on aspects other than current output, but we are concerned with the relation of the current output to welfare, and properly abstract from other aspects. Use of formula (1) is to be read in this light.

Data on national income, of course, are supposed to be of the "real" sort in "constant prices." Thus, for the simple community considered, we know $\Sigma p_0 X_0$, $\Sigma p_0 X_1$, $\Sigma p_1 X_0$, and $\Sigma p_1 X_1$. Here X_0 and X_1 refer respectively to the community's consumption of any product in position 0, where the new measure has not been introduced, and in position 1, where it has been introduced. Also, p_0 and p_1 are the corresponding prices. Some data are also at hand on income distribution. Ideally, these might take the form of measures for different households of the same sort as are available for the entire community on income in the two sets of constant prices. Thus, for any one household we might wish to know $\Sigma p_0 x_0$, $\Sigma p_0 x_1$, $\Sigma p_1 x_0$, and $\Sigma p_1 x_1$. Here x_0 and x_1 represent the

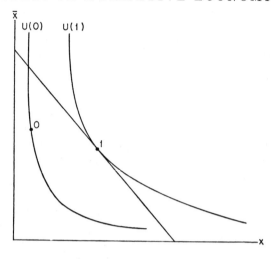

FIGURE 1

consumption of any particular good by the household in position 0 and position 1 respectively, and p_0 and p_1 are as before. Such data, however, are hardly likely to be available in practice.

Let us recall first the familiar essentials concerning the relation of income in constant prices and utility for any one household:

(i) $\quad \sum p_1 x_1 \geq \sum p_1 x_0$ implies $U(1) > U(0)$;

(ii) $\quad \sum p_0 x_1 > \sum p_0 x_0$ implies $U(1) \gtrless U(0)$;

(iii) $\quad \sum p_0 x_1 \leq \sum p_0 x_0$ implies $U(1) < U(0)$;

(iv) $\quad \sum p_1 x_1 < \sum p_1 x_0$ implies $U(1) \gtrless U(0)$.

The first of the four relations, for the case where $\sum p_1 x_1 > \sum p_1 x_0$, is illustrated in a well-known way in Figure 1, and the third might be shown similarly. As indicated, the income data in (ii) and (iv) are inconclusive.

To turn to income and welfare for the community: In Figure 2 are shown for a community comprising two households the utilities enjoyed by them in positions 0 and 1, and the corresponding "point" utility possibility schedules, Q_0Q_0 and Q_1Q_1. Each schedule, therefore, shows alternative utilities that would be en-

134

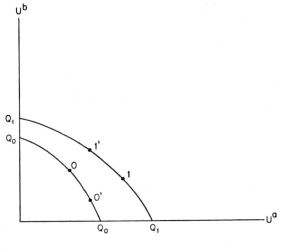

FIGURE 2

joyed by the two households if an unchanged bill of goods were redistributed between them so that the two households remain on their "contract curve." In an open market such a redistribution might be accomplished by "lump-sum" transfers of money income. Prices, too, would have to vary in response to resulting changes in demand for different commodities.

Also shown are $0'$ and $1'$. The former is the position on Q_0Q_0 where the marginal rate of substitution, in terms of the community's welfare, between a dollar of A's income and a dollar of B's would be the same as it is at 1. The position $1'$ is determined similarly in relation to Q_1Q_1 and 0. The positions $0'$ and 1 will be said to be on the same "expansion path," and the positions 0 and $1'$ will be described similarly. Along any one expansion path, the distribution of the "real" national income is understood to be unchanged. As was implied, marginal rates of substitution such as are in question are in principle given by appropriate value judgments.

The volume of "real" national income evidently is constant for variations along any one utility possibility schedule, for such variations entail only redistributions of the same bill of goods.

Along such a schedule, however, note that the community's welfare is *not* constant; rather, as the same bill of goods is redistributed among households, welfare almost inevitably varies. Hence, as the community shifts from one utility possibility schedule to another along any one expansion path, the gain in welfare may not be comparable to that accruing from a corresponding shift along another such path. Indeed, a gain along one path may go hand in hand with a loss along another. These facts are of interest for reasons that will appear later.

With national income data at hand in terms of both 0 and 1 prices, there are various cases to consider. Figure 2 is intended to illustrate one where $\Sigma p_1 X_1 \geq \Sigma p_1 X_0$ and $\Sigma p_0 X_1 > \Sigma p_0 X_0$. Thus, from the former relation we know that $0'$ must be southwest of 1, as shown. This is so because, with some redistribution of the 0 bill of goods which leaves the community on $Q_0 Q_0$, the relation $\Sigma p_1 x_1 \geq \Sigma p_1 x_0$ must hold for each household. Since each household then would be worse off than it is at 1, $Q_0 Q_0$ must be southwest of 1 in the vicinity of 1. Although the expansion path is determined by appropriate value judgments, no one will dispute that $0'$ will be on $Q_0 Q_0$ in this region, and hence that $0'$, too, will be southwest of 1.

The impact of the new measure on welfare, then, depends on the evaluation of the redistribution of income that would occur as a result of a hypothetical change from 0 to $0'$. If this is regarded favorably, necessarily $W(1) > W(0)$, for with the change from $0'$ to 1 everyone gains, so that $W(1) > W(0')$, and a favorable view of the redistribution means $W(0') > W(0)$. If the redistribution is regarded unfavorably, welfare still might increase, but for this the gain in welfare from the shift from $0'$ to 1 would have to be regarded as more than sufficient to offset the loss from the redistribution.

The foregoing follows from the relation $\Sigma p_1 X_1 \geq \Sigma p_1 X_0$. Hence, the impact of the new measure on welfare might be judged without reference to the further relation $\Sigma p_0 X_1 > \Sigma p_0 X_0$. Moreover, the latter relation, like the corresponding one for a single household, is not very informative in any event. When $\Sigma p_1 X_1 \geq \Sigma p_1 X_0$, however, it is of interest that the corresponding calculation in 0 prices also shows an increase in "real" national income, though the alternative case where it does not show an increase need not lead to any different finding regarding welfare. But I consider the latter case in a moment.

The case where $\Sigma p_0 X_0 \geq \Sigma p_0 X_1$ and $\Sigma p_1 X_0 > \Sigma p_1 X_1$ is conceptually parallel to that just discussed. Hence it need not be explored here.

The next case to consider is $\Sigma p_1 X_1 \geq \Sigma p_1 X_0$ and $\Sigma p_0 X_1 \leq \Sigma p_0 X_0$. As is well known, such "conflicting" relations in income in constant prices for a single household could occur only if the household's preferences either were inconsistent or had changed under the impact of the new measure. For the moment I am passing by such possibilities, but the conflicting relations in *national* income are still possible so far as the new measure may affect the distribution of income. Should the values defining W be consistent, however, we should in principle be able to gauge, as we did before, how it varies from either of the two national income comparisons in question. But, so far as these comparisons are here in conflict, they might seem to lead to inconsistent inferences, and it is of interest to see how such inconsistency would have to be avoided.

Suppose, then, that by reasoning as before from $\Sigma p_1 X_1 \geq \Sigma p_1 X_0$, one were led to conclude that 1 is preferable to 0. Suppose, too, that the redistribution involved (the shift from 0 to 0' in Figure 3) were viewed favorably, and hence as compounding the gain resulting from the shift along an expansion path from 0' to 1. If one is to be consistent, how must he reason from the relation $\Sigma p_0 X_1 \leq \Sigma p_0 X_0$? Evidently, since there is now an adverse shift along an expansion path from 0 to 1', the associated redistribution (the shift from 1' to 1) must be considered not only favorably but as more than offsetting the loss in volume.

And this is not implausible, but suppose the initial decision in favor of 1 on the basis of $\Sigma p_1 X_1 \geq \Sigma p_1 X_0$ were made despite an unfavorable view of the associated redistribution (the shift from 0 to 0'), and in the belief that the gain from the shift from 0' to 1 was more than offsetting. Would it not be inconsistent now to view favorably the alternative redistribution (the shift from 1' to 1)? Moreover, if the judgment on this were now adverse, is it not implied that 0 is preferable to 1 after all, which is again a contra-

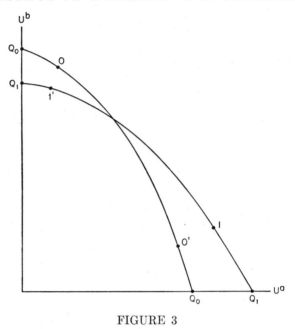

FIGURE 3

diction? The answer in both instances is in the negative, for if there is any paradox here it is purely geometric and is dispelled at once if we consider the fact referred to above: the utility possibility schedule is not a locus of constant welfare. If a redistribution from 0 to 0' reduces welfare, it is not at all precluded that a redistribution from 1' to 1 would increase it. In order clearly to see this the reader may wish to elaborate Figure 3 by drawing in alternative sets of loci for which W might be constant at different levels.

By reasoning from $\Sigma p_1 X_1 \geq \Sigma p_1 X_0$ one might possibly have concluded that 0 is preferable to 1, but what might be said about this further possibility will be evident.

Our final case is $\Sigma p_0 X_1 > \Sigma p_0 X_0$, and $\Sigma p_1 X_1 < \Sigma p_1 X_0$. Apparently the national income data are here indecisive.

Reference throughout has been to the evaluation of two alternative economic states, 0 and 1, one prevailing without, and the other prevailing with, a new public measure. If other alterna-

138

tives should be open—for example, if $0'$ and $1'$ were not simply hypothetical but could be achieved in fact—the appraisal necessarily would have to consider these as well. However, if $\Sigma p_1 X_1 \geq \Sigma p_1 X_0$, $0'$ could never be favored over 1. Similarly, if $\Sigma p_0 X_1 \leq \Sigma p_0 X_0$, $1'$ could never be favored over 0.

But if alternatives have to be evaluated in the foregoing manner, is the procedure not likely to be taxing in respect of the value judgments required? Thus, would it not be too much to expect that anyone could meaningfully compare conflicting consequences for welfare of a "real" income redistribution, on the one hand, and a shift along an expansion path, on the other? And this says nothing of the need to supply value judgments defining an expansion path to begin with. Would not the delineation of such a path really be out of the question for any likely source of value judgments, even an economist?

Although it has seemed in order to formulate the appraisal precisely in terms of expansion paths, there is no need to suppose that these paths could be delineated precisely in fact. Rather, the requirement is only that one be able somehow to evaluate a redistribution such as that in question, and I do not think this need be overly taxing, at least not always. For example, in the first case considered (Figure 2), one need not know precisely where $0'$ is. All that is required is that one knows whether a shift along $Q_0 Q_0$ in the direction of a distribution more or less similar to 1 would be to the good. If it were not to the good, it is true that the new measure could be definitely evaluated only if one were able to compare the loss from the redistribution with the gain realized otherwise, but this surely would sometimes be possible. Still, if it were not, admittedly it would be impossible to say whether the new measure is a good thing or not, but this is a limitation not of the procedure, but of one's values. Other cases I believe need not always be unduly taxing either, though here too some choices will no doubt be indeterminate. This is especially likely where there are conflicting comparisons of national income in terms of alternative prices.[2]

---

[2] Where the source of value judgments is unable to appraise alternatives, should we not conclude, not that the ranking of the alternatives is indeterminate, but that the source is simply indifferent between them? Such

Redistributions such as those in question would entail not only lump-sum transfers but appropriate adjustments in prices to assure that the market is always cleared of available supplies. This means that the reallocation of supplies must be less marked than the money transfers might suggest, for, necessarily, prices would tend to increase for things purchased especially by those whose money income increased, and to decrease for those purchased especially by those whose money incomes decreased. But, while this aspect too would have to be considered in the evaluation of the income redistribution, it should not pose any serious problem. The price changes could never be so large as to cause the redistribution of "real" income to be in the reverse direction from that in money income.

Granted that the needed values would often be available, the appraisal assumes that, ideally, data in constant prices are at hand not only on national income but on incomes of different households. From the latter sort of data, would it not be possible to appraise the new measure without reference to any hypothetical alternative positions, and indeed even without reference to the national income data, but simply from a consideration of the gains and losses to different households? No doubt it sometimes would be, but reference to national income seems only to simplify a complex task, and once national income is considered, reference to hypothetical positions is logically inherent in the appraisal. Reference to national income data, one suspects, is likely to be the more in order where available data on distribution are less than ideal, though in this case confidence in the appraisal may diminish too.

---

usage no doubt has some merit, but if one were to adopt it he might encounter anomalies. Thus, consider three social states, A, B, and C. In terms of A's prices, the "real" national income of A is greater than that in either B or C, but because of adverse changes in income distribution the source of values is in doubt whether A really represents an improvement over either alternative. In accord with the proposed usage, then, the source is held to be indifferent between A and B and A and C. What, however, if in B's prices "real" national income in B is greater than in C, while income distribution of a B-like sort is also judged preferable to that in C? By implication B is preferable to C, although both states are equivalent to A.

NATIONAL INCOME AND WELFARE

ALTERNATIVE FORMULATIONS

Anyone who inquires into the relation of national income to welfare, as represented by formula (1), must soon come to be heavily in debt to the pioneer work of Pigou, Kaldor, Hicks, Scitovsky, and Samuelson. In order to relate the foregoing discussion to previous analyses, however, it may suffice to explain that I take as a point of departure Little's famous criterion for an increase in welfare.[3]

According to this, a change is economically desirable,[4] "if (a) it would result in a good redistribution of welfare, and if (b) the potential losers could not profitably bribe the potential gainers to oppose the change."

This criterion is rather abstract and can become useful only if it is specified how we may determine whether (b) is satisfied. But, as Little makes clear, one way in which this can be done is by reference to national income data. Particularly, a sufficient condition for (b) to be satisfied in 1 compared with 0 is simply that $\Sigma p_1 X_1 \geq \Sigma p_1 X_0$. Similarly (b) is satisfied in 0 compared with 1 if $\Sigma p_0 X_1 \leq \Sigma p_0 X_0$. Hence for the case where $\Sigma p_1 X_1 \geq \Sigma p_1 X_0$ and the distribution is deemed better in 1 than in 0, my finding is the same as Little's. This is also true for the case where $\Sigma p_0 X_1 \leq \Sigma p_0 X_0$ and the distribution is deemed better in 0. I have also followed Mr. Little so far as I have referred to hypothetical positions in elaborating the logic of the appraisal.

Mr. Little's criterion, however, provides a basis for appraisal of welfare only in these cases. Admittedly, other cases where the redistribution is in conflict with the pertinent national income data may be difficult to gauge, but appraisal must often be possible, nonetheless. After all, the redistribution itself is apt to be complex, and if one is able to appraise it, it seems odd to suppose that one must always balk if asked to take a further step and judge whether an increase in "real" national income may not sometimes be to the good even though the associated redistribution is bad; or whether a decrease in "real" national income may

[3] I. M. D. Little, *A Critique of Welfare Economics*, 2nd ed. (Oxford, 1957), chapters 6, 7, 12.

[4] *Ibid.*, pp. 123, 275.

not sometimes be to the bad even though the associated redistribution is to the good.

Little is not very explicit as to when an income distribution referring to one bill of goods might be deemed equivalent in terms of welfare to one referring to another bill of goods. In elaborating his criterion I have sought to be clear in this regard. Also, Little focuses especially on the case where, if a redistribution from (say) 0 to 0' (Figure 2) is good, so also is one from 1' to 1. Other cases are also possible, though their appraisal probably presupposes an especially discriminating source of value judgments.

Little's criterion is now the subject of numerous writings.[5] Their authors' concern, however, is more with the meaning and logic of the criterion, as such, than with its application by reference to national income data. But one aspect debated is whether Little's hypothetical positions need be on a point utility possibility schedule. It should be observed, therefore, that, as Mr. Sen has urged, they need not be generally, but are appropriately conceived as on such a schedule, as Mr. Mishan has argued, when the criterion is applied by reference to national data. One may wonder to what extent there are likely to be interesting applications involving hypothetical positions otherwise located, but this is another matter. For the case where use is made of national income data, I have already sided with Little against Kennedy on the question of whether consideration of hypothetical positions is in order to begin with. The present analysis conforms to a desideratum of Professor Meade, however, so far as appraisals are made, even where there are conflicting changes in "real" national income and its distribution.

CONSUMER IRRATIONALITY, INTERRELATEDNESS, AND CHANGING TASTES

Use of formula (1) to represent social welfare means that variations in a household's consumption are valued in terms of its own

[5] For the early literature, see E. J. Mishan, "A Survey of Welfare Economics," *The Economic Journal*, June 1960. For more recent contributions, see the review by Meade of the second edition of Little's book in *The Economic Journal*, March 1959, and the communications by Robertson, Little, Meade, Mishan, Kennedy, Dobb and Sen in issues of the same journal for March 1962, June 1963, December 1963, June 1964.

overt preferences. At least this is so when its overt preferences are also taken to indicate its utility from consumption. However, the principle of "consumers' sovereignty" as thus understood has been questioned on two grounds: (i) The household often does not know what is "good" for it. Hence, its overt preferences may fail to indicate its utility from consumption if such utility is understood in a normative (as distinct from descriptive) sense, such as is proper when it is an argument in the formula for social welfare. (ii) A household's utility depends not only on its own consumption but on that of other people. In formula (1) no account is taken of such interdependence.

Whether a household knows what is good for it is a familiar theme on which I cannot embark here,[6] but, as frequently observed, even if one questions the household's overt preferences, it does not follow that one knows any better what is good for the household. Still less does it follow that in the appraisal of a public measure such preferences should be disregarded, for the violation might be felt repugnant and, in a deeper sense, itself injurious to the household's interest.

In any case, if overt preferences were questioned only exceptionally and in spheres rather remote from the new governmental measure, national income data might still be used to appraise it, and indeed in the same way as where overt preferences are not questioned at all. Even if circumstances were otherwise, reference might usefully be made to national income data, but one would have to consider how the calculations might be affected if different commodities were valued, not at market prices reflecting overt preferences, but at some other prices deemed to be more appropriate.

I wonder whether in economics the phenomenon of interdependence has not been somewhat overstressed. Granting that interdependence is pervasive, nevertheless, for the bulk of consumers' goods, the effect on the community's welfare of variations in a household's consumption would still seem properly gauged primarily by reference to the utility of the household in question.

---

[6] On consumers' sovereignty generally, see the essays of Tibor Scitovsky and Jerome Rothenberg, and the comments by Abram Bergson, Stanislaw Wellisz and William J. Baumol in *American Economic Review*, May 1962, No. 2. See also Chapter 3.

Interdependence, however, is no doubt often consequential, and should the new measure have much impact in spheres where it is, the interdependence must be considered in the appraisal. Reference to national income data may still be useful, but it is necessary to consider how the outcome might be affected when account is taken of the interdependence. Possibly the latter aspect could sometimes be quantified through special inquiry; otherwise its import must somehow be judged along with that of extra-economic aspects already alluded to (above, p. 131).

As is not always understood, interdependence is a complex phenomenon. Thus, different households may be interdependent because the satisfactions of one depend on another's consumption of one or another good (for example, one derives satisfaction from a neighbor's lawn); because the satisfactions of one depend on another's consumption generally (the household's prestige and status in the community, for example, depend on its relative income); because the satisfactions of one depend on another's satisfactions (one simply derives satisfactions from another's dissatisfactions).[7]

In considering interdependence as it affects the import of national income data for welfare, I have had in mind interdependence of the first of these three types. As for interdependence of the second type, this does not really represent any departure to speak of from formula (1). In any case, so far as its import can be judged, such interdependence is to be considered in the evaluation, not of individual commodities, but of alternative income distributions. Interdependence of the third type also is consistent with formula (1) so long as one household derives satisfactions, rather than dissatisfactions, from another's satisfactions; and one hardly is disposed to consider interdependence otherwise, though in principle it too could be taken into account in the evaluation of income distribution.

Interdependence even of the first type has different facets. Thus, where a household's utility is affected by consumption of one or another good by others, its preferences among different goods may or may not be affected. I have been referring thus far

---

[7] See Chapter 3, n. 5.

to cases where such preferences are not affected. If the household's preferences are affected, often what will count is not so much the consumption of the good in question by other households individually, but the total consumption of the community generally. Here the appraisal may proceed more or less as before. Thus, for any given total supplies, market prices are still indicative of the relative marginal utilities of different commodities to households, and national income data correspondingly still indicate welfare, though necessarily the data only register benefits and losses that households experience from changes in their own personal consumption. A complete appraisal must also consider additional benefits and losses which, as a result of interrelatedness, the households experience from changes in the consumption of the community generally. So far as the community's total consumption of a good varies, however, and the preferences of different households vary correspondingly, alternative index numbers in terms of prices relating to different situations may possibly conflict not only for the community generally but for individual households. Such an eventuality surely would be awkward. But what might be said about it I think will be sufficiently evident from what has been said already about conflicting index numbers and what will be said about another matter to which I now turn: changes in tastes.

Thus far I have tacitly assumed that a household's "tastes," that is, its overt preferences, are the same in 1 as they are in 0. What if instead they should change? Professor Hicks long ago answered this question in a way that is still widely accepted:[8]

For my part, I should distinguish the question of economic welfare from any conceivable broader question of welfare generally by the rule that comparisons of economic welfare must proceed under the hypothesis of *constant* wants. It is only under this hypothesis that quantitative comparisons are possible. In order to be able to compare the positions of a particular individual in two different situations, we must assume that his wants are the same in the two situations. If this assumption cannot be granted, the question of whether he is better off in one situation or in the other loses all economic meaning. If he has undergone a

[8] J. R. Hicks, "The Valuation of Social Income," *Economica*, May 1940, p. 107.

spiritual conversion in the interim, so that he has given his goods to feed the poor, the question of his relative well-being in the two situations is a spiritual question, not an economic one. Comparisons of economic welfare are comparisons of welfare in general, under the assumption of unchanged tastes. They are significant so far, and only so far, as we judge the assumption of unchanged tastes to be a tolerable assumption with reference to any particular actual comparison.

Since this essay deals with the appraisal of some government measure, we are in effect concerned, not with a *historical* variation in welfare, such as actually occurs with the lapse of time, but with a *virtual* variation, such as might occur at any one time, depending on whether a new measure is adopted or not. As seems rarely considered, changes in taste are unlikely to be as consequential from the latter as from the former standpoint. In respect of a historical variation, any and all changes in tastes matter; in respect of a virtual variation, we need be concerned only with changes that might be induced by the new measure.[9]

Moreover, while changes in tastes are often difficult to observe, they are apt to be especially so where reference is only to those pertinent to a virtual variation in welfare. Thus, for different households, changes in tastes over a period of time are manifest in "real" income data if there are conflicting index numbers, but not otherwise. For the community generally, even conflicting index numbers may not be incisive, for these may be due also to income redistribution, though whether this is likely to be so might sometimes be inferred from further information on income redistribution. Where reference is to virtual changes, however, the relevant income data must themselves have the character of projections. This is true of the calculation for 0, representing what income would be without the new measure, as well as of the calculation for 1, representing what income would be with the new measure. Hence, the income data could be indicative of a change of tastes to begin with only if such a change is otherwise observable, and as so observed is considered in calculating the prices and quantities on which the income projections are based.

[9] Without considering virtual changes in tastes, Arrow in his review (*American Economic Review*, December 1951) of the first edition of Little's *Critique of Welfare Economics* is explicit that historical changes need not be relevant in the context of policy appraisal.

Yet a new measure may induce taste changes, and in one way or another these may be observed in some degree. Thus something might be learned about them from a study of the impact of similar measures at other times and places. And so far as taste changes are induced and observable, we surely cannot ignore them. But the moral then would seem to be somewhat different from that drawn by Professor Hicks. It follows, not that quantitative comparisons of welfare cease to be possible, but that there is now one more factor affecting welfare that is beyond the reach of national income data but must somehow be considered in the appraisal: the change in tastes.

To evaluate this aspect from the standpoint of welfare, however, might be difficult, and if it is, there are in principle additional sorts of national income data from among which we may be unable to choose very meaningfully. Thus, national income projections for both 0 and 1 might conceivably be made not only in terms of alternative prices but from the standpoint of alternative tastes. So far as available information on the change in tastes permits, comparisons might be made of national income in the two periods in terms of the tastes prevailing without the new measure and of either the corresponding 0 prices or the corresponding 1 prices; and also in terms of the tastes prevailing with the new measure and either the corresponding 0 prices or the corresponding 1 prices. Moreover, each sort of comparison would have a claim to be considered. The appraisal would be facilitated, however, by acceptance of two further principles: If a new measure increases welfare according to national income projections reflecting both tastes prevailing without and tastes prevailing with the new measure, the new measure should be adopted. If the change in tastes is expected to be irreversible, it suffices that projections reflecting tastes prevailing with the new measure should show an increase in welfare.[10]

While not unassailable, the first principle might be viewed as something of a corollary, for the case of changing tastes, of the

[10] Compare Sidney Schoeffler, "Note on Modern Welfare Economics," *American Economic Review*, December 1952; Jerome Rothenberg, *The Measurement of Social Welfare* (Englewood Cliffs, N.J., 1961), pp. 52ff.

principle of consumers' sovereignty, and surely is appealing. As for the second, this requires that priority be accorded to tastes prevailing after, over those prevailing before, an irreversible change, and this too perhaps is a not unappealing extension of consumers' sovereignty. After all, the consumer with all his foibles might tend to learn from his experience, and in this way to come to know better what is "good" for him. But this is a philosophic matter, on which opinions may often differ.

The government measure in question has been supposed thus far to be such that its adoption involves the introduction of no new products. If new products are introduced, national income may be calculated as before at prices prevailing under the new measure, but for the corresponding calculation at prices prevailing without the new measure, appropriate prices are lacking for the new products. As Professor Hicks has explained,[11] however, in this calculation new products should be valued at prices such that the demand for them would be zero. From this, something may be inferred as to the change in national income at prices prevailing without the new measure, though this may not be very helpful.[12] I leave it to the reader to consider the problem posed when the new measure affects population numbers.

In the simple community considered, consumers' goods supposedly have been made available to households at prices which are at clearing levels; at least they limit demand to quantities at or below available supplies. To the extent that consumers' goods are distributed otherwise than at prices conforming to clearing levels, the national income data necessarily are distorted. How-

---

[11] *Economica*, May 1940, p. 110.
[12] By deflation, the index of change in national income at such prices is given by the formula: $(\Sigma p_1 X_1 / \Sigma p_0 X_0) \div (\Sigma p_1 X_1 / \Sigma p_0 X_1)$. The first fraction represents the ratio of total money outlays in the two periods and is known. If the second is calculated for all goods other than new products, the resulting measure of price change should overstate the increase or understate the decrease in prices, for in relation to other prices the prices of new products should have declined from the level at which demand would be zero. Unfortunately, national income measurements in 0 prices could be incisive only if the indicated index were equal to or less than unity. If it were actually less than unity without allowance for new products, one might be in doubt whether it still would be with such an allowance.

ever, with supplementary information on the comparative state of the market for different products and the comparative changes in the volume of their output, something might be inferred about the direction of the bias, or possibly even the amount.

COMMUNAL CONSUMPTION AND COLLECTIVE AND INVESTMENT GOODS

While the simple community considered produces only consumers' goods that are made available to households individually at money prices, in the real world consumers' goods usually are also supplied to households communally, that is, free of charge, and such supplies must also be included in national income viewed as a category indicative of welfare. How are they to be valued?

If consumers' goods are supplied to households communally, the supplier almost always is the government, and such supplies usually are valued in national income at the cost to the government of supplying them. This procedure has also been held by Hicks to have some merit:

> Here I can see no alternative but to assume that the public services are worth, to society in general, at least what they cost; and that this principle holds also at the margin. One may well feel considerable qualms about such an assumption—it is obvious that the government spends far too much on this, far too little on that; but if we accept the actual choices of the individual consumer as reflecting his preferences . . . , then I do not see that we have any choice but to accept the actual choices of the government, even if they are expressed through a Nero or a Robespierre, as representing the actual wants of society.[13]

In practice, valuation of consumers' goods supplied communally at cost is difficult to avoid, but, as we see from Professor Arrow's analysis of political decision-making,[14] the interpretation of such a valuation as reflecting some collective preference scale may encounter logical difficulties. Also, if one is at all dissatisfied with the existing allocation to communal consumers' goods, one

[13] *Economica*, May 1940, p. 116.
[14] Kenneth J. Arrow, *Social Choice and Individual Values*, 2nd ed. (New York, 1963).

149

cannot expect national income data which include them at cost to be reliably indicative of welfare from one's own standpoint. Valuation at cost, of course, is inappropriate in any case where the concern is to appraise a new measure directed to change the resources devoted to communal supply of consumers' goods. Rather, reference must be made to some other values deemed appropriate. Whether one should then trouble at all to aggregate communal with other supplies in order to calculate national income, however, is open to question. Very likely the appraisal could be made just as well by reference to alternative mixes of the two sorts of supplies.

Why not seek to value consumers' goods supplied communally, like those supplied at money prices, in accord with consumers' sovereignty? To ascertain household overt preferences in the absence of a market would not be easy. Moreover, even though they are distributed free of charge, consumers' goods are understood here to be supplies which physically are made available to different households individually. Given this, consumers' sovereignty could not provide a clear basis for valuation even in principle. Unless the demand of all households were satisfied at the zero price, valuation conforming to their preferences would have to vary with the household. Again, the decision to supply consumers' goods communally often reflects misgivings about household preferences for the products in question. If these misgivings are shared, one would hesitate to be guided by consumers' sovereignty in any case.

In addition to consumers' goods, the government of almost any community will also supply communally and without charge diverse collective goods, that is, goods which because of their physical nature cannot be made available to households individually. Like consumers' goods supplied communally, collective goods usually are valued in national income at cost, though in principle much the same considerations apply for the latter as for the former. In contrast to a consumers' good, a collective good must be distributed communally because of its nature. Hence, in the decision to supply collective goods in this way no determination is implied to overrule consumers' sovereignty, but in reference to a collective good conformity to this standard presumably would mean that a marginal unit should be valued at the sum which all households together would pay for it. One might hesitate to value collective goods in this way even if this were practicable, which is unlikely.

Depending on the standpoint, it may possibly be felt that a collective good sometimes has only a zero value in terms of welfare. In this case it should not be included in national income to begin with.[15]

Ordinarily the community also produces investment goods, representing an increase in its capacity to produce consumers' and collective goods in the future. Professor Fisher would have excluded such goods from national income, but where the latter category is taken as indicative of welfare, as Professor Pigou held long ago, investment goods are properly included in it.[16] Yet opinions diverge regarding the appropriate valuation. According to Professor Kuznets, investment goods are properly valued at their own prices. Hence, national income at constant prices is calculated by valuing all goods, including investment goods at the corresponding prices of the year to which the constant prices refer.[17] According to Mr. Little, national income at current prices include savings, and hence presumably investment goods at current prices, but saving at constant prices is to be computed by deflation by a price index for consumers' goods only.[18]

For purposes of measuring welfare, I believe Professor Kuznets' procedure is the correct one. Imagine a community in which investment goods are purchased directly by households who wish to save. Suppose also that the community produces only such goods, together with consumers' goods made available to households individually at money prices. Furthermore, when calculated by the Kuznets procedure, national income in the prices of (say)

---

[15] To return to the valuation of a collective good conforming to consumers' sovereignty, the total amount households together would pay for a marginal unit would seem to be the value indicated, but if national income were calculated with collective goods valued in this way, I believe it still could indicate welfare only if income distribution were optimal.

[16] A. C. Pigou, *Economics of Welfare*, 4th ed. (London, 1948), pp. 34ff.

[17] Simon Kuznets, "On the Valuation of Social Income—Reflections on Professor Hicks' Article," Part I, *Economica*, February 1948, pp. 12–14.

[18] *Critique of Welfare Economics*, pp. 235–236.

1, is found to be greater in 1 than in 0. In other words,

$$p_1^c X_1^c + p_1^i X_1^i > p_1^c X_0^c + p_1^i X_0^i. \qquad (2)$$

The community is supposed to produce in periods 0 and 1 only one consumers' good in amounts X_0^c and X_1^c, and only one investment good, in amounts X_0^i and X_1^i, while p_1^c and p_1^i are the corresponding prices in 1. Evidently, if a relation corresponding to (2) should prevail for any one household, the household could have acquired the 0 mix of goods in 1 for less money than was actually spent. Hence the 1 mix must be preferable to the 0 one, and with due regard to redistribution, we may reason as before from (2), to the welfare of all households together.

Suppose, however, that a similar change is observed in national income in period 1 prices when the calculation is in accord with Mr. Little's procedure:

$$p_1^c X_1^c + p_1^i X_1^i > \frac{p_1^c}{p_0^c} (p_0^c X_0^c + p_0^i X_0^i), \qquad (3)$$

Given the corresponding relation for a single household, the household might have been able to acquire the 0 mix in 1 at a reduced outlay, but then again it might not have. It would have been able to if $(p_1^i/p_0^c) \cdot p_0^i \geq p_1^i$, but it might not have otherwise. Hence, nothing may be inferred from (3) as to the community's welfare.

In fact, households do not purchase investment goods when they save, but I believe nothing is changed in principle if households purchase equities with their savings and the sales of equities in turn finance the purchase of investment goods. Calculated by the Kuznets method, however, national income inclusive of investment goods would tend to be less indicative of welfare the less effective and competitive are the markets for capital and investment goods. Also, I am assuming that consumers' sovereignty serves as a standard for defining welfare in choices between present and future. From this standpoint the reliability of national income as a measure of welfare is likely to be further impaired when savings are undertaken by business enterprises in behalf of households, and when, because of public fiscal policy, private savings generally may differ from the volume of investment goods produced.

The volume of investment goods to be included in national income is supposed to be that currently produced less an allowance for the loss in value of pre-existing stock of such goods that is associated with their current use. As for the nature of this allowance, Professor Pigou's careful formulation still seems reasonable to me,[19] but he apparently focuses primarily on historical changes in welfare and national income. It should be observed, therefore, that, where the concern is rather with virtual variations, the calculation is in principle somewhat simplified. Thus, what matters is only the degree to which introduction of the new measure itself might affect the volume of future services obtainable from the pre-existing stock, and in this way the value of this stock at prices congruent with those used in valuing national income generally. Actually, the change in stock as so understood should often be negligible.

Finally, a community also produces "intermediate" goods, representing supplies not valued for their own sake which are used up currently in the production of other supplies. Such goods, of course, must be omitted altogether from the calculation of national income.

Reference has been to various categories of goods analytically distinguished: consumers' goods distributed to households individually at money prices; consumers' goods distributed communally or without charge; collective goods; investment goods, and intermediate products. It is understood that the classification of any actual products among these different categories must depend on the use made of them. Also, any actual product might in this way be classified in more than one category. In practice such a classification is often difficult to make, and appeal understandably is made to one or another convention. For present purposes, only the division between intermediate and all other goods matters, but there are difficulties here as well: for example, in the treatment of various sorts of government services. I do not think, however, that I need pursue this familiar theme here.

---

[19] *Economics of Welfare*, pp. 43ff.

HISTORICAL CHANGES IN WELFARE

I have been focusing throughout on the use of national income data to gauge virtual changes in welfare. In conclusion, it should be observed that where the concern is the alternative one of gauging historical changes, the appraisal in principle may proceed much as in the former case. Yet difficulties already encountered seem only to be compounded when the concern is with historical changes, especially if the latter span a lengthy interval. Among other things, we must now consider not only changes in tastes induced by a new measure, but any and all changes in tastes; and over a lengthy period these are apt to be consequential. Indeed, as time passes the consumers will tend increasingly to be different people from those present initially. Associated with the change in tastes there will very likely be changes also in the nature and importance of interdependence. If the interval considered is one in which there are marked changes in the relative volume of communal supplies, the arbitrary evaluation of these at cost could also become a source of significant distortions; and changes in the share of savings by business enterprises and government might have a similar effect.

In sum, national income hardly is precisely indicative of welfare whether the concern is with virtual or historical changes, but the relation between the two categories becomes especially obscure in the latter case. Even so, national income data can still serve as a point of departure for speculation about historical changes in welfare, and on such a complex theme this must be to the good.

I refer to the use of national income data to appraise the impact on welfare of historical changes in the volume and disposition of current output. As before, changes in these aspects are likely to be associated with political, cultural, and economic changes affecting welfare that are quite beyond the reach of national income data. Indeed, over any lengthy interval the latter are likely to be especially consequential, and obviously to speculate how, together with changes in the volume and disposition of output, they might affect welfare, could not be a very meaningful or fruitful exercise. When reference is to historical changes in welfare, however, the more basic concern apparently is often to gain insight into the dynamics of the historical process, and so far as the national income data sum up the impact on welfare of changes in the volume and disposition of current output, they might still be helpful in this regard. Thus, they might often illuminate the sources of changing attitudes and behavior in the community, and, so far as they do, they surely would be of value.

In respect of historical as of virtual variations, I have been assuming that the aim is to determine whether—as it is affected by changes in the volume and disposition of current output—welfare is greater or less. In a thoughtful essay, however, Professor Abramovitz has urged that in the study of economic growth this does not suffice.[20] "We want to be able to say not only that welfare in II is greater than in I, but also that the improvement from II to III is greater or less than that between I and II, and so on." From comparative changes in national income, therefore, it is such comparative changes in welfare that we wish to infer, and this Professor Abramovitz argues we are unable to do.

I agree that from national income data we generally cannot hope to infer the comparative magnitude of changes in welfare, but wonder why such inferences are so vital. If national income data serve only to indicate whether welfare has been increasing or decreasing, they surely would illuminate the historical process on this score alone. If welfare were not only ordinally but cardinally measurable, and we knew its relation to national income, our understanding of the historical process might be greater, but this is not essential.

In studying economic growth with the aid of national income data, it is true, we often compare rates of growth in different periods, but as may not have been considered such comparisons can be meaningful and useful even though welfare cannot be assumed to vary commensurately. By studying how the rate of growth of national income varies at different times, and the underlying causes of the variation, we may gain insight into

---

[20] Moses Abramovitz, "The Welfare Interpretation of Secular Trends in National Income," in *The Allocation of Economic Resources* (Stanford, California, 1959), pp. 9–10.

comparative rates of growth that might result from alternative policies *now* being weighed. And, in seeking to choose between such policies, we need be concerned only that national income be ordinally indicative of welfare in the context where the policies are to be applied. Whether it may also have measured welfare cardinally over historically observed intervals is an interesting issue, but not germane to current policy appraisal.

7

ON THE APPRAISAL OF

INDIVISIBILITIES*

In his efforts to rehabilitate consumers' surplus, Professor Hicks has surely achieved a very real success.[1] Among other things, the analysis is now seen not to require the cardinal measurability of utility, which Marshall assumed, but only ordinal measurability. With this, the objectionable Marshallian requirement of a constant marginal utility of money is also supplanted by that as to the absence of "income effects."

What, however, if such effects are present? Among the various uses to which consumers' surplus analysis is put, by far the most important is that where the aim is to appraise, from the standpoint of welfare, indivisible changes in the capacity to produce some product. For commodities for which the income-elasticity of demand is "low," or which constitute only a "small" fraction of the household's budget, we are told that the finding as to whether such an indivisible change is meritorious is still likely to be valid. As with Marshall, however, the analysis still employs only information on the household's price-demand schedule. Curiously, as seems not to have been considered, where information is available on the household's price-demand schedule it usually is available also on the corresponding income-demand schedule. Indeed, the price-demand schedule represents the relation of demand to

* I have benefited from helpful comments by Professors Pieter de Wolff, Hendrik S. Houthakker, and Clopper Almon. For my instruction, Mr. Yoel Haitovsky kindly carried out, by use of an electronic computer, several illustrative computations such as are referred to below, p. 160.
[1] See J. R. Hicks, *A Revision of Demand Theory* (Oxford, 1956).

price when income is constant, and except rarely this relation is only determinable where that between demand and income is determined as well. Moreover, it becomes almost immediately apparent that rather than neglect income effects it should be possible on this basis to take them into account to begin with in the calculation regarding the indivisibility.

This essay re-examines the appraisal of indivisibilities with a view to treating income effects in this manner. Admittedly no reason is found to question the presupposition that such effects ordinarily should not be very consequential. But it should be useful to be able to integrate them in the appraisal.

ALTERNATIVE METHODS OF DELIMITING THE INDIFFERENCE MAP

Barring cardinality, the appraisal of an indivisible change requires that we determine whether, as a result of the change, the household might move to a preferred position. To do so, we must somehow delimit the household's "indifference map," at least as it bears on choices between the product that is especially affected by the indivisibility and all other products. As is still not always grasped but nevertheless is readily seen from Hicks' analysis, this is the import of the attempt to determine through consumers' surplus analysis the amount of a household's "all-or-none offer" for the product that is especially affected, or, rather, for the expected increment of that product. So far as the all-or-none offer is determined, the indifference map is delimited for relevant choices. Indeed, in the absence of income effects, the delimitation is precise.

The delimitation of the indifference curve, therefore, must also be the concern where income effects are to be taken into account. To achieve such delimitation, on the basis of the information that is supposed to be available, must reduce formally to a problem of integration, and one which might be approached in various ways, but it should be generally feasible and often convenient to employ a procedure where reference is made to two formulae, one familiar and one perhaps less so. This is the familiar formula:

$$\overline{E}_{xp} = E_{xp} + \frac{px}{I} E_{xI}. \tag{1}$$

Here x is the amount of X, the commodity on which attention is focused, which is consumed by the household; p is its price and I is the household's income. Also E_{xI} is the household's income elasticity of demand for X, and E_{xp} its price elasticity of demand for X. $\overline{E}_{xp}$ is the household's compensated price elasticity of demand for X—that is, the percentage change in demand induced by a one percent change in price, where income varies concomitantly so that the household remains on the same indifference curve so far as concerns choices between X and all other goods. The latter are measured with a dollar's worth at constant prices as the unit, and for convenience p will be understood to represent the price of X in terms of other goods as so measured.

Formula (1), of course, is the famous Slutsky equation expressed in terms of elasticities. The second formula in mind is simply the counterpart of this, where the relation of the consumption of all other goods and the price of X is in question:

$$\overline{E}_{yp} = -\frac{px}{y}\,\overline{E}_{xp}. \tag{2}$$

Here $\overline{E}_{yp}$ is the elasticity of the schedule of the compensated demand for all other goods Y, in respect of the price p of X; and y is the volume of Y consumed.[2]

To repeat, for purposes of appraising an indivisible change, we wish especially to delineate the facet of the household's indifference map bearing on choices between one product on which attention focuses and all other products. Also, only one indifference curve is immediately relevant, namely, that passing through the position initially occupied by the household. We are supposed to know the household's demand function for the product singled out; that is, the relation of the household's demand for the product to the price of that product and the household's income. The indifference curve corresponding to any initial position, then, might readily be determined from formulas (1) and (2).

---

[2] We have

$$\frac{dy}{dp} = \frac{dy}{dx}\frac{dx}{dp},$$

where all differentials are taken along a given indifference curve. Hence, $dy/dp = -p(dx/dp)$, and (2) follows.

Thus, to consider the most general case, suppose E_{xp} and E_{xI} vary, depending on the magnitude of X and Y, and hence on p and I, and that the nature of the relationship in each case has been determined statistically. Starting, then, from any initial magnitudes of X, Y, p and I, and corresponding values of E_{xp} and E_{xI}, we may determine approximately from (1) and (2) the corresponding magnitudes of X and Y lying on the same indifference curve but associated with (say) a one percent reduction in p. From the new magnitudes of X and Y and the reduced value of p we may also calculate a new value for I. For these magnitudes there are corresponding new values of E_{xp} and E_{xI}. Using in (1) and (2) the new values of X, Y, p, I, E_{xp} and E_{xI}, we may repeat the calculation for another one percent reduction in p. The household's indifference curve corresponding to any initial position is traced out by successive computations of this sort.

While in this way we may delineate the indifference curve of particular interest, evidently the same procedure may be used to delineate any other curve, and hence the indifference map generally, as it bears on choices between X and Y. In the case of each indifference curve, some initial position must be taken as a point of departure, but the initial magnitudes of X and Y may be specified arbitrarily, and the corresponding magnitudes of p and I should be determinable from the demand function for X and the requirement that outlays correspond to income.

Formulas (1) and (2), of course, are differential equations relating to the household's indifference map. I have done no more here, therefore, than set forth a numerical procedure for solving these equations. As with any such procedure, that described can only approximate the desired solution, but it should be possible to make the approximation sufficiently accurate.[3] One can often

---

[3] As described, the procedure would involve delineation of the indifference curve through successive one percent cuts in the price of X. Depending on the magnitude of the successive percentage price-cuts actually considered, the delineation might be made more or less accurate, but since calculations of the sort in question may readily be made on electronic computers, there should be no difficulty in making the percentage price-cut so small as to assure a satisfactory approximation. I shall refer in a moment to special cases where one may derive an analytic formula of a conventional sort for the indifference curve. In order to judge the accuracy of the numerical procedure where reference is made to successive percentage price-cuts of different magnitudes, it should be useful to compare

derive for the differential equations relating to the household's indifference map, however, an explicit solution of a conventional analytic sort. The indifference curve of interest may then be delineated simply by reference to this solution, and without resort to the numerical procedure described.

To refer, for example, to a special but very tractable case, suppose that E_{xp} and E_{xI} were found within the relevant range to be minus and plus unity respectively. From (1)

$$\frac{y'}{xy''} = E_{xp} - \frac{y'x}{y - y'x} \cdot E_{xI}, \tag{3}$$

where $y' = dy/dx$, and $y'' = d^2y/dx^2$, both differentials being taken along an indifference curve, and it is understood that

$$p = -\frac{dy}{dx}. \tag{4}$$

Taking $E_{xp} = 1$ and $E_{xp} = -1$, and letting $u = v/x$ and $v = y'$, this reduces to

$$\frac{du}{dv} - \frac{u}{v} = 0. \tag{5}$$

Solving,

$$\frac{u}{v} = A, \tag{6}$$

where A is a constant of integration, and this in turn yields the equation,

$$y = Bx^{1/A}, \tag{7}$$

where B is also a constant of integration. A presumably would be <0, but, for the indifference curve passing through any initial position, the magnitudes of A and B would be determined from the initial magnitudes of X, Y and p. The formula for an indifference curve is general, however, and might be used to derive the indifference map as a whole. As it turns out, the marginal rate of

the results of such calculations in such special cases with those obtained directly from the analytic formula for the indifference curve. I understand, however, that the error in a numerical procedure such as that in question may be controlled generally.

substitution between X and Y is constant for any given mix of X and Y, that is, for any ray through the origin of the preference field.[4]

With cardinal measurability of utility, $E_{xp} = -1$ would mean that the marginal utility of money is constant as the consumption of X changes in response to a change in p.[5] This has sometimes been thought of as coming to the same thing as an absence of income effects, as understood by Hicks, and hence as providing the basis for use of consumers' surplus analysis in the appraisal of indivisibilities. This, of course, is not so, but the case in question is of some theoretic interest. Curiously, as may be seen from formula (5), the elasticity of substitution between X and Y is unity.

Where income effects in the sense pertinent to consumers' surplus analysis are indeed absent, however, an explicit solution of a conventional analytic sort can still be derived. At least, this is so, if (as must often be the case) E_{xp} is constant within the relevant range. Here, we have

$$\frac{d \log x}{d \log p} = k. \tag{8}$$

For any given I, the term on the left represents the elasticity of the uncompensated price demand schedule, but from (1), in the absence of income effects, the differential may also be viewed as relating to the compensated price-demand schedule, and hence as being taken along an indifference curve. Solving (8), we have

$$p = Ax^{1/k}, \tag{9}$$

[4] In the case in question, in order to derive an explicit analytic formula for the indifference map, I have taken equation (1) as a point of departure. The analysis thus conforms to the numerical procedure that was employed for deriving the indifference map. It should be observed, however, that so far as the demand function for X is known, one might take this as a point of departure in deriving an analytic formula. Moreover, this procedure is somewhat more elegant than the one employed, since, while equation (1) is of the second order, the demand function is of the first. The demand function might also be taken as a point of departure in an alternative type of numerical calculation, such as I alluded to above, p. 158, though at this point I do not think this procedure would ordinarily have any advantages over that employed. As will be evident, these remarks also apply to the case considered below where $E_{xI} = 0$.

[5] The utilities from X and Y must also be independent. This itself, however, is a sufficient, though not necessary, condition for cardinality.

162

where A is a constant of integration. With p taken as the dependent variable, formula (9) represents both the uncompensated and the compensated price-demand schedule for x. But combining (9) and (4) and integrating again, we have

$$y = - \frac{A}{\left(1 + \dfrac{1}{k}\right)} x^{(1+1/k)} + B. \qquad (10)$$

Here B is a second constant of integration, and (10) represents any indifference curve in terms of the two constants, A and B.

We also have here the familiar result that, in the absence of income effects, the marginal rate of substitution between X and Y depends only on consumption of X, while different indifference curves are parallel where the consumption of X is given.

In the absence of income effects, formula (10) represents the indifference curve provided $k \neq -1$. If $k = -1$, this formula obtains instead:

$$y = -A \log x + B. \qquad (10a)$$

A and B are again constants of integration.

APPLICATION TO INDIVISIBILITY APPRAISAL

Reference has been to the delineation of the household's indifference map. It may be well to be explicit as to how the indivisible change might be appraised on this basis. Assume, as before, that X is the product especially affected by the indivisibility, and that Y represents all other products measured in units of a dollar's worth at constant prices. Since the introduction of additional capacity to produce X entails a withdrawal of inputs from Y, however, the indivisible change entails not only an expansion in the output of X but a reduction in the output of Y. Assuming that, for any household, the changes that would occur in consumption of both X and Y are known, evidently we could tell at once whether these would represent a gain simply by reference to the indifference curve corresponding to the household's initial mix of X and Y. Thus, the household would benefit, be unaffected, or suffer, depending on whether

$$y_1 >, =, \text{ or } < \bar{y}, \tag{11}$$

where x_0, y_0 is the household's initial and x_1, y_1, its final consumption mix, and x_1, $\bar{y}$ is a mix that is indifferent to x_0, y_0.

In the appraisal of indivisibility, reference usually is to a change affecting not one household alone but a group of households or an entire community. The appraisal, of course, might still proceed in the manner described if all affected households should have the same tastes and income, but so far as they do not, some attempt would have to be made to classify them, if only in a crude way, by income and taste categories. One might then determine for each category separately whether the indivisible change was beneficial. So far as some households gain and some lose, the final evaluation of the indivisibility necessarily would entail reference to some principle of equity.

In consumers' surplus analysis as reformulated by Professor Hicks, attention similarly is focused in the first instance on the individual household. Thus, the concern is initially to approximate the individual household's all-or-none offer, in terms of all other goods, for some one good that is especially affected by the indivisibility. Although it is not usually made very explicit, this approach, no less than the one being explained here, requires, at least in principle, that, in appraising an indivisible change for the community generally, reference be made separately to the experience of different income and taste categories. This must be done, on the one hand, to ascertain in the light of each category's income and tastes the all-or-none offer that it would be prepared to make for the increment of X that is added to its consumption, and, on the other, in order to evaluate, from the standpoint of some principle of equity, the incidence of the indivisible change on "real" income distribution. [6]

[6] Where an indivisible change is appraised by consumers' surplus analysis in its Marshallian form, one usually takes as a point of departure the price-demand schedule of the community generally for the commodity especially affected by the indivisibility. Assuming no income effects, it is true that the all-or-none offer for an increment in the community's consumption of X, which is implied by the community's price-demand

I have been assuming that the amount of Y that must be given up by the community in order to expand the supply of X by any given amount is known. What, however, if one merely knows the cost of producing the increment of X? I have also been tacitly assuming that the relative prices of other goods are not perceptibly affected by the expansion of X,[7] and this might be so under diverse circumstances, but, in the simplest case, prices elsewhere would equal marginal cost, production would occur under conditions of constant average, and hence, marginal cost, and factor prices generally, would be unaffected by the expansion of X. Here the cost of the increment of X would exactly indicate also the sacrifice in Y, in units of a dollar's worth at constant prices, that would be required. In other circumstances, the cost of the increment in X might not measure the sacrifice in Y required, but it might be sufficiently indicative of the latter for purposes of the appraisal. Alternatively, the appraisal would require additional information on the sacrifice of Y.[8]

In consumers' surplus analysis the cost of the increment of X, rather than the sacrifice of Y, is usually taken as a point of

---

schedule, corresponds to the sum of the all-or-none offers that would be made by households for the increments of X they would consume in response to the same change in price as would generate the aggregate increment in X. Hence, should an indivisible change in the community's consumption of X require a sacrifice of Y less than the all-or-none offer indicated by the market price-demand schedule, there must be some distribution of this sacrifice such that all households would benefit by the change.

In judging whether the change should be made, however, one presumably would still wish to know to what extent different groups of households might gain or lose. For this purpose, reference must be made in principle to the separate price-demand schedules of households with different tastes. If there are no income effects, differences among households in their incomes would be immaterial.

[7] Although the volume of Y is measured with a dollar's worth at constant prices as the unit, it will be evident that for purposes of the analysis the prices of other goods need be stable in fact only relative to each other and not absolutely.

[8] Should Y be produced under conditions of rising marginal cost, as is readily seen, the cost of the increment of X would tend on this account to overstate, when deflated by the *ex post* price of Y, the volume of Y sacrificed. Should the price of Y be subject to a percentage markup over marginal cost, however, the effect would be the opposite.

departure, but evidently the appraisal ultimately must presuppose as much knowledge of the sacrifice of Y as has been presupposed here.

While I have assumed that the relative prices of all other goods are unchanged, the analysis admits of extension to other cases. Thus, suppose again that X is especially affected by the indivisibility, but that a change in its price affects to a relatively marked degree the price of Y, a close substitute or complement. Among all other goods, Z, relative prices are still unchanged. Assuming the demand functions for all three products are known, one might evaluate the indivisible change in this way: from the demand functions, one is able to delineate the indifference curve between X and Z, Y constant, that corresponds to the initial position, x_0, y_0, z_0. Thus, one can determine how much of Z could be sacrificed for the realized increment of consumption of X without any loss to the household. One can also delineate an indifference curve between Y and Z, X constant, that corresponds to the new position $\bar{x}, y_0, \bar{z}$, that is thus defined. In this way, one determines the further change in Z that would be required to compensate for the change that actually occurs in Y. The indivisibility is evaluated by comparing the actual change in Z with the hypothetical one so arrived at. [9]

The stability of relative prices of goods other than the one especially affected by the indivisibility is also assumed in con-

[9] Let the demand functions be:

$$x = H(p, q, I),$$
$$y = L(p, q, I),$$
and
$$z = M(p, q, I).$$

Then it may be shown that

$$\left(\frac{dx}{dp}\right)_{U,y} = H_1 - \left(\frac{x + (L_1/L_3)}{y + (L_2/L_3)}\right) H_2 + \left(\frac{x - y(L_1/L_2)}{1 + y(L_3/L_2)}\right) H_3,$$

where $(dx/dp)_{U,y}$ represents the change in the demand for X that would occur for a unit change in p, when q and I vary so that Y is constant and the household remains on the same indifference curve in respect of X and Z. The corresponding formula for Z is simply $-p(dx/dp)_{U,y}$. Similar schedules may be derived for the impact of changes in q on the consumption of Y and Z, X constant. From these schedules, one may delineate by numerical procedure the indifference curves of interest.

sumers' surplus analysis, but Hicks has outlined a technique for extending this method to other cases as well.[10]

I have now described a procedure for appraising indivisible changes, which, in contrast to consumers' surplus analysis, takes account of income effects. While, as already stated, such effects are not apt to be very consequential, their magnitude may now be calculated in any particular case. Also, by selective application, our "indifference map" procedure should provide a better basis than was available previously to judge the import of income effects generally. One or two calculations, for the special case where $E_{xI} = 1$ and $E_{xp} = -1$, may be suggestive. With A in formula (7) equal to $(-)10$, I find that, as calculated from the uncompensated demand schedule, a household's all-or-none offer for an added 100 units of X would be 13.863 units of Y, or 3.5 percent greater than the true all-or-none offer indicated by the household's indifference curve. The household initially consumed 100 units of X, requiring an outlay of 9.1 percent of its income. With A equal to $-(10/3)$, the household's all-or-none offer for the same increment of X would be 41.589 units of Y, according to the uncompensated demand schedule, or 10.8 percent more than the corresponding true all-or-none offer. Here the household's initial consumption of X requires an expenditure of 23.1 percent of its income.

A single product, of course, rarely constitutes as much as 23.1 percent of a household's budget, and even one for which outlays are as large as 9.1 percent of the total must be unusual, but the cited examples may be suggestive of magnitudes that obtain where the income elasticity of demand is high or where reference is to a group of related products.[11]

---

[10] *A Revision of Demand Theory*, pp. 168ff.

[11] For both cases considered, x_0 and y_0 are 100 and 200 respectively, while p_0 and I_0 are .2 and 220 in the first case and .6 and 260 in the second. The uncompensated demand schedule, with I held constant at I_0, is $x = 20/p$ in the first case, and $x = 60/p$ in the second.

From the Slutsky equation, we see that for the first case $\overline{E}_{xp}$ is but $(-).909$. Hence E_{xp} is 10 percent greater than $\overline{E}_{xp}$. In the circumstances, the fact that the all-or-none offer indicated by the uncompensated demand schedule exceeds the true all-or-none offer by only 3.5 percent may seem paradoxical, but the paradox, I believe, is resolved when we consider that we are comparing areas under the two demand schedules, uncompensated

At a time when the rehabilitation of consumers' surplus was already far advanced, Professor Samuelson still considered that the analysis serves no useful purpose that could not be better served otherwise:[12]

> If one were to begin afresh to give answers to the following problems, in no one of them would consumers' surplus be necessary or desirable: Should Robinson Crusoe, a Socialist state, or a capitalist economy build a particular bridge? Should discriminatory prices be allowed if uniform prices will not keep an activity in business? Should the number of firms producing differentiated products be reduced, and in what way? Should a particular small industry be expanded or contracted by means of a tax or subsidy? etc., etc. Aside from their extraneous interpersonal aspects, all of these questions can more conveniently (and more honestly!) be answered in terms of the consumers' ordinal preference field.

Little has demurred at this: "This is a rather surprising passage. It implies not only that all individuals are 'economic,' but also that we have a copy of everyone's preference field filed away."[13]

I wonder if both writers would not agree that, properly viewed, the purpose of consumers' surplus analysis is simply to obtain observations on the household's indifference map. From this standpoint, the alternative approach that has been set forth here has the merit that the observations obtained are more accurate. In formulating the indifference-map approach, it is true, I have abandoned altogether the notion of a "surplus," but, as Samuelson implies, this is not really integral to consumers' surplus analysis

---

and compensated, where the increment in X is taken as given and the same for both schedules. The relative magnitude of the two elasticities should bear more directly on the comparative areas under the two schedules, where the change in p is given and is the same for both schedules, and where in each case reference is only to sectors lying between the initial and final price levels. The relation of the latter areas will ordinarily differ from that of the areas under the two schedules where the increment in X is the same for both schedules. One must read similarly the fact that in the second case $\overline{E}_{xp}$ is but $(-)$ .769, so that E_{xp} is 30 percent greater than $\overline{E}_{xp}$. Yet the all-or-none offer indicated by the uncompensated demand schedule exceeds the true all-or-none offer by but 10.8 percent.

[12] Paul A. Samuelson, *Foundations of Economic Analysis* (Cambridge, Mass., 1947), p. 197.

[13] I. M. D. Little, *A Critique of Welfare Economics*, 2nd ed., (Oxford, 1957), p. 181.

either. In any event, I must allow the reader to judge for himself to what extent the appraisal proceeds "more conveniently (and more honestly!)" when, as has been done here, such a notion is abandoned.

If we know not only the increment in X, the good especially affected, but also the decrement in Y, all other goods, and the change in relative prices, we need rely on neither consumers' surplus analysis nor the indifference map approach, in order to appraise the indivisibility. Rather, the appraisal may be based simply on the computation of index numbers. The latter sort of computation, however, is not always incisive, and it is precisely where it is not that recourse to consumers' surplus analysis has been in order. The indifference map procedure, therefore, is also to be employed in such circumstances.

Thus, for simplicity, suppose again that the prices of all other goods are unaffected by the introduction of the indivisibility, and for the reasons stated above. Hence, the additional cost incurred in the provision of the increment of X also measures the decrement in Y, in units of a dollar's worth. It suffices to refer to two interesting cases. In the first, the additional revenue from the sale of X covers the additional cost, whether revenue is measured in either *ex post* or *ex ante* prices; thus, we have

$$p_1(x_1 - x_0) > y_0 - y_1, \tag{12}$$

and

$$p_0(x_1 - x_0) > y_0 - y_1. \tag{13}$$

By implication,

$$p_1 x_1 + y_1 > p_1 x_0 + y_0, \tag{14}$$

and

$$p_0 x_1 + y_1 > p_0 x_0 + y_0. \tag{15}$$

According to index-number theory, if relations such as these obtain for a community generally, the introduction of the indivisibility is in order, provided there is no adverse change in income distribution.[14] It also follows that neither consumers' surplus analysis nor indifference map procedure need be applied.

[14] See Chapter 6.

In the second case, the additional revenue from the sale of the increment of X covers the additional cost when sales are valued in terms of *ex ante* prices, but falls short of costs when they are valued in terms of *ex post* prices. In other words, equations (13) and (15) obtain as before; but in place of (12) and (14) we have

$$p_1(x_1 - x_0) < y_0 - y_1, \qquad (12a)$$

and

$$p_1 x_1 + y_1 < p_1 x_0 + y_0. \qquad (14a)$$

Here index-number theory fails us, but evidently an appraisal is still possible by use of either consumers' surplus analysis or the indifference map procedure.

Where there is an indivisibility, of course, index numbers may turn out to be of the sort given by (14a) and (15), as well as of the sort given by (14) and (15). Applications, therefore, are by no means lacking for the consumers' surplus or indifference map procedure. Admittedly, however, if (14a) and (15) obtain, an indivisibility that passes muster according to either procedure might be considered dubious on the practical ground that it would not be "self-financing." But this is a familiar theme that need not be pursued here.[15]

[15] To return to the relation of the two alternative procedures to index number theory: according to Samuelson, p. 196, after the concept of consumers' surplus "has been renovated and altered, it *is* simply the economic theory of index numbers in the Pigou, Könus, Haberler, Staehle, Leontief, Lerner, Allen, Frisch, Wald tradition." If the reasoning set forth in the text is correct, it would seem more accurate to say that index number theory can often supplant consumers' surplus analysis, but that the latter still differs from the former. This is also true of the indifference map procedure. Under the consumers' surplus and indifference map procedures we delineate, implicitly in one case and explicitly in the other the shape of the indifference curve. On this basis, appraisals may be possible even where index numbers are not incisive. So far as consumers' surplus analysis and the indifference map procedure are thus more potent than index number theory, this, of course, reflects the difference in information employed. In index number theory, one seeks to rank two budget points from information on prices and quantities for the two budget points alone. In the alternative procedures, one takes as a point of departure instead the demand function for a product on which attention is focused. In effect, such a function provides us with price-quantity data not only on the two budget points of interest but on others as well.

Probably, however, I have understood the theory of index numbers differently from Professor Samuelson. Or rather he may be referring to index-number theory in the sense where, for purposes of comparing two budget points, information is available on prices and quantities not only for the two points but for intermediate points as well, that is, as in a chain index. In this case, the appraisal by use of index numbers could more often be incisive, but the information required tends to become essentially the same as with the alternative procedures.

PART III. SOCIALIST ECONOMICS

8

PRINCIPLES OF SOCIALIST WAGES*

The determination of wages under socialism is a familiar theme, but one that is rarely analyzed systematically. In the empirical inquiry into the Soviet wage structure that is to be attempted, I propose to take as a point of departure a particular set of wage principles. The principles studied should sound no new note to the reader, for they are none other than the principles usually applied to wages under capitalism, at least in its competitive form. This fact is no bar to their application to socialist wages as well. Indeed, there is strong support for the view that Marx, among others, foresaw in essentials just such an eventuality.[1] But before plunging into the complex Soviet world, it is well to inquire whether, in general, there is any reason for focusing attention on capitalist wage principles rather than on any others.

ACCOUNTING WAGES

The administrators of the socialist economy, it may be assumed, will wish to extract as high a value product as possible from the resources at their command. Just what procedures they will resort to in order to attain this objective is nevertheless not a

---

* Originally published as Chapter II in Abram Bergson, *The Structure of Soviet Wages* (Cambridge, Mass., 1944). As explained, in republishing this essay, I have rather extensively rewritten it, primarily in order to assure a necessary degree of clarity and coherence. The rewriting has affected chiefly the parts on accounting wages, social services, and the tax or dividend.

[1] Marx's treatment of the problem of socialist distribution is discussed below, pp. 188ff.

ready subject for generalization. Indeed, an omniscient planning board with the powers of Superman might arrive at an effective use of resources without recourse to any working arrangements to speak of. The conditions for an effective use of resources might be perceived at once, and then realized as well without more ado. Administrators who are not Jovian will be greatly aided in their task, however, if a system of accounting records is maintained by the various production units into which the community is organized. Such records not only serve to record the past, but also help the administrators to reach decisions as to the future, to delegate authority, and to fix responsibility. To be useful the accounting records must be kept in some unit of account, the output of each enterprise being valued at an established price, and the inputs of labor as well as of other productive factors recorded at predetermined wages and prices. Insofar as these practices are observed, the incidental result is that socialist wages, at least as an accounting category, can exist outside the minds of non-Jovian administrators.

While accounts are supposed to be kept in terms of prices of different products, the manner in which these prices might be fixed is left to separate inquiry, though something will be said about one aspect to appear later. But the administrators presumably would seek to maximize a value product that is calculated by reference to such prices, and it should be observed that this endeavor would be more or less meaningful depending on the degree to which the prices indicate the rates at which the administrators would be willing to substitute one commodity for another in the community's output, if a choice had to be made.

If available resources are to yield a maximum value product, labor must do so as well, and in seeking this end, the administrators should find themselves circumscribed in respect to wages. At least, having troubled to account for labor inputs at established wages, the administrators might be expected to calculate in these terms. So far as they do, they might approach an effective use of available labor supplies by seeking to satisfy two conditions, and it is not easy to see how they could hope to do so otherwise. The first condition is that for any given set of accounting wages, the total wage bill required to produce any given value product must be a minimum. The second is that the actual wage rates must be such that, for some given value product, the numbers of the different kinds of workers required to operate at a minimum cost equal respectively the numbers of the different kinds of workers available for employment. In other words, at the given wage rates there must be full employment of the available labor resources.

To formulate these conditions, needless to say, is a much easier task then to realize them. The socialist "leap to plenty" is hardly automatic. Even able administrators cannot hope to do more than approximate an effective utilization of the labor available to an entire community. But, to whatever extent the conditions for such a use of labor are approximated, wages are to that degree restricted. Though nothing is implied as to the administrative or market procedure through which the conditions are approached in practice, they are logically equivalent to the conditions of supply and demand which determine capitalist wages in a competitive market. To the extent that the conditions are satisfied, furthermore, the accounting wages of the different types of labor in the socialist state must be proportionate to or within limits set by the productivity—more precisely, the "marginal value productivity"[2]—of the different types of labor. This familiar principle of capitalist wages follows directly from the fact that wage costs are minimized. For, if wages were not proportional to productivity, the substitution of workers whose wages were low relative to productivity for workers whose wages were high relative to productivity would always reduce costs. More of the low-paid and fewer of the high-paid workers would be required than were actually employed.[3]

In a position in which the available resources are fully employed the most effective use of labor, it is true, could also be attained if

[2] The marginal productivity of any particular type of labor employed in a particular production unit is the increment of product associated with the employment of the last worker of that type in the production unit in question. Marginal value productivity is simply the value of the increment of product. It is usually inderstood that both before and after the addition of another worker all resources in the production unit are employed as efficiently as possible.

[3] Strictly, in a position of minimum cost, wages will only be proportional to productivity if the production process is highly flexible, so that with the employment of additional workers in a particular occupation, the successive increments of output do not differ sharply. Ordinarily this is probably

wages were not proportional to productivity—*provided* the disproportion for any particular type of labor were the same in every use.[4] Socialist administrators, enamored of the beauties of logic, might find it pleasant to try to devise administrative rules to make possible an approximation to this elegant result. But in view of the manifest simplicity of the administrative rule of equating supply and demand, it is justifiable to regard it as a highly likely, if not necessary, element in a socialist production policy designed to assure effective resource use.

But workers do not eat accounting categories, and so far it is only to accounting wages that capitalist wage principles appear to apply. Once having determined accounting wages it is not unlikely that both administrative convenience and political pressure would impel the socialist administrators to keep one set of books rather than two, and to distribute to consumers claims against goods corresponding to their accounting wages. However, the effective utilization of the available labor resources implies nothing as to the economics of such a distribution. In the case of machinery and land, clearly, no personal claims against real income are established in the socialist state by any sums that might be recorded in the state's books for their employment. Though interest and rent may continue as accounting categories, they need not be categories of consumers' income. Whether or not this is likely to be so in the case of labor, too, is a matter to be determined.[5]

---

not the case, and relative wages are only determined within limits set by marginal value productivity. If such limits are wide, therefore, the value of this condition as a determinant of wages is much reduced. But it may be hazarded that if a whole industry or a whole economy is taken into account the limits are quite restrictive.

[4] The essential requirement is that in a position in which all resources are employed the productivity of a particular type of labor is the same in every use.

[5] The conclusion stated in this section as to the determination of accounting wages in the socialist state is contained in the more general conclusions as to the determination of prices of the factors of production which have been advanced in O. Lange, "On the Economic Theory of Socialism," *Review of Economic Studies*, October 1936, February 1937, particularly pp. 60ff. in the October issue, and in H. D. Dickinson, *Economics of Socialism* (Oxford, 1939) chap. iii. The argument supporting the conclusion, however, differs somewhat from those of Lange and Dickinson.

WAGES AND CONSUMERS' CLAIMS

If, as was implicitly assumed in the preceding section, the supply of different types of labor were fixed, the problem of distribution under socialism would be a quite distinct problem economically from that of production. Indeed, distribution would not be an economic problem at all. The same would be true if the supply of the different types of labor were variable, but the variation were not subject to administrative control, or if the supply could be varied by administrative action, but without the incurrence of any social cost that would otherwise be avoided.

In fact, however, with respect to but few workers might these conditions be said to have a counterpart in reality. Artists, musicians, and poets, it is often said, are called to their occupation at an early age and would serve in no other. This view may be only romantic, but to the extent that it is factual the supply of these workers is not subject to administrative control. Their reward is akin to an economic rent, and its magnitude is to be determined solely by consideration of ethics, politics, and administrative convenience.

But for most types of labor the situation confronting the socialist administrators is otherwise: the supply of workers can be influenced by administrative action. The overzealous administrator who neglects this fact would surely err. The "just shares" distributed to the populace by such an official would turn out, at least in the long run, to be woefully shrunken shares.

In the solution of the problem, however, much depends on the manner in which the costs of varying the supply of the different types of labor are determined. The most obvious procedure, and one which the socialist administrators might find as politic as it is simple, is to determine these costs from the workers' own preferences for the different types of work. If this is done, the cost of shifting a worker from one occupation to another, in which he is able to perform, is simply the additional claim on consumers' goods necessary to compensate the worker for any additional risk, responsibility, training, or physical and mental hardship or disagreeableness involved in the change. The cost of employing a new worker in one occupation rather than another is established similarly.

179

In determining costs in this manner, of course, the socialist administrators would again not break any new ground. Under capitalism, costs are determined thus wherever workers have freedom of choice and the labor market is competitive—probably now a rather limited sphere. Freedom of choice and the determination of costs from a consideration of individual preference, however, are not one and the same thing. Conceivably, if the socialist administrators were sufficiently cognizant of the preferences of different workers, a free labor market in which the workers could express their preferences would be unnecessary so far as the determination of costs is concerned. Or, vice versa, the workers might be allowed to express their preferences in a free market and these preferences be disregarded in administrative calculation. [6] In practice, however, it is questionable whether, if there were any large and continued inroads on freedom of choice, costs would continue to correspond with individual preference in the socialist state.

No principle is certain to prevail, but socialist administrators might well find it desirable, or at least expedient, to reckon labor costs in conformity with the workers' own evaluations of alternative employments. Even a supremely egocentric administrator might hesitate to undertake the administrative task of establishing and applying values of alternative occupations other than those of the workers actually engaged in them. And this is to say nothing of the adverse political reaction which such a course might provoke.

If labor costs under socialism are determined in the manner described, socialist distribution policy is immediately restricted. For it follows that the community would gain by any shift in labor from one occupation to another for which the additional claims necessary to compensate the workers for the shift were less than the addition to the community's value product due to the change. Shifts in employment for which the added value product was less than the additional claims, *pari passu*, would result in a loss. Thus, if the claims paid workers in the different

---

[6] The analogous possibility in the case of the market for consumers' goods has been discussed by Lange, *Review of Economic Studies*, October 1936, pp. 68ff.

occupations differ by more or less than the productivity[7] of labor in those occupations, a change in claims up to the point where the two correspond always will result in a social gain as long as the supply of labor in the different occupations is altered by the change.[8] Should the consumers' claims differ by more or less than productivity, the supply of labor will not adjust itself fully to the opportunities to acquire income which the economy affords.

Thus, the effective utilization of resources in the socialist community requires that differences in the claims paid workers for different types of work equal differences in the contribution of the different types of work to the community's value product. Again, the socialist principle is also a capitalist principle.

It is clear also that if the wages recorded in the socialist books are to measure labor costs correctly, accounting wages must differ from a worker's claim against consumers' goods, if at all, only by a fixed sum, which does not vary with the workers' accounting wage. On this sum, properly designated as the worker's "tax" or "dividend," as the case may be, more is said below. By the same token, wages—they are no longer simply accounting wages—must be not only proportional but equal to productivity, if the resources of the community are to be utilized as effectively as possible.[9]

INEQUALITY UNDER SOCIALISM

The magnitude of wage differentials. The morrow of the revolution, it appears, must prove disappointing to those among the socialists—and there have been and doubtless still are many—who

---

[7] Strictly, it is "marginal value productivity" which is in question.

[8] This assumes that "freedom of choice" prevails in the socialist labor market. The conclusions as to socialist distribution which are derived, however, would still be valid in the unlikely case that the administrators accept the workers' evaluations of alternative occupations as indicating differences in labor cost, but do not grant the workers freedom of choice.

[9] The principles of socialist wages stated in this section are the same as those advanced in Lange, *Review of Economic Studies*, February 1937, pp. 123ff., and which are supported in Dickinson, chap. iv. However, the argument advanced here may make clearer than has been done heretofore the value content of the principles. The argument is stated more exactly, with respect to the general problem of attaining an effective utilization of all resources, in Chapter 1.

regard equality of reward as a prime revolutionary objective. At least, so far as the effective use of labor is a matter of concern, socialist wages could not be equal wages. A convinced equalitarian who by chance found himself in the saddle after the revolution and who attempted immediately to equalize the rewards of labor would soon find that in consequence both the community's income and his political power were much deflated.

The determination of socialist wages in accord with capitalist principles, however, does not imply that socialist differentials must be the *same* as capitalist differentials. Even an equalitarian, if a patient one, might become reconciled to operating within a capitalist framework.

For, first of all, if the socialist administrators succeed in relaxing the monopolistic restrictions on the supply of skilled labor established by unions under capitalism, the wage differentials corresponding to productivity will be reduced. The vested interests of specially privileged workers are a political rather than an economic force in the socialist state. Also, under socialism, general and vocational education might well be made more accessible to able citizens than is the case under capitalism, where the costs of education are an important obstacle to the acquisition of the higher skills. One important barrier between the noncompeting groups of economic theory thus might be broken down, and in the long run wage differentials could be reduced on this account.

To be reckoned with, too, is the possibility that socialist workers of ability might be stimulated to produce more, to undergo special training, or to assume responsibility by incentives other than an increased supply of material goods for their own use. The desire for power and a position of prestige and honor in the community are at least partial motives for the performance of numerous tasks in a capitalist society. It is a prevalent belief that the so-called nonpecuniary incentives will be even more influential in a socialist society. The common ownership of the means of production, the knowledge that every value created by the worker "ultimately redounds to the benefit of himself, his own kind and class" has been presented specifically as the basis for a far-reaching change in the worker's attitude toward labor. This view perhaps assumes a greater plasticity in human nature than is justified, but to the extent that workers can be stimulated by nonpecuniary incentives the pecuniary differentials prevailing under socialism may be reduced.

Wages and the disutility of labor. It is an oft-quoted paradox of capitalist wage differentials that many occupations which seem in all other respects unattractive are also poorly remunerative, and that many occupations which seem highly attractive are also highly remunerative. Heavy, dirty labor rather than light, clean labor, monotonous labor rather than varied labor, disciplined labor rather than autonomous labor, often draw the blanks in the capitalist lottery. Many critics of the inequality of reward prevailing under capitalism are chiefly indignant at this anomaly. Differences in remuneration which merely correspond to differences in the disutility of labor are, if at all, not nearly so provoking

The paradox of capitalist remuneration is largely resolved, of course, by the fact that under capitalism the disutility of different types of labor is not the only factor which limits the supply of workers in the different occupations. The cost of education, trade union and professional restrictions on the labor supply, and finally ability, are also limiting factors.

The application of capitalist wage principles under socialism, thus, does not imply that the anomalous differentials of capitalism must remain intact. If education is supplied free, and the monopoly power of unions and professional organizations is broken, and wage differentials are reduced on this basis, the resulting differences in reward will approximate more nearly the differences in the disutility of labor. The equalitarian socialist might derive some comfort from this fact.

But that the socialist wage structure will continue to be encrusted with anomalous disparities is not unlikely. Though many workers who are incompetent for the task might be pleased to shift to a more remunerative occupation for less than the prevailing differential, the differential cannot be reduced on this account. Furthermore, the disutilities of a particular type of work are not the same for all workers who can be employed productively at that task. Among the workers able to accept responsibility and to undergo training for more skilled work, for example, some will relish these tasks more than others. It is to workers on the margin of choice between occupations that wage differentials are directed under capitalism, and so they must continue to be under socialism, if labor resources are to be used as effectively as possible.[10]

Conceivably, the socialist administrators might discriminate in fixing the wages of different workers in the same occupation, paying more to workers on the margin of choice than to other workers. In this manner the large value products of specially endowed citizens might be extracted in some measure for the benefit of the community as a whole. The administrative burden of such a wage policy, however, is imposing, and the chances of success are by no means clear. The discrimination, too, might arouse such political opposition as even a relatively secure administrator could not afford to ignore.

For the persistence of anomalous rewards under socialism is an economic rather than a political paradox. The principle of rewarding labor in accord with its contribution to the social product will have all the support under socialism that its long prevalence in the capitalist era has given it.

Social services. Parallel to the problem of recruiting labor that confronts the socialist administrators is that of distributing available supplies of consumers' goods, and the procedures employed in respect to the latter should often be similar to those used in respect to the former. Thus, having paid the worker a money wage, the socialist administrators can hardly refrain from allowing him also to acquire goods by expending it, and should the administrators allow the household to exercise freedom of choice as to employment they might be expected ordinarily to allow it to do so also as to consumption. Given this, it is easy to see that the administrators would also find reasons to seek to fix prices which would assure that available supplies are distributed in an orderly manner, that is, prices that clear the market and limit demand to available supplies. In any event, the wage received by the socialist worker must be more or less significant for him, depending on the degree to which such circumstances obtain,

[10] Lange argues that, ideally, wage differentials must correspond to differences in the disutility of different occupations as well as to differences in productivity (*Review of Economic Studies*, February 1937, p. 124). This could be true, however, only for workers who are on the margin of choice between occupations. It could not be true of the bulk of the workers, who are intramarginal.

and the socialist administrators must consider this fact in determining wages.

The goods and services obtained by the worker through these arrangements, however, will presumably not comprise his entire real income. Some goods and services will be made available to him as social services, without charge. In any modern community certain services, owing to their physical nature, must be distributed in this manner. In the case of police protection, national defense, and to an extent, sidewalks, roadways, parks, and sanitary measures, it is either impossible or impracticable to determine the extent to which individual citizens avail themselves of these services, and to charge them accordingly. Further, if freedom of choice prevails in the socialist consumers'-goods market, it will be undesirable to distribute in this market goods which have a very high social value, but a low, or zero value to a sizeable minority of the citizens. As is the case in capitalist communities, infectious diseases should be treated without charge. And if many parents do not give the education of their children nearly the value consonant with its importance to the community, a free distribution of this service, or a compulsory distribution of it, or both, may be desirable.

The distribution of goods and services without charge necessarily equalizes real incomes beyond what they would be in the absence of such a distribution. Indeed, a prevailing ethic in favor of greater equality within the framework of a private property system is probably one of the motives for the distribution of goods and services as social services under capitalism. An equalitarian ethic might also prevail, and perhaps would have more political weight, under socialism, but here large property incomes are no longer an influencing factor. The scope of the social services may well be expanded in a socialist community, but the force of the equalitarian argument for such a distribution should be diminished. Indeed, an attempt on the part of the socialist administrators to substantially equalize real incomes through an expansion of the social services would more than likely be self-defeating. The inequality in the distribution of the remaining goods purchased in the consumers'-goods market would have to be all the greater to attract workers in the different occupations in the proper proportions.

The tax or dividend. While social services, like other goods, require the payment of wages for their production, they realize no values for the state in the consumers'-goods market. This is likewise true for any investment goods production undertaken by the administrators. To finance these wage payments, the socialist administrators will have available the rent, interest, and depreciation reserves on the state's resources—these items, it should be expected, will appear as accounting categories in the state's books—and any voluntary saving undertaken by members of the community. But it is unlikely that these two sums will coincide, and the administrators will have to finance the difference.[11]

One course open to the socialist administrators is simply to adjust the prices of marketable consumers' goods, upward if the wage payments for the social services and new investment are in excess, and downward if the converse. There is little danger that this procedure will entail the alarming consequences that some economists have predicted in similar circumstances for a capitalist economy. Once having engaged in, say, a new investment program, and having adjusted the prices of consumers' goods upward, it is unlikely that the large consumers' goods profit will rouse the administrators to abandon their investments, and rush again to the production of consumers' goods, with a cumulative contraction process following.[12] Nevertheless, this tempting course is objectionable. The socialist administrators, we have supposed, would find it expedient to calculate costs in terms of the households' own evaluations of work done. In determining resource use generally, the administrators must also value goods, and possibly here, too, the households' own evaluations will be guiding. If so, the prices of consumers' goods must be fixed equal to costs.[13] Alternatively, goods might be valued according to

---

[11] While I speak of "finance," it should be observed that the problem of finance of concern is purely one of consistently arranging the state's accounts. It should be noted that the balance struck in the text does not include all items that might be relevant.

[12] See F. A. Hayek, *Prices and Production* (New York, 1932).

[13] More accurately, marginal costs. This is equivalent to the requirement that wages equal marginal value productivity. Where workers are producing goods for future rather than present consumption, the marginal value productivity must be discounted, but the insertion of this element does not affect the argument of the text. The discount should be determined by an independent appraisal of the values of present and future income.

some other principle, but prices then must be fixed in accordance with this principle. In either case, the arbitrary adjustment of consumers'-goods prices upward to allow for investment and social service costs, if substantial, would imply in the long run an ineffective utilization of resources. Differences in wages would not correspond to differences in value productivity, and not as many workers as is socially desirable would be attracted into the more arduous, the more responsible, and the more skilled occupations.

While price manipulation is an economically objectionable means of financing the investment program, it has all the advantages of indirection possessed by a sales tax under capitalism. Consequently it might prove an irresistible political expedient even for socialist administrators. Should the administrators not be aware of the economic consequences of such acts it would not be surprising, when we consider that economists themselves have not always clearly grasped the problem.[14]

The alternative to an over-all price increase which first suggests itself is a proportionate income tax. But in a socialist state such a tax, too, is likely to be objectionable. To whatever extent marginal workers take account of the tax in weighing the merits of alternative occupations, the wages recorded as costs no longer correspond to social costs, and an insufficient amount of labor will be attracted to the more remunerative occupations.[15] The effect of a progressive income tax on the utilization of resources necessarily would be more adverse than that of a proportionate tax. The progressive tax might be felt to have a redeeming quality, however, so far as it expropriates part of the economically unnecessary gain accruing to workers who are not on the margin

[14] Lange has advocated that the socialist administrators levy a proportionate income tax (or pay a proportionate dividend) to balance the state's outlays and revenues. See *Review of Economic Studies*, October 1936, pp. 64, 65. As will appear, this procedure is undesirable. The objectionable character of Lange's solution was first pointed out by A. P. Lerner in a note appended to Lange's article (pp. 72ff). But Lerner himself regards as arbitrary the over-all level of prices relative to costs, and thus implicitly admits the possibility of a proportionate adjustment of prices as a means of financing the state's investment program. See *Review of Economic Studies*, October 1936, pp. 75, 76; October 1938, p. 71. More recently, Dickinson (pp. 136, 137) has fallen into Lange's original error.

[15] This assumes that freedom of choice prevails in the socialist labor market. But even if it does not, the income tax is inconsistent with the acceptance of individual preference as a measure of social cost.

of choice between occupations.[16] In view of the political and administrative obstacles to the adoption of a discriminatory wage policy, this may be a consideration of some import.

The only method of adjusting the state's financial position that is economically unobjectionable, however, is through the lump-sum tax or dividend that was referred to earlier. This share might prove politically unpalatable, but its allocation would in no way bar attainment of an optimum use of resources. Despite the tax, differences in wages still would correspond to the marginal workers' evaluations of alternative employments, and the adjustment of wages to equal value productivity would be favorable to the attainment of an optimum utilization of resources.

The use of a lump-sum tax to finance the state's investment and social service program does not preclude its use to redistribute income. Such a redistribution, however, is limited by the nature of the share. As a means of recouping the larger incomes paid to skilled workers, for example, the tax could not serve in the stead of a progressive tax. But other things being equal it would be quite consistent for a worker with a small family to be taxed more heavily than a worker with a large one. In principle the levying of heavy taxes on individuals with special native abilities also would not be precluded, for so far as such individuals were bent on entering one occupation only, their wage would in some degree be indeterminate; and if their product were automatically (through the administrative procedure used) imputed to them as a wage, the tax might conceivably extract some of the "rental" return on their abilities for distribution among the members of the community. The tax would have to be levied, however, so as not to discourage effort or special training, and it is not easy to see how such a result could ever obtain in practice.

MARX ON SOCIALIST DISTRIBUTION

The conscientious reader will find in scattered references the relation of the present inquiry into socialist distribution to other recent ones. It is advisable, however, to consider in some detail

[16] See above, p. 183.

one early contribution to the subject which has had much influence on the wage policy of the lone modern state where socialist symbols are the accepted political ones.

A theory of the distribution of income in a socialist state was developed by Karl Marx as early as 1875 in a criticism of the draft program of the congress of the German Workers' Party held at Gotha in that year.[17] The passages which relate to distribution are short, and the essentials can be set forth briefly.

Marx argued that, contrary to the view implied in the Gotha program, inequality of income would persist in the socialist state. As in a capitalist community, the relative shares of the workers in consumers' goods (aside from the products reserved for communal satisfaction of needs) would be proportionate to the quantity of labor supplied by them. Marx regarded the principle of distribution simply as an expression of the "bourgeois right," which would still prevail in the socialist society, that each producer should receive back from society the value equivalent of what he contributed to it. The equivalents are determined simply by an extension to labor of Marx's theory of commodity values:

> Here obviously the same principle prevails as that which regulates the exchange of commodities, as far as this is an exchange of equal values ... So much of labor in one form is exchanged for an equal amount of labor in another form.

But quantity of labor is not to be measured simply by labor time. Differences in intensity, and differences "in individual endowment and thus productive capacity," Marx was careful to add, are also to be recognized.

Inequality of reward, according to Marx, could be liquidated only with the higher development of the socialist economy:

> In a higher phase of a communist society, after the enslaving subordination of individuals under division of labor, and therewith also the antithesis between mental and physical labor, has vanished; after labor from a mere means of life, has itself become a prime necessity of life; after the productive forces have also increased with the all-round de-

---

[17] Karl Marx, *Critique of the Gotha Programme.* Quotations are from the International Publishers' edition (New York, 1938), pp. 6ff.

velopment of the individual, and all the springs of coöperative wealth flow more abundantly—only then can the narrow horizon of bourgeois right be fully left behind, and society inscribe on its banners: from each according to his ability, to each according to his needs.

To those who continue to identify equalitarianism with Marxism this argument should be evidence of their error. But it must be acknowledged that Marx's brief analysis of socialist distribution leaves much to be desired. The relative rewards of different workers in a capitalist society, and in a socialist society, cannot be explained simply in terms of the quantity of labor they supply; this is not the *bourgeois* right. It is true and important that for Marx the quantity of labor depended on intensity and individual capacity as well as on duration. But the gap between the Ricardian labor theory of value that Marx used and the modern theory that relative rewards are determined by the productivity of labor—and more generally, by value productivity—could be bridged only by applying sufficient patches to the definition of quantity of labor for the concept to contain implicitly the latter theory. In this case the labor theory would be redundant. Without such patching the essential difference between the two theories is clear: in one case relative rewards are determined by the characteristics of the workers, while in the other case they depend as well on the state of technique, and on the demand for the various commodities produced.

Furthermore, the reason for the persistence of capitalist principles of distribution in the socialist state is left obscure by Marx. Is the explanation, as the expression "bourgeois right" might imply, simply that there is an ethical lag in the socialist community? Do capitalist principles continue to prevail simply because of the pressure of the vested interests of privileged workers? Or, as the passage on the conditions for full communism implies, are there economic forces at work? These questions are raised but not resolved by a reading of Marx's discussion.

Whatever the shortcomings of his analysis, the fact that Marx proceeded to develop a concrete theory of socialist distribution attests once again to his grasp of the scientific approach to social phenomena. Whether it is a tribute to his analytic power or to his intuition, his conclusion that inequality will persist in a socialist state has gained rather than lost support in the thought and events of ensuing years. The weight of Marx's authority has also served in good stead the administrators of the socialist state with which we are concerned, even if conditions affecting the demand for and supply of labor obtrude in their considerations. But this is a matter for the empirical inquiry that is to follow.

9

SOCIALIST ECONOMICS*

This survey focuses on recent theoretic studies of the economic problems of socialism and, so far as they bear on these problems, on recent inquiries in the cognate field of welfare economics. These writings, which are notably abstract, might be considered as providing a theoretic basis for the work of a Central Planning Board seeking to rationalize the planning system of a socialist state. Reference is of course to a socialist state which has not yet reached the era of unlimited abundance; in other words, one which still faces, like its capitalist predecessor, the fundamental problem of allocating scarce resources among alternative uses. In the light of whatever ends the Board serves, its task is to assure as far as practicable that the available resources are utilized to the optimum advantage. My chief aim is to appraise summarily the contributions which have been made to the solution of the Board's task.

Among the studies to be considered, of course, are the recent contributions to the debate, provoked originally by Mises' famous article,[1] as to whether socialism can work at all, and how well. By now it seems generally agreed that the argument on these questions advanced by Mises himself, at least according to one

* Reproduced from Howard S. Ellis, ed., *A Survey of Contemporary Economics* (Philadelphia, 1948). The essay benefited from valuable comments by Professors Frank D. Graham and Abba P. Lerner. The very dated third paragraph in the original version has been omitted.

[1] "Die Wirtschaftsrechnung im sozialistischen Gemeinwesen," *Archiv für Sozialwissenschaften*, April 1920, pp. 86–121. A translation, to which references are made in this survey, has been published in F. A. Hayek, ed., *Collectivist Economic Planning* (London, 1935).

interpretation, is without much force. I shall try here to arrive at an understanding as to just what has been settled and just what remains unsettled in this debate.

THE ENDS

Of the writings to be surveyed, a considerable number are concerned with one large problem: to define (in a sense that will become clear) the allocation of resources that would be an optimum. On this problem the basic works were all published some years ago. Mention is to be made particularly of the writings of Pareto[2] and Barone[3] in the field of socialist economics and of Marshall[4] and Pigou[5] in the field of welfare economics. These studies provide all the essentials of a solution to the question just posed. In more recent studies, however, much has been done to clarify and elaborate the analysis.

Marshall, Pigou, Pareto, and Barone on "ends." The definition of the optimum allocation involves, for one thing, the formulation of a scale of values, on the basis of which the alternative uses of resources are to be evaluated. In the present context this scale of values might be considered as representing the ends which the Central Planning Board serves. In order to describe the recent doctrinal developments relating to this aspect of the analysis, it is necessary to refer briefly to the formulations in the basic works just mentioned.

In the case of Marshall and Pigou, the needed scale of values is given immediately in their proverbial conception of "welfare" as the sum of the utilities of the individual households in the

---

[2] V. Pareto, *Cours d'économie politique*, II (Lausanne, 1897), pp. 90ff., 364ff.

[3] E. Barone, "Il ministerio della produzione nello stato colletivista," *Giornale degli Economisti e Rivista di Statistica*, September and October 1908, ser. 2a, pp. 267–293, 391–414. A translation has been published under the title "The Ministry of Production in the Collectivist State," in F. A. Hayek, ed. *Collectivist Economic Planning*. References made to this paper are to the translation.

[4] A. Marshall, *Principles of Economics*, 1st ed. (London, 1890); 8th ed. (London, 1920).

[5] A. C. Pigou, *Economics of Welfare*, 1st ed. (London, 1920); 4th ed. (London, 1934).

community.[6] For different persons of equal sensitivity the marginal utility of income supposedly is the same when incomes are equal. The optimum allocation of resources, then, is one which maximizes welfare in this sense. One condition for the attainment of the optimum is immediately apparent: incomes must be equal.

In the case of Pareto and Barone, the criterion for an optimum allocation of resources is somewhat more complex: it must be impossible by any reallocation of resources to enhance the welfare of one household without reducing that of another.[7] If a reallocation which would lead to this result were possible, it is reasoned, the resources of the community could be used to better advantage by making it; in the optimum such opportunities must already have been completely exploited.

For Pareto, this formulation had one outstanding virtue: it is possible to define the optimum allocation of resources without assuming (as Marshall did) that the welfare is the sum of the utilities of individual households. This assumption Pareto considered objectionable, on the ground that the utilities are incommensurate: "nous ne pouvons ni comparer ni sommer celles-ci, car nous ignorons le rapport des unités en lesquelles elles sont exprimées."

As Pareto and Barone recognized, however, their formulation provides a necessary but insufficient criterion for the definition of the optimum allocation. The question remains, how to decide between different allocations which make some households better off and others worse off—that is, where there is a redistribution of income. This matter Pareto disposes of simply by assuming that incomes are distributed "suivant la règle qu'il plaira d'adopter." Similarly, Barone supposes that the distribution of incomes is on the basis of some "ethical criterion."

Alternative ends. One of the recent doctrinal developments concerning ends involves the introduction into the analysis of variants of the scales of values of Marshall and Pigou, and

---

[6] For references to the pertinent passages in the works of Marshall and Pigou, see Chapter 1.

[7] This is the verbal equivalent of a mathematical criterion which Pareto introduced. Pareto himself misinterpreted his criterion; the correct interpretation given here is due to Barone.

Pareto and Barone. All these writers, evidently, consider the case where alternative uses of resources are evaluated on the basis of the preferences of individual households—the preferences of the households, as they see them, are to count. If such a scale of values is in operation, consumers are "sovereign." Interest has focused recently on the variants of this case that arise where the Board itself undertakes to determine, to a greater or lesser extent, what is good for consumers, and allocates resources on this basis.

An important precedent for the consideration of this variant is found in the well-known argument of Pigou that consumers do not correctly weigh their own interests in decisions on savings; that, as a result of a defective telescopic faculty, they tend to undervalue future, as compared with equivalent present, satisfactions. From this it follows at once that if consumers are sovereign in respect of questions of saving and investment, the aggregate saving will be less than is socially desirable. There is a case for disregarding consumers' preferences in this sphere.

This particular argument has recently been extended to socialist economics. Thus Dobb[8] now argues that the socialist Board must disregard consumers' preferences on the question of savings and observe instead the principle that future satisfactions be valued equally with equivalent present satisfactions. Lange[9] introduces the same postulate.

Under this assumption, as I understand it, the Board would value equally a marginal "dollar" of present and future income, provided that income is constant. To the extent that income is expected to rise as a result of the investments undertaken, presumably the marginal dollar in the future would still be valued less than in the present. This would result from the operation of the law of diminishing utility within each income period and has nothing to do with the defective telescopic faculty referred to by Pigou. Thus, in deciding on the amount of investment, the Board presumably would strike a balance between two opposing consid-

[8] M. Dobb, *Political Economy and Capitalism* (New York, 1940), pp. 298–299, 311–312.

[9] "On the Economic Theory of Socialism," in B. Lippincott, ed., *On the Economic Theory of Socialism* (Minneapolis, Minn., 1938), pp. 90ff. This is a revision of two articles which were published originally in the *Review of Economic Studies*, October 1936 and February 1937, pp. 53–71, 123–142. Unless otherwise indicated, references are to the revision.

erations: on the one hand, the fact just mentioned, that with a rising level of income the marginal dollar in the future would be worth less than in the present; on the other hand, the fact that by investing a marginal dollar now an agio might be earned as a result of the supposedly greater productivity of roundabout processes.

Dobb[10] envisages that under socialism there will be many other exceptions to the principle of consumers' sovereignty. He considers that consumers are to a greater or lesser extent irrational in many decisions other than that on saving; and furthermore, that in many cases (for example, education, health care), even if the consumer chooses rationally from his own point of view, his decision may not be in accord with the social interest. Dobb refers also in this same connection to goods (as, for instance, police protection) which by their very nature cannot possibly be allocated among households in accord with their individual preferences.[11]

---

[10] *Political Economy and Capitalism*, pp. 309ff. See also *idem*, "Economic Theory and the Problems of a Socialist Economy," *Economic Journal*, December 1933, pp. 588–598.

[11] One other case to which Dobb refers as indicating the need for a departure from consumers' sovereignty requires special comment. This is the case where the individual consumer's desire for a thing depends on the fact of others possessing or not possessing it. "Conspicuous consumption" is the familiar example of this sort of situation.

As Paul Samuelson observes in his *Foundations of Economic Analysis* (Cambridge, Mass., 1947), p. 224, the welfare analysis as it is usually formulated assumes that the individual's preferences depend only on the amounts of goods he consumes and not on the amounts consumed by others. In the case of "conspicuous consumption," one must restate the principle of consumers' sovereignty so that the utility of any household depends not only on the amounts of goods it consumes, but also on the amounts consumed by others.

The Board might consider, however, as Dobb implies, that because of their "conventional" character consumers' preferences in this case should be overruled. If the Board did so, there would indeed be a departure from the principle of consumers' sovereignty.

But of more interest perhaps is the fact, which Dobb does not bring out, that even if the Board determines to adhere to the principle of consumers' sovereignty in this case (where the tastes of different households are interdependent), there would be very real difficulties in implementing it. It can be shown that in a free market where consumers take prices as parameters (see below, the discussion of the distinction between consumers' sovereignty and freedom of choice), the allocation of goods as between consumers could never be an optimum one. If an effective barter

If a free market prevailed for consumers' goods generally, then many commodities such as are covered by the foregoing considerations presumably should be distributed communally in the form of "social services." The question of the types of goods that should be distributed in this fashion also is discussed by Dickinson.[12]

The welfare function. In another recent development, to which the writer has endeavored to contribute,[13] the concern has been to clarify the question of the number and nature of the decisions on ends required to formulate the needed scale of values. This important question is left in doubt by the various writings, both old and new, that have been cited.

From the formulation of Marshall and Pigou, and of recent writers who follow them in using the utility calculus, one might gain the impression that in reality only one such decision is involved, that is the decision to maximize "welfare." Once this decision is taken it would seem that all else is determined, that is, it remains only to settle, presumably by empirical investigation, whether consumers do or do not value future satisfactions "accurately," whether or not they are "rational" in one or another kind of choice, whether they are indeed equally "sensitive" or if not just how their "sensitivity" varies, and so on.

These, however, are rather startling implications, and it is not surprising that followers of Marshall and Pigou are in doubt as to their validity. This I take it is what Dobb[14] and Kahn[15] after him

---

market could be arranged, where consumers could trade among themselves, however, it would seem that in theory the optimum might be attained. The individual household in the former case (the free market) would disregard and in the latter case (barter) take into account the effects on its welfare of changes in the consumption pattern of other households which might be induced by its own choices.

The work of Samuelson, referred to above, unfortunately reached me too late to be taken fully into account in this essay. On a number of points, Samuelson presents a more exact formulation of the welfare analysis than hitherto has been available.

[12] H. D. Dickinson, *Economics of Socialism* (Oxford, 1939), pp. 51ff.

[13] See Chapter 1; also O. Lange, "Foundations of Welfare Economics," *Econometrica*, July-October 1942, pp. 215–228.

[14] *Economic Journal*, December 1933, p. 594.

[15] R. F. Kahn, "Some Notes on Ideal Output," *Economic Journal*, March 1935.

wish to convey when they express the suspicion that the welfare that is being maximized may be entirely "subjective" after all, like a "black hat in a dark room."

Pareto and Barone, as has been mentioned, are explicit that the question of income distribution must be the subject of a decision on ends. In view of their silence on the question of consumers' sovereignty, however, one inevitably is led to wonder how *this* question is settled. Uncertainty on this score is only increased by recent efforts, such as that by Hicks,[16] to establish by use of the Pareto-Barone formulation welfare principles that are in some sense "positive" or "scientific." By implication, such principles would require no decisions on ends for their derivation.

In dealing with this whole question, it has seemed useful to introduce into the analysis a welfare function, W, the value of which is understood to depend on all the variables that might be considered as affecting welfare: the amounts of each and every kind of good consumed by and service performed by each and every household, the amount of each and every kind of capital investment undertaken, and so on. The welfare function is understood initially to be entirely general in character; its shape is determined by the specific decisions on ends that are introduced into the analysis. Given the decisions on ends, the welfare function is transformed into a scale of values for the evaluation of alternative uses of resources.

On this basis, it has been argued, decisions on the following questions on ends are involved in the welfare formulations that have been outlined:

Consumers' sovereignty. According to the welfare function analysis, the question of whether and to what extent consumers will be sovereign involves one such decision or a complex of such decisions. If one understands "welfare" to *mean* that consumers are sovereign, the question is, of course, already decided when it is determined to maximize welfare; but nothing in substance is gained by this type of implicit theorizing, in which many economists seem to engage. Whether by definition or otherwise, a decision on ends must be introduced. Furthermore, differences in

16 J. R. Hicks, "Foundations of Welfare Economics," *Economic Journal,* December 1939, pp. 696–712.

opinion as to consumers' "rationality," the accuracy of their evaluation of future satisfactions, etc., *are* seen as often turning at least in part on divergences in ethics and hence as not easy to resolve by empirical investigation.

If the decision is in favor of consumers' sovereignty, the welfare function may be expressed in the form,

$$W = F(U^1, U^2, U^3, \ldots). \qquad (1)$$

Here U^1, U^2, U^3, etc., represent the utilities of the individual households as they see them and W, the welfare of the community, is understood to be an increasing function of these utilities. The welfare of the community, then, is constant, increases, or decreases, according to whether the utilities of the individual households are constant, increase, or decrease. If the decision is against consumers' sovereignty, the welfare function must be expressed by a formula in which the Board's own preference scales are substituted for the utility functions of the individual households.

Evidently, the formula in (1) is nothing more nor less than a generalization of the Marshall-Pigou formulation; according to the latter, W is the *sum* of the utilities U^1, U^2, U^3, etc. Also, to maximize W would satisfy the criterion of Pareto and Barone. Indeed, this function might be considered as an explicit formulation of the scale of values implicit in their criterion.

Income distribution. The analysis in question follows Pareto in holding that utilities are incommensurable,[17] and agrees with Robbins[18] that, because of this, principles of income distribution cannot be deduced from the utility calculus either by the rules of logic or by empirical demonstration. The familiar appeal (in which Lerner[19] and Lange[20] now join) that we must "assume" the

---

[17] Their incommensurability is reflected in the appearance of a dimensional constant in empirical measures of utility.

[18] L. H. Robbins, *Nature and Significance of Economic Science*, 2nd ed. (London, 1935), chap. vi; "Inter-personal Comparison of Utility," *Economic Journal*, December 1938, pp. 635–641. The latter article replies to R. F. Harrod, "Scope and Method of Economics," *Economic Journal*, September 1938.

[19] A. P. Lerner, *Economics of Control* (New York, 1944), pp. 24–25.

[20] *On the Economic Theory of Socialism*, p. 100, n. 54.

comparability of utilities in order to establish a basis for normative precepts is seen as not meeting the issue.

But all of this is regarded as saying nothing more than that here, too, a decision on ends is involved. Ends are essentially principles for the evaluation of alternatives that otherwise are incommensurable. That is why an *evaluation* is needed. Once an evaluation is made, the alternatives are indeed commensurable. Given the ethical principle according to which incomes are to be distributed, the marginal welfare per "dollar" for different households necessarily is the same *in the light of this principle* when the distribution is realized.

Interrelations in the welfare of different households. Insofar as Marshall and Pigou conceive of welfare as the sum of the utilities of different households, their formulation is seen to involve an additional decision on ends, namely, one to the effect that the interrelations in the utilities of the different households have a zero social value. The magnitude of the change in the community's welfare resulting from a change in the budget position of any one family does not depend at all on the living standards enjoyed by other households.

For purposes of analyzing the optimum allocation, however, it has been found unnecessary to refer to this special and obviously very dubious case; all propositions of interest have been deduced from the more general function in the formula given above. The demonstration of this point would seem to be one of the more interesting doctrinal gains resulting from the introduction of the welfare function into the analysis.

From this standpoint, Pareto's criticism of the Marshall-Pigou formulation is misdirected. From a purely formal point of view the objection to the Marshall-Pigou formulation is not (as Pareto implied) that incommensurate utilities are added, but that their aggregation involves a redundant and indeed dubious assumption.[21]

[21] As Samuelson makes clear (*Foundations*, pp. 224–226), the assumption of the independence of the contribution of each household to total welfare is distinct from and additional to the assumption, referred to above, n. 11, regarding the independence of the *structure of tastes* of the different households. All that independence in the latter sense implies is that each household's marginal rates of substitution depend only on the quantities

In the writings under review, the principle of consumers' sovereignty usually is interpreted as referring to the households' preferences not only as between consumers' goods but also as between jobs. Hence, the utility functions in the formula should be considered as representing for the different households the balance of utilities from consumption and of disutilities from work done.

It has been found convenient, following Pareto and Barone, to distinguish between the "wage" that a household earns, and its "income," which differs from the wage by the amount of a social "dividend" or "tax," as the case may be. On balance, the aggregate amount of the dividends and taxes for all households equals the aggregate amount of "profits" (including "interest" and "rent," if charged) available to the community after provision is made for capital accumulation and communal consumption. Given the wages of the different households, a decision on the dividend or tax is, in effect, a decision as to the optimum distribution of income, that is, the distribution for which the marginal welfare per "dollar" is the same for different households.

For purposes of analyzing the distribution of income in terms of these two income categories (wages and the dividend or tax) it is necessary to introduce a further assumption on ends, which is not clear in the writings under review. The assumption is that the comparative marginal welfare per dollar for different households would not be changed by a change in the composition of their budgets (including changes in work done) for which their own total utilities are unchanged.[22] This requirement, a fundamental one, assures that the decision on the distribution of income is consistent with the principle of consumers' sovereignty. As we shall see, it means in effect that differences in disutilities must be taken into account in the distribution of income.

---

of goods it consumes and not at all on the quantities consumed by other households; conceivably this condition might obtain at the same time that the household felt its total utility affected by general changes in living standards of other households.

[22] See below, p. 205.

OPTIMUM CONDITIONS

Given the scale of values, the definition of the optimum allocation is formulated in these terms. In accord with familiar theoretic procedures, technical knowledge and tastes are taken as given, that is, it is assumed that they are not affected by the changes under consideration; also, the question of the resources to be allocated to research is left out of account. On this basis it is possible to derive from the given ends a series of conditions ("equations") which must be satisfied if the optimum allocation is to be achieved. The optimum conditions are sufficient in number to determine the amounts of each and every sort of goods and services allocated to each and every use (the "unknowns"). Thus, if the scale of values implied by the ends were known in complete detail (that is, if all the utility functions were known), and detailed information were available on techniques and on the stocks of resources on hand, it would be possible, at least theoretically, to solve this system of equations for the concrete values of all the unknowns.[23]

With respect to this aspect of the analysis, recent writings have been concerned chiefly to formulate explicitly the optimum conditions (which are not in every case clearly stated in the works of Marshall, Pigou, Pareto, and Barone) and to develop the analysis to deal with various complexities. These aims have been pursued by several writers, especially Lerner.[24]

For convenience, I present below a brief inventory of the more interesting optimum conditions as they have come to be formulated. That the conditions listed are indeed requirements for an

---

[23] As far as I know, Barone is the only writer in the field of socialist or welfare economics who has counted up and matched equations and unknowns. Much the same ground has been covered many times, however, in discussions of the determinacy of competitive equilibrium.

[24] See A. P. Lerner, "The Concept of Monopoly and the Measurement of Monopoly Power," *Review of Economic Studies*, June 1934; "Economic Theory and Socialist Economy," *Review of Economic Studies*, October 1934; "A Note on Socialist Economics," *Review of Economic Studies*, October 1936; "Statics and Dynamics in Socialist Economics," *Economic Journal*, June 1937; *Economics of Control*. Also Chapter 1 of this volume; Hicks, *Economic Journal*, December 1939; Lange, *Econometrica*, July–October 1942.

optimum, the reader should be able to satisfy himself without too much difficulty. My brief comments are intended only to be suggestive on this score. Except as indicated, the conditions listed are either stated or implied in one or another of the basic works to which reference has already been made.

The main conditions, then, are as follows:

(i) *The ratio of the marginal utilities (the marginal rate of substitution) for each pair of consumers' goods must be the same for all households.* If this is not the case there is always the possibility of an exchange of goods between a pair of households which would increase the utility of both, and accordingly, assuming consumers' sovereignty, would increase welfare.

(ii) *In every industry factors must be combined in a technologically optimum manner* in the sense that it is not possible technologically to dispense with any amount of any factor without a reduction in output.

(iii) *The marginal value productivity of each factor must be the same in every industry.* The "prices" at which marginal productivities are valued are understood, for the time being, to represent not market prices but merely indexes of the comparative social values of alternatives. In the case of consumers' goods, the "prices" are proportional to the common values for all households of the marginal rates of substitution. If, in terms of these prices, the marginal value productivity of a factor were larger in one industry than in another, this would mean that by a shift in resources it would be possible to realize an exchange of consumers' goods which would enhance the utilities of some or all households without any concomitant losses.

In the case of capital goods, it is supposed that the "prices" represent "present values," where the present value of any particular capital good is the discounted value of its marginal value productivity in the consumers' goods industries. The rate of discount is the rate at which the Board discounts future in comparison with present income.[25] This presupposes of course that the

[25] If it is assumed that the capital goods are used up fully within one accounting period, these conditions lead to a very simple relation, namely that the marginal product of an increment of a capital good employed in

Board has a fixed single rate of discount. One might more realistically conceive the case where the Board's rate of time preference varies with the amount of savings undertaken; or there might be multiple rates, each relating to a comparison of present income with income at some specified future date. This latter case has been treated in detail by F. P. Ramsey.[26]

(iv) *In the optimum, there must be no possibility of shifting a worker from one occupation to another to increase the value of output by more than would be required to compensate the worker for the change.* This assumes that all commodities are valued according to principles already stated and that consumers' preferences govern not only as between consumers' goods but also as between jobs.

(v) *Occupational wage differentials must correspond at one and the same time to differences in marginal value productivity and, for marginal workers, to differences in disutility.* When the marginal worker is shifted from one job to another, then, he *actually* is paid the amount that is necessary to compensate him for the change in jobs. If freedom of choice prevails, this must be the case; but it is not clear that this is desirable. The desirability of this principle of wage determination follows from the assumed ends. Given that the marginal welfare per dollar for a given household is unaffected by any change in its budget position which leaves its

---

the industry producing this capital good must equal the increment of the capital good employed plus interest on this increment. Let $A_c\Delta C$ be the marginal product of an increment of capital good in consumers' good industry A, P_A be the price of the consumers' good, A, $C_c\Delta C$ be the marginal product of the capital good in the industry producing this capital good, and P_c be the price of this capital good. It is required that

$$P_A A_c\Delta C = P_c C_c\Delta C.$$

Since $P_c = P_a A_c/(1 + r)$, it follows at once that $(1 + r)\Delta C = C_c\Delta C$. Since the marginal value productivity of capital is the same in every use, it follows also that the rate of interest earned on marginal investments of capital is the same in every use, and equal to the rate established by the Board.

[26] "A Mathematical Theory of Saving," *Economic Journal*, December 1928.

total utility unchanged, the worker must be compensated fully for any extra disutility incurred as a result of a change in jobs.[27]

(vi) *The social dividend or tax, however, must be determined independently of the workers' occupation or earnings.* This principle, advanced by Lerner,[28] also follows directly from the principle that marginal economic welfare per dollar is unaffected by any budget change which leaves the total utility of the household unchanged. Given any initial allocation of "profits," no change is called for if a marginal worker is shifted from one job to another for which the additional wage just compensates him for the extra disutility. An attempt to offset the established wage differentials by the use of the tax or dividend would be out of place. The amount of the dividend or tax might be established on any of a variety of principles: for example, it might be fixed as an equal lump sum for all households; it might be made to vary with the size of the household, and so on.

In the foregoing we have made use of the distinction, which Lange recently has clarified,[29] between "consumers' sovereignty" and "freedom of choice." Consumers' sovereignty is an "end." Freedom of choice may also be an end, in and of itself, but is also an administrative procedure. The principle of consumers' sovereignty might conceivably be accepted, while some procedure other than freedom of choice was used to ascertain consumers' preferences (statistical inquiries for instance); to distribute goods

[27] In theory, though hardly in practice, the possibility is not precluded that different wages be established for workers in the same occupation, workers who are not on the margin of choice between occupations being paid less than those who are. In this way, the household's "producer's surplus" would be extracted for distribution in the community at large. This in no way would conflict with the principle of consumers' sovereignty.

[28] In the original version of his essay, "On the Economic Theory of Socialism" (*Review of Economic Studies*, October 1936, pp. 64, 65), Lange assumed that the dividend should be distributed proportionately to wages. The objectionable character of Lange's solution was pointed out by Lerner in a note appended to Lange's article, and Lange has since corrected his argument. Both Lange and Lerner assume freedom of choice as well as consumers' sovereignty. As a result, it is not brought out clearly that the stated principles of wage determination and taxation follow from the principle of consumers' sovereignty alone.

[29] *On the Economic Theory of Socialism*, pp. 95–96.

among the different households (as in rationing); and to recruit workers for different jobs (conscription). Under what circumstances, if any, this might be advisable is a matter for consideration. Conceivably, also, freedom of choice might prevail without the acceptance of the principle of consumers' sovereignty. While households might be permitted to spend their incomes as they wish, at established prices, their demands might be disregarded in decisions on production.

Though it is not always made clear in the writings under review, for the purposes of defining the optimum position the assumption of consumers' sovereignty alone is sufficient. For the sake of logical clarity, the conditions are formulated here on this assumption and without regard to whether freedom of choice also prevails.

Lange has discussed also the case where consumers' sovereignty is abandoned or modified.[30] Conceptually, this case is readily dealt with. All that needs to be done is to rephrase the preceding argument to take into account the fact that the pertinent marginal rates of substitution are those decided on by the Board rather than by individual households. Thus, in terms of *these rates*, the requirement that the marginal value productivity of a factor be the same in every use still holds.

If consumers' sovereignty were abandoned, however, it is open to question whether the Board would be concerned to elaborate its preference scale with any great precision. Very possibly there would be significant ranges of choice within which the Board itself would be indifferent as to allocations. To whatever extent this is so, the optimum position is in the last analysis indeterminate.

"MARGINAL COST" VS. "AVERAGE COST"

It is an easy matter to restate the foregoing optimum conditions in terms of "costs." The total cost incurred in the production of the optimum output must be at a minimum and, in the optimum, price must equal marginal cost (costs being understood here to comprise material costs, interest, and wages). The reader may

---

[30] *Ibid.*, pp. 90ff.

readily verify that if the stated requirements regarding costs are met the following optimum conditions will be satisfied: the condition that the factors employed in each firm be combined in a technologically optimum manner, the condition that marginal value productivity of a factor be the same in every use, and the condition that differences in the wages of different kinds of labor equal differences in their value productivity. Conversely, it can readily be shown that if the stated requirements do not hold for all firms alike, one or another of these optimum conditions will be violated.[31]

The requirement that the total cost of producing the optimum output be a minimum means, of course, that the average cost incurred in the production of *this* output is a minimum. If there is no barrier to using at one scale of output the same combination of factors that may be used at any other, then presumably one and the same combination of factors will be the most efficient at all scales of output. We deal, then, with the case of *constant costs*. Marginal cost and average cost are constant and equal for all levels of output.

For various well-known reasons, however, the case of constant costs may not prevail in the real world. For one thing, there is the case of the so-called "fixed factors"; for another there is the case of indivisibilities in the factors employed or in the production unit (for example, bridges, railways, utilities, etc.). These two cases pose a variety of theoretic questions, which recently have been discussed in some detail by Lerner[32] and Lewis.[33] What is of concern here is that in both cases—in the former case, for the duration of the service life of the "fixed" factor; in the latter case, indefinitely—only a relative optimum combination of factors can be attained at any level of output, that is, only the amounts of factors other than those that are fixed or indivisible can be

---

[31] At this stage where no specific planning scheme is in mind, it is a matter of convention just where the line is drawn between wages and dividends or taxes. As long as *differences* in wages correspond to *differences* in marginal value productivity, all is well. For our present purposes the convention may be adopted that in some one firm and for some one occupation, wages *equal* marginal value productivity. A similar assumption is needed with respect to the prices of capital goods.

[32] *Economics of Control*, chap. xvii.

[33] W. A. Lewis, "Fixed Costs," *Economica*, November 1946.

adjusted as output varies. It is usually assumed that under these circumstances the average cost varies with output according to a familiar U-shaped pattern, and, hence, that marginal cost and average cost will be equal only at one scale of output, that for which average cost is at a minimum. In the case of indivisibilities, however, the possibility has also to be reckoned with that because of the very heavy overhead and the relatively limited importance of variable costs, average cost per unit will not follow the familiar U-shaped pattern, but instead will continue to decline for a wide range of output variations. Marginal cost may be below average cost for the entire relevant range of operations.

To repeat, the rule for the attainment of the optimum is that price must equal *marginal* cost. This principle is perfectly general: it holds regardless of the relation of marginal and average cost, regardless of whether price is above average cost and there are "profits" (as might be so in the case of "fixed factors"), or below average cost and there are losses (as might be so also in the case of "fixed factors," and very likely would be so in the case of large indivisibilities).

For this very fundamental proposition, we are indebted chiefly to Marshall and Pigou, who long ago advanced it boldly even for cases of decreasing costs. In recent years, however, the rule has had to be defended and reaffirmed on a number of occasions in the face of recurring confusion. In this connection, mention should be made of the contributions of Lerner[34] and Hotelling.[35] Both

[34] *Review of Economic Studies*, June 1934; *Economics of Control*, particularly chaps. xv, xvi, xvii.

Lerner takes pains to make clear that "marginal cost" must be understood as the increment of costs at *given* factor prices. Only on this understanding does the condition that price equal marginal cost correspond to the optimum conditions set forth on pp. 204ff. Only then is it assured that any factor will be equally productive in every use. Lerner's stipulation, however, requires elaboration. If variations in output that are very small in relation to the supply of factors are under consideration, then for all practical purposes factor prices will be constant anyhow, so the stipulation is not necessary. On the other hand, if there are large indivisibilities, so that the changes in output do affect factor prices, the changes in factor prices would have to be taken into account. The special problems arising when large variations in output are under consideration are discussed below in the text.

The foregoing refers to marginal variations in the output of a given production unit, as distinct from variations in output due to the opening up or shutting down of the production unit itself. For purposes of formu-

writers, Lerner with special vigor, have championed the Marshall-Pigou position against doctrinal deviations.

Part of the confusion seems to stem from the fact that the distinction is not always kept clearly in mind between the definition of the optimum allocation and the problem of realizing this optimum in practice. As Schumpeter has observed, the stated principle follows from the general logic of choice;[36] its validity does not depend at all on the possibility of devising an administrative procedure under which the optimum might be approxi-

lating optimum conditions, the concept of a production unit as distinct from an industry is purely conventional—except in the case of large indivisibilities, it is always possible to conceive of an industry as comprising a large number of very small production units, so that within the scale of operations of this production unit, no variations in output, whether marginal or total, have any significant effect on the prices of factors. If, however, the production units are taken to be large—let us say there is only one production unit in the industry—one more item must be added to the list of causes of a departure from constant costs, the rising supply prices of the factors. Average and marginal costs will diverge on this account even if there are no fixed factors of indivisibilities. But the optimum condition still is as before, that prices equal the marginal costs incurred at *given* factor prices.

These remarks, of course, bear directly on the controversy stirred up by Pigou, concerning the case of increasing supply price. This controversy seems no longer to be active, but it may be advisable to suggest a standpoint on the main issues. First, so far as the nature of the optimum is concerned (this seems to have been one of the questions arising), my view is as above. Second, so far as concerns the question of whether the optimum would be realized under perfect competition (this apparently was the main issue), the logic, as Pigou himself came to recognize, is overwhelmingly in favor of the affirmative as advanced by Young and Knight and against the negative originally advanced by Pigou. Regardless of whether factor prices rise with increasing output in the industry, the relevant marginal cost under perfect competition necessarily is one for which factor prices are given for any one firm. The optimum condition that price equal marginal cost *in this sense* is satisfied. Any divergence that persists in the long run between price and average cost, of course, will be absorbed by rent.

A brief review of the literature in this controversy is presented in Howard S. Ellis and William Fellner, "External Economies and Diseconomies," *American Economic Review*, September 1943.

[35] Harold Hotelling, "The General Welfare in Relation to Problems of Taxation and of Railway and Utility Rates," *Econometrica*, July 1938.

[36] J. A. Schumpeter, *Capitalism, Socialism, and Democracy*, 2nd ed. (New York, 1947), p. 176, n. 5. Schumpeter should have said that the principle follows from the logic of choice *and* given ends (see below, n. 44).

mated in practice. One important question posed by indivisibilities in the latter connection is referred to below pp. 220ff.[37]

The confusion concerning the principle of equating price and marginal cost seems to stem also from a further confusion as to the fiscal implications of the welfare principles. In particular it is often suggested that if losses are not offset by profits elsewhere, the stated principle could not be applied.[38] The optimum conditions that have been outlined, however, are fully consistent with either "profits" or "losses" for the system as a whole. The fiscal counterparts of these "profits" or "losses" are the subsidy and tax that have been mentioned. At least on a theoretic plane, a logically satisfactory fiscal device for financing the losses or disposing of the profits of the socialist economy is always at hand.

In the long run, of course, "fixed factors," too, become variable and mistakes in investments may be rectified. The rule is the same as before: price must equal marginal cost. Now, however, it is "long-run" rather than "short-run" marginal cost that is of concern. Account is to be taken of whatever increment of cost is incurred in producing an increment of output under the condition that the "fixed factors," too, are variable.

[37] Attention may be called here, however, to the article of E. F. M. Durbin, "Economic Calculus in a Planned Economy," *Economic Journal*, December 1936, which raises several practical objections to the Lerner-Hotelling condition; to Lerner's article cited in n. 24 above (*Economic Journal*, June 1937), which disposes of these objections; and finally to the recent article of R. H. Coase, "The Marginal Cost Controversy," *Economica*, August 1946, which again raises practical objections to the Lerner-Hotelling condition.

While Coase accepts the Lerner-Hotelling condition as a valid principle, he argues that in practice it might be desirable to use a multi-part price system, in which consumers are charged one price to cover overhead and another to cover marginal costs. While in the special case he considers (where the overhead actually can be imputed separately to different households) his scheme is unobjectionable, in any more typical case of indivisibility the lump sum tax scheme we have discussed, I believe, would be a preferable means of covering overhead costs.

Incidentally, under socialism this tax might be used without ill effect to offset any important unfavorable effects on income distribution such as Coase argues would result from the charging of prices below costs to some consumers. In the same way, the Board might decide to pay an extra dividend to spaghetti eaters in seasons when the price of spaghetti was abnormally high.

[38] See Durbin, *Economic Journal*, December 1936, p. 685.

This is to say that in practice what we have to reckon with is not a unique marginal cost for a given level of output, but a complex of marginal costs, each of which is pertinent to a particular period of time. As a longer period of time is considered, more of the "fixed factors" become variable. Because of this greater flexibility in the production process, long-run marginal cost will generally be less than short-run marginal cost. Lewis discusses in detail the complexities that would be encountered on this account in determining marginal costs in the real world.

In the case of the indivisible production unit, the stated rule has to be reformulated. If the production unit is large, its introduction may affect the structure of prices (marginal rates of substitution) and wages. The optimum conditions listed on pp. 204–206 are all formulated in terms of the prices and wages appropriate to a *given* allocation of resources. In the case of indivisibility, this is no longer possible.[39]

How is it to be decided whether or not to introduce the production unit to begin with? In place of the requirement that price equal marginal cost, one may advance here the more general requirement that the social value yielded must equal the additional social cost. But how is it possible to tell when this condition obtains?

The solution of this problem advanced by Pigou still is generally accepted. This involves the use of the dubious consumers' surplus concept,[40] and so seems methodologically objectionable, but it is hardly likely that subsequent work will overthrow Pigou's important conclusion that it might pay to introduce the production unit even though it were known in advance that losses would be incurred. Lerner presents a systematic exposition of this aspect of the problem of indivisibility.[41]

The general rule, I have said, is that price must equal marginal cost. What if prices are merely proportional to marginal cost?

[39] Cf. Lerner, *Economics of Control*, p. 176: "The indivisibility is significant when it is large enough to destroy perfect competition."

[40] A. C. Pigou, *Economics of Welfare*, 3rd ed. (London, 1929), p. 808. It should be possible to handle this question without using the consumers' surplus concept. Essentially, what is involved is an index number problem, the objective being to compare the community's real income in two different situations with different price structures.

[41] *Economics of Control*, chap. xvi.

Would this not suffice? In the face of a good deal of authority for the affirmative, I have argued that the correct answer is in the negative.[42] If prices are proportional but not equal to marginal costs, optimum conditions will be violated. In particular, the differences in value productivity of different types of labor will no longer equal differences in wages, and hence will not correspond to differences in disutility. A reallocation of resources, involving the shift in marginal workers from one occupation to another, would be in order.

THE CONCEPTUAL FRAMEWORK

Before going further, let us try to understand the contribution that the foregoing analysis might make to the solution of the Board's task. As I see it, what has been done is to construct a conceptual framework which might serve two purposes. On the one hand, it in effect poses for the Board a series of questions on ends, that is, on consumers' sovereignty, saving and investment, communal consumption, and income distribution. In this way the analysis might assist the Board to formulate a conceptually satisfactory scale of values to guide the economy, one that is internally consistent and, in principle at least, covers the bill. Insofar as the particular questions posed are such as the Board might be expected to deal intelligently with, this would be all to the good.

On the other hand, the analysis establishes the implications of the given ends. These implications are the optimum conditions. In this way the analysis might assist the Board to allocate resources consistently in accord with the given ends. The establishment of these implications would seem to be a prerequisite for the construction of a planning scheme which might approximate the given ends in practice. It happens that the criteria for the optimum that have been set forth are conceptually simple and, for the cases where small adjustments are possible, require for their application only facts which actually might be experienced in a given situation (the marginal rates of substitution, marginal

---

[42] See Chapter 8, pp. 186ff, which refers incidentally to the writings of Lerner and Dickinson on this question. Lerner, who is cited as having supported the erroneous view that proportionality is sufficient, has since corrected himself: *Economics of Control*, pp. 100ff.

productivities, etc.). For purposes of planning, this too is clearly all to the good.

How useful this particular framework might be, however, would depend on whether the Board would feel that the particular questions posed are the right ones for it to decide, that is, whether in this sense the underlying aim is welfare. A rather different conceptual framework might be needed if the Board's aim were, say, to build up military potential. In this case, it might be necessary at least to pose for the Board a series of questions concerning the amounts of subsidies to be allowed to particular heavy industries. If the Board took a more or less absolutistic view on such matters, it might find these questions also unsuitable: in view of the uncertainties that inevitably would surround any attempt to control output via taxes and subsidies, the Board might wish to fix directly specific goals and priorities for key industries. In the case considered, moreover, the question at issue might not be what was good for the consumers from either their point of view or the Board's, but their efficiency, which need not come to the same thing.

Conceivably, there might not be any one set of questions which was right for any length of time. We have phrased the foregoing discussion as if the decisions on ends were taken by the Board. Whether this is so, or the ends are formulated through democratic political processes, they hardly will reflect ethical considerations alone. Questions of power relations inevitably will obtrude. Probably such questions would be the more important the greater the division of opinion on ends in the community. Under certain circumstances, the Board might be compelled to do a good deal of the work of planning on an *ad hoc* basis.[43] In the light of changing political conditions, the Board might find it expedient to give a higher priority to the manufacture of farm implements on one day and to the production of automobiles on another.

What has been said as to the limitations on the relevance of the ends necessarily applies also to the optimum conditions which are

[43] The problems that arise for planning as a result of the existence of divisions on ends are one of the principal grounds for the argument, made familiar by F. A. Hayek, that democracy and planning are incompatible. See his *The Road to Serfdom* (Chicago, 1944), chap. v.

deduced from the ends. Any particular optimum conditions are relevant only in contexts to which the corresponding ends are relevant. Thus the proposition that the marginal value productivity of a factor must be the same in every use—it being understood that values are proportional to the marginal rates of substitution of the individual households—clearly obtains only if the principle of consumers' sovereignty prevails as an end.

Of course, if, as is often the case, the optimum conditions are formulated in more abstract terms, the context in which they are relevant is broadened correspondingly. The condition that the marginal value productivity of a factor must be the same in every use might be formulated without specification of whether the marginal rates of substitution are those of the household or of the Board. This precept for socialist economic calculation is valid, then, no matter whether the principle of consumers' sovereignty prevails or not.[44]

In saying that the analysis outlined in preceding sections poses questions on ends for the Board, we do not mean to imply that the Board would not be interested in the views that the various writers have themselves expressed on these ends. The Board

---

[44] It still does not follow, however, that this is a universally valid precept, or, what comes to the same thing, that it is, as often supposed, a matter of pure logic. The point is that the derivation of the optimum conditions that are listed on pp. 204-206 requires a set of valuations not yet specified, namely that a shift in any factor from one use to another does not make any difference from the point of view of welfare, except in respect of the resulting difference in the value of output. In other words, a zero social value is assigned to such phenomena as "factory smoke," differences in a worker's attitude toward different industries (as distinct from different occupations), etc. Only in this case is it rational to determine the allocation of any factor simply on the basis of a comparison of the value of output in different uses. The condition of equality of marginal value productivity, far from being universally applicable, applies only where the foregoing values prevail.

The prevalent confusion on this matter seems to have arisen in part from a tendency, for which I believe Robbins is chiefly responsible, to speak of alternative uses of a factor as if they always were alternative *indifferent* uses. Unless there are alternative *indifferent* uses, in the sense that nothing but differences in the value of output counts for welfare, there is no basis at all to speak as Robbins does of "ends" as distinct from "means." Insofar as "factory smoke," etc., have a negative social value, the optimum conditions that have been outlined must be reformulated along the familiar lines marked out by Pigou.

might well be glad to have the advice of economists on the basic question of ends. It might wish to hear also from sociologists, dieticians, psychiatrists, and others. Whether in offering such advice economists are acting in their capacity as *economists* or in some other capacity (which is the issue raised by Robbins[45]) is a question not necessary to debate here.

THE PROBLEM OF ADMINISTRATION

The foregoing analysis in itself provides a conceptual basis for the use of a method of successive approximations to the optimum position, at least to the extent that small adjustments are in order. On the basis of the stated criteria for the optimum allocation of resources it is readily possible to establish whether and in what respects any given allocation deviates from the optimum position. Provided it had at its disposal the necessary facts, the Board might focus attention first on one pair of alternatives and then on another, and, in the light of these criteria, try to distribute any given resources to the best advantage between each pair of alternatives in turn. There is no need even at this stage to suppose, as sometimes is suggested, that the Board would have to solve at one blow "millions of equations."[46]

That there is facing the Board any substantial administrative task is due to several facts. First, the vast stock of detailed knowledge that would be needed to decide on the myriads of alternatives that have to be dealt with is not immediately available to the Board; to the extent that it is available at all, it is scattered throughout the community—and indeed the amount of knowledge actually available will depend on the particular administrative procedure used. Second, even if such knowledge were available to the Board, it would be physically impossible for the Board within any finite period of time to decide successively on all the alternatives to be dealt with. Finally, even if the Board could specify how every sort of resource should be used, the task of controlling the execution of its directive would still remain.

[45] *Nature and Significance of Economic Science*, chap. vi.
[46] L. C. Robbins, *The Great Depression* (London, 1934), p. 151.

It is necessary, then, to devise a planning scheme to approximate the optimum allocation in practice. This must also take into account: the basic limitations on the knowledge and executive capacities of the Board and of any other decision-making units under it, the cost of running the planning scheme itself (some procedures might be too costly to operate), and finally the fact that "means" are also "ends." The choice of administrative procedure (for example, as between rationing and freedom of choice) cannot be made solely from the standpoint of efficiency.

A number of recent writings on socialist economics grapple with this interesting administrative problem, though without always making clear its precise nature. To these writings I now turn.

THE COMPETITION SOLUTION: MAIN FEATURES

The optimum conditions that have been devised for the case of consumers' sovereignty will be familiar to the reader of any elementary textbook on economics. With certain exceptions, they are the same as the equilibrium conditions of "perfect competition" under capitalism. The exceptions are (1) the conditions relating to income distribution and the rate of investment (insofar as this is determined without regard to the time preference of households), and (2) the case of decreasing cost, where, as the textbooks show, competition breaks down.

For well-known reasons revolving partly around the exceptions just stated, this correspondence of the optimum with the competitive equilibrium does not necessarily mean that perfect competition is itself an optimal system. The correspondence is the basis, however, for one much-discussed solution of the question in hand. This is the so-called Competitive Solution.

The correspondence of the optimum and the competitive equilibrium was noted in all the early writings to which we have referred. Indeed, this was one of the main points of Pareto and Barone. However, Pareto and Barone did not follow out this lead. The Competitive Solution is the work of a number of later writers,

among whom Taylor, Dickinson, and Lange are the chief con-
tributors.[47]

The essentials of this planning scheme may readily be set forth.
Reference is mainly to the very systematic exposition of Lange,
and, for the moment, to the case where consumers are sovereign.

(i) All transfers of goods and services among production units
and between production units and households are recorded in
terms of an accounting unit, all goods being valued at established
prices, and services at established wages. Both the prices and
wages initially are arbitrary. In the case of transfers of goods and
services between households and production units there may be
a transfer of "cash."

(ii) Freedom of choice is allowed households in respect of both
the work they do and the goods they consume.

(iii) Each production unit is instructed to conduct its operation
in accord with two basic rules. For any given scale of output, it
must seek to combine the factors of production in such a way as,
at the established prices, to minimize the average cost per unit of
output. Second, it must seek to fix its output at the point where
the established price for its goods equals marginal cost.

(iv) The capital that is required for these purposes is made
freely available to the production units at an established rate of
interest, which is to be reckoned among the elements in cost.[48]

(v) On the basis of well-known theoretic arguments, it can be
shown that, at the established prices, wages, and rate of interest,
the aggregate demand for and supply of each and every sort of
goods and services on the part of *all* households and production
units is determined. There will also be some given demand for
capital at the established rate of interest. One of the functions
which the Board itself must perform is to adjust prices and wages
from time to time in order to bring the demand for and supply of

[47] F. M. Taylor, "The Guidance of Production in a Socialist State," *American Economic Review*, March 1929, reprinted in B. Lippincott, ed.,
On the Economic Theory of Socialism; H. D. Dickinson, "Price Formation
in a Socialist Economy," *Economic Journal*, December 1933; *idem*,
The Economics of Socialism; Lange, in *On the Economic Theory of Socialism*.
Mention is to be made also of the studies of A. P. Lerner, cited above,
n. 24; and of Durbin, *Economic Journal*, December 1936.
[48] See Lange, in *On the Economic Theory of Socialism*, p. 84.

goods and services into line. Where the demand for a product exceeds supply (this would be evidenced in the case of goods by a depletion of stocks), the price must be raised; where supply exceeds demand (as evidenced in the case of goods by an accumulation of stocks), the price must be reduced. The Board is also supposed to determine the rate of investment. The rate of interest is fixed so that the aggregate amount of new capital demanded equals the aggregate amount of new investment that the Board wishes to have undertaken. The Board allocates the dividend, and presumably decides on the amount of resources to be devoted to communal consumption.

Under this scheme, then, socialist households, like those in a perfectly competitive capitalist system, are autonomous in respect to the acquisition of consumers' goods and sale of their services. Accordingly, they may be expected to act in agreement with the same principles in these respects as apply under competition. Likewise, under the established administrative rules, the socialist production units are called upon to act in the same way, with respect to the purchase of factors and the determination of output, as enterprises in perfect competition. Under perfect competition each enterprise is such a small element of the market that it has no power over prices and accordingly must take prices as given so far as its own decisions on production are concerned: it seeks to maximize profits at the established prices. Under the established rules, the socialist production unit would tend to do likewise.

This is as far, however, as the analogy goes. Under the Competitive Solution, the Board supplants the capitalist market as the integrator of the decisions of the households and production units. The Board rather than the market adjusts prices to bring supply and demand into line.

Lange considers that the Competitive Solution might be adapted also to the case where the Board undertakes to determine what is good for the households.[49] In this case the Board might introduce a system of taxes and subsidies on consumers' goods, to express the divergencies between its preference scale and those of

[49] *Ibid.*, pp. 90ff.

consumers. In other words, there might be a two-price system in the consumers' goods market, one for the purpose of distributing goods to the households and the other, based on the Board's preference scale, to guide production. Freedom of choice would still prevail, even though consumers' sovereignty had been abandoned. Alternatively, freedom of choice might be abandoned also, and consumers' goods rationed and jobs filled by assignment. For the rest, the scheme would be as above.

THE COMPETITIVE SOLUTION: AN APPRAISAL

Assuming that the socialist economic system were administered in accord with the very general principles and procedures outlined, to what extent might an optimum allocation of resources be approximated? For the moment we try only to provide a brief inventory of the more important factors which might have to be considered in forming a judgment on this central question.

Managerial controls and incentives. To begin with, there is the fundamental question of how the success of the managers of the production units is to be tested. Lange does not deal explicitly with this question. Dickinson refers to it briefly.[50]

The obvious test is profits. As Dickinson recognizes, however, this is not an altogether satisfactory criterion. For one thing, there is the case of decreasing cost due to large indivisibilities. If the scale of operations for which price equaled marginal cost were one for which price was below average cost, there would be losses, and the manager would be disinclined to engage in any additional investments, even though they might be socially desirable. The maximization of profits (or minimization of losses) in this case would lead in the long run to the restriction of output below the optimum. If profits were the test of success, managers, in order to succeed, would be compelled to violate the rules. (The case of decreasing cost, then, constitutes an exception to the statement that has been made that under the established rules the socialist like the competitive firm maximizes profits.)

Managers would be tempted to violate the rules also if their production units were large in relation to the market served by

---

[50] *The Economics of Socialism,* pp. 213–219.

them. In order to make a large profit they might try to take into account the effects of their actions on the Board's decisions on prices. In this case they might restrict output in much the same way as monopolists do in a capitalist economy. The Competitive Solution might not be so competitive after all.

In such cases, then, there might be no alternative but for the Board to do as Dickinson suggests: to look into the cost records of the individual production units. This, however, would raise an administrative question of some dimensions. If carried to any length, therefore, this practice would be in conflict with an essential aim of the Competitive Solution, to decentralize decision-making.

Hayek[51] seems to argue that in fact the Board would have to look into the cost records of individual firms in any and all circumstances. This will not be a "perfunctory audit," but a full-fledged study to check whether the managers have operated as efficiently as possible. This would seem to exaggerate the difficulties of the problem. Where, for example, profits might be used effectively as a control, probably much could be accomplished by tying incentives to profits and by comparing the profit records of similar firms and of one and the same firm over a period of time. A detailed examination of the costs of each and every firm would not seem to be essential.

Provided the question of controls could be disposed of satisfactorily, the question of managerial incentives probably would not present any serious difficulties. Given the possibility of fixing policy on dismissals on the one hand and on rewards on the other, it should be feasible to establish a climate in which the managers evaluate risks in whatever is considered to be the proper manner. There is no reason to suppose that they would necessarily be too venturesome or, as Hayek argues, too cautious.[52]

Errors in forecasts of managers. Lange refers to his method as a "trial-and-error" method. Dobb[53] considers that an important

---

[51] "Socialist Calculation: The Competitive Solution," *Economica*, May 1940, p. 141.

[52] *Ibid.*, pp. 141–142.

[53] M. Dobb, "Saving and Investment in a Socialist Economy," *Economic Journal*, December 1939, pp. 726–727.

source of error would be the forecasts made by individual managers concerning future market conditions. Even supposing that profits were the test of success, that there were no cases of decreasing costs, and that the managers did not seek to influence prices, they still would have to estimate the prospective behavior of prices. This is necessary for purposes of deciding on investments. Under conditions of perfect competition, managers are supposed to take prices as "given" (parameters) insofar as their own actions are concerned; but they still must form estimates of future market conditions in deciding on investments.

Errors in forecasts presumably would be the greater, the more dynamic the economy. In considering their possible magnitude under socialism, however, account must be taken of the fact that the Central Planning Board might run a comprehensive information service for the benefit of the managers. In supplying this service, the Board would presumably not hesitate to express its own opinion and sentiments on market conditions, in much the same way as central banks of capitalist countries have been doing for the markets they control.

Rigidity; undue standardization; other errors of the Board. Hayek[54] also argues that the Board itself would be unable to cope effectively with its responsibilities. For one thing, it would be impracticable for the Board to adjust prices promptly in accord with the ever-occurring changes in supply and demand. Prices will be adjusted only periodically or from time to time. For a longer or shorter period of time, then, they will not correctly measure the "true" values of alternatives. For another, the Board hardly will be able to fix in detail prices for all the infinite varieties of goods produced in a modern industrial society. Inevitably, there will be a tendency to fix prices only for broad categories of goods, with the result that on this account, also, the prices will not provide an accurate measure of alternatives in particular circumstances.

Both these deficiencies apparently would stem from two limitations on the Board's executive capacities: its limited physical powers, which restrict the number of decisions it might deal with

---

[54] *Economica*, May 1940, pp. 135–136.

effectively, and the limitations on the amount of detailed knowledge of time and place which can be placed at its disposal. Elsewhere[55] Hayek emphasizes this latter limitation. He explains that:

the sort of knowledge with which I have been concerned is knowledge of the kind which by its nature cannot enter into statistics and therefore cannot be conveyed to any central authority in statistical form. The statistics which such a central authority would have to use would have to be arrived at precisely by abstracting from minor differences between things, by lumping together, as resources of one kind, items which differ as regards location, quality, and other particulars, in a way which may be very significant for the specific decision.[56]

These remarks of Hayek's would seem to provide a wholesome antidote to the tendency among many writers on socialism to regard the Central Planning Board as a committee of supermen. In judging how important these limitations might be in practice, however, it must be considered that the Board could set up a more or less elaborate administrative apparatus just for the purpose of fixing prices. The apparatus might be broken down functionally and geographically; it might even have regional offices to take local conditions more fully into account.[57] Presumably the Board would establish general directives to guide its subordinates.

Inequality of income. Lange[58] argues that under his scheme income might be distributed on essentially equalitarian principles. While there would be differentials in wages to accord with differences in marginal value productivity, these differentials would correspond at the same time to differences in disutility. If the dividend itself were, say, equal for all households, then aside from differences in well-being due to personal variations in need, all households would in reality be equally well off. It is understood that education and training would be free for all.

[55] "The Use of Knowledge in Society," *American Economic Review*, September 1945.
[56] *Ibid.*, p. 524.
[57] This, of course, is what is actually done in the Soviet Union.
[58] In *On the Economic Theory of Socialism*, pp. 100–103.

Lange recognizes that this would not be so in the case of persons with unusual natural talents (artists, musicians, etc.). For these persons, payment on the basis of value productivity might lead to differences in income all out of proportion to differences in disutility. These exceptions might be more numerous than is commonly assumed—for example, what of the personnel in high-level jobs in the bureaucracy? But Lange observes correctly that in such cases a high tax might be levied without any adverse effect on the supply of these services. There would be no conflict (such as was noted above) with the principle of consumers' sovereignty.

Disparities of this sort, however, might be widespread purely as a result of dynamic factors. Workers in occupations where there is short supply might for protracted periods receive a "rent" over and above what is required to attract them into these occupations. If freedom of choice prevails, it would be out of the question to extract this rent by taxation devices. Also, as we have already observed, the equation of disutilities and value productivities holds strictly only for persons on the margin of choice between occupations. Depending on their preferences, intra-marginal workers would likewise receive a rent, which it probably would be administratively impractical to extract if freedom of choice prevailed. Thus, given freedom of choice, the departures from egalitarian principles might be much greater and more numerous than Lange envisages.

Instability; unemployment. Dobb[59] raises and answers the question as to whether under the Competitive Solution there might be any high degree of instability and large-scale unemployment of resources. He observes that a reduction in the rate of interest designed to encourage investment on the part of managers of firms might lead to a cycle of expansion and contraction: as the investments take place, there is an expansion in purchasing power, the prices for consumers' goods rise, there is a secondary increase in the demand for capital, and so on. An attempt to put an end to this process by increasing the rate of interest might lead to a cumulative movement in the opposite direction, resulting in unemployment. Dobb recognizes, however, that the Board would be able to control the volume of purchasing power directly

[59] *Economic Journal*, December 1939.

through its fiscal powers. The Board presumably would plan its policy on taxes and dividends to assure as far as possible that the volume of purchasing power in the hands of consumers was just sufficient to buy at prices covering marginal costs the volume of consumers' goods it was desirable to produce.

Errors certainly would be made here as elsewhere in the operation of the Competitive Solution. Whether these errors would be so serious as to constitute a telling point against the Competitive Solution, as Dobb implies,[60] is open to question.

Referring to socialism in general and not to any particular planning scheme, Wright[61] argues that there might be cyclic disturbances because of a tendency to overbuild the durable-goods industries. The capacity required to build up stocks of durable goods might exceed that required to maintain these stocks after they were built up. Insofar as the conclusion is that at one time or another there might be excess capacity in one or another durable goods industry, there can be no dissent from this argument. It is difficult to see, however, why this necessarily entails "waste" in any economic sense, as Wright implies. If the capacity is built up with a full knowledge of the implications, including the fact that at some future date it will be excessive, then presumably this represents an optimum use of the resources in question: the "value" of the capacity would be fully written off by the time it is released. Furthermore, it is not at all clear why the release of capacity in different industries should tend to occur merely simultaneously and thus engender a general cycle. The release of excess capacity in one industry or another might be entirely consistent with a balanced and even development of the economy as a whole. Finally, the workers released from one or another durable-goods industry would be unemployed only during the time needed to retrain them for employment elsewhere. For this reason it is difficult to see why there should be mass unemployment which Wright would expect.

Transition problems. Lange[62] seems to argue that the Competitive Solution would work not only in an established socialist society but also in the period of transition. The proviso is made

---

[60] *Ibid.*, pp. 723–726.
[61] D. M. Wright, *The Economics of Disturbance* (New York, 1947), chap. vi.
[62] *On the Economic Theory of Socialism*, pp. 121ff.

that the private sector of the economy must be small, that competition must reign in it, and that small-scale production must not in the long run be more expensive than large-scale production. This last condition is presumably to assure that the private small-scale enterprise can survive; why this is desirable or necessary under socialism, however, is not clear. Lange hints that political and other factors might also raise special problems for planning in the transition period.

In a more adequate treatment of this very important question, I suspect that the difficulties in applying the Competitive Solution would loom a good deal larger than Lange implies. For one thing, insofar as, in the years following the transfer of power, political considerations might have an overwhelming importance, the usefulness of the conceptual framework that has been outlined (and by the same token the usefulness of the Competitive Solution) might be seriously impaired. The reasons for this have already been stated. For another, there is the important question of the loyalty of old—and the efficiency of new— managerial personnel, which would have to be taken into account in deciding on the responsibilities to be delegated to them. This would presumably be a pressing problem in the transition period.

Schumpeter[63] argues that the political problems of transition would be more or less difficult according to whether the capitalist society from which socialism emerges is in an early or late stage of development. Thus, it is said that in a late stage of capitalist development resistance is likely to be weak and the revolution might be accomplished in an orderly manner. If we may judge from the Soviet experience, however, a most favorable moment for the socialist revolution is at an early stage of capitalist development, when the middle class still is weak and the proletariat has not yet tasted the fruits of capitalism.

But in this case, if the Soviet experience serves at all, there would be pressing economic as well as political problems to deal with after the seizure of power, and it is easy to see that on account of problems of both sorts there might be very real difficulties in the way of applying the trial-and-error Competitive

[63] *Capitalism, Socialism, and Democracy,* chap. xix.

Solution. Consider only the matter of high-tempo industrialization, and the rapid shifts in demand and production schedules that would be associated with this process. In such a situation, the errors involved in the operation of the Competitive Solution might well be formidable; and evidently experience could not be very helpful in rectifying them. Whether there is any alternative planning procedure that might work more effectively in such circumstances is a question that has to be considered.

In referring to the foregoing considerations under the heading of transition problems, it is not implied that there ever would be a period in which they would be entirely absent, or, at any rate, that there ever would be such a period short of the era of unlimited abundance. Lange is not explicit on this matter.

AN ALTERNATIVE APPROACH TO SOCIALIST PLANNING

We must now consider the special case of "fixed coefficients" dealt with by Pareto and Barone: for technical reasons and regardless of their relative values, the different factors must be employed in amounts that bear a constant relationship to output. [64] In this case there is no basis for speaking of the marginal productivity of any one factor. It is necessary to formulate the analysis of the optimum conditions, as Pareto and Barone originally did, in terms of the fixed coefficients and without the use of the marginal productivity concept. With fixed coefficients, as in the case where the coefficients are variable, a scale of values is needed to decide on optimum output and the distribution of income; it turns out, however, that, for the rest, the allocation of resources is entirely a technical question.

It is easy to see that, if this case obtained, the practical work of planning might be simplified considerably. Lange[65] says that

---

[64] "Fixed coefficients" is itself a special case of the genus "limitational factors." Lange (*On the Economic Theory of Socialism*, p. 67, n .15; p. 94, n. 46), distinguishes two types of limitational factors, according to whether the amount of the limitational factor that must be employed is a function of output or of the amount of another factor employed. If all factors are limitational in the first sense, we have the case of fixed coefficients.

[65] *Ibid.*, p. 94, n. 46.

here "no prices and no cost accounting whatever are needed" in allocating resources. All is decided by considerations of technical efficiency. This is true only if, as Lange assumes, the demand for consumers' goods is in the form of fixed quotas. If demand is variable, prices and costs still would have to be taken into account in the allocation of resources among different consumers' goods industries. There would be no need, however, to rearrange production methods in the different industries in response to each and every change in the relative scarcities of the different factors of production.

If the Competitive Solution were in operation in this case, the managers of the individual production units would not have to change their production methods in response to changes in the price structure. On this account it might seem that the process of trial and error would be shortened appreciably. So far as the Competitive Solution is concerned, however, this case has an important adverse feature. If the coefficients are fixed, marginal and average costs are constant. The administrative rules established by Lange no longer provide a definite basis for managerial decisions. If prices were above marginal costs, for example, the managers would know that they should expand, but would be quite in the dark as to how much. The possibility is still open that by the manipulation of prices the Board could assure that the total output of the industry was brought in line with demand; there might be a "neutral" equilibrium such as it is supposed might be attained under capitalist perfect competition in the case of constant costs. But there would be no satisfactory basis for moving toward the equilibrium by successive approximations. As a result, the trial-and-error process might turn out to be very protracted, despite the simplification of the work of choosing between different production methods.

I turn to an alternative planning scheme which seems to be inspired in part by emphasis on this case of fixed coefficients.

The alternative planning procedure, which may be referred to as the Centralist Scheme, has been sketched only in very general terms. Under the Competitive Solution the operations of individual production units and households are integrated through a market process. Under the Centralist Scheme it is proposed that, to a greater or lesser extent, these operations be integrated directly by the Board. The managers of individual production units, it is supposed, will submit to the Board the data required for this purpose. Under this scheme the process of trial and error takes place on paper rather than in the market place.

A planning scheme of this sort is suggested by Dickinson, who presents it merely as a possibly practical alternative to the Competitive Solution.[66] Dobb, however, advocates it as a preferable procedure.[67] It is in Dobb's writings that the case of fixed coefficients seems to be linked with the Centralist Scheme. Dobb emphasizes the importance of technological factors in the determination of the optimum allocation.[68]

The advocates of the Centralist Scheme, no doubt, have drawn their inspiration partly from the Soviet planning procedure, the distinguishing feature of which is a comprehensive plan that purportedly integrates the whole economy. This integration is accomplished by the so-called "Method of Balanced Estimates," by which the planned requirements of different commodities and services are checked against planned supplies.[69] Soviet economists have published very little in a theoretic vein concerning their planning system[70]—perhaps because they are too much preoccupied with practical work. From scattered writings, however, one gains the impression that they emphasize the importance of technological factors in resource allocation, and that this emphasis plays a part in their thinking about planning procedures.

It is not surprising, then, that another well-known feature of the Soviet economic system is incorporated in Dobb's program. Dobb contemplates that there might be numerous cases where the Board would overrule consumers' preferences.[71] This seems to be

---

[66] *The Economics of Socialism*, pp. 104–105. Dickinson's position on this scheme in this book seems to represent a retreat from the rather positive views he expressed earlier in *Economic Journal*, December 1933.

[67] M. Dobb, *Economic Journal*, December 1933; "A Reply," *Review of Economic Studies*, February 1935; *Economic Journal*, December 1939; *Political Economy and Capitalism*, chap. viii.

[68] See especially *Political Economy and Capitalism*, pp. 331ff.

[69] For a brief description of this procedure, see Alexander Baykov, *The Development of the Soviet Economic System* (Cambridge, Eng., 1946), chap. xx.

[70] For references to some of the Soviet sources on planning, see *ibid.*

[71] *Economic Journal*, December 1933, pp. 591ff.; *Political Economy and Capitalism*, pp. 309ff.

a prevailing practice in the USSR. It should be observed, however, that the Centralist Scheme itself is not tied logically to a system in which consumers' preferences are overruled or indeed tied to any particular ends. Dickinson has in mind a system designed to satisfy the demands of consumers as they see them.

The main objection to the Centralist Scheme is that it imposes an impossible administrative burden on the Board. Large-scale waste, it has been said, is inevitable if planning is on this basis. We find ourselves again confronted with the problem of solving "millions of equations."

In general, much weight would seem to attach to this objection; but the difficulties clearly are reduced in the case of fixed coefficients. Here relative prices do not make any difference for much of the work of planning. It is not necessary to suppose that the case holds strictly. To whatever extent it is approached, any technologically feasible allocation will, to that extent, approach the optimum.

So far as the Centralist Scheme is feasible, the choice between it and the Competitive Solution presumably would revolve about the nature of the ends sought and the stage of political, social, and economic development that has been reached. One might imagine, for example, that in a highly dynamic economy a Centralist allocation of investment might lead to fewer and smaller errors than a Competitive allocation. While under the Centralist Scheme the Board might err, there would seem to be a better prospect of meeting the requirements of technical consistency with respect to complementary industries. If technical rigidities are present, the chances are diminished that under the Competitive Solution the errors of individual firms would cancel out.[72] In other words, the Centralist Scheme might be able to deal more effectively than the Competitive Solution with the problem of bottlenecks and excess capacity.

To what extent does the case of fixed coefficients hold in a modern industrial society? Lange considers it to be very exceptional.[73] This is probably the view also of most "orthodox"

---

[72] This point was suggested to me by A. Erlich, with whom I have had many profitable discussions.
[73] In *On the Economic Theory of Socialism*, p. 94, n. 46.

economists. Lange seems to refer, however, only to situations where the case holds strictly. Clearly, it is a matter of very great interest how closely it is approximated: the more nearly it is approached, the more limited is the range within which price calculations matter. On the basis of numerous recent cost studies,[74] it would appear that, for a considerable range of short-run output variations, marginal costs for the individual firm tend to be constant. This suggests that at least in the short run the proportions are indeed fixed between labor and other variable elements in marginal costs. Mention should also be made of Leontief's study of the structure of the American economy.[75] Leontief found it practicable to assume that for broad industrial groups the production coefficients are constant. The prevailing preconception on this whole question may have to be revised as more empirical data become available.

The degree of emphasis on technological as compared with economic factors in resource allocation, by the way, might be one basis for a distinction which is now somewhat difficult to make, between the "orthodox" and "Marxian" theory of planning.

There is no need here to go into the question of the validity of the labor theory of value as a basis for socialist calculation. Mises[76] has shown clearly enough its deficiencies in this respect. What is to be noted is that there now appears to be a diversity of opinion even in Marxian circles as to the applicability of the labor theory to socialism. Indeed, it is difficult to find in any quarter unqualified support for the labor theory in this connection.

Dunayevskaya[77] and Sweezy consider that the labor theory of value does not and was not intended by Marx to apply to social-

---

[74] See the very careful evaluation of these studies issued by the Committee on Price Determination (E. S. Mason, Chairman) of the National Bureau of Economic Research, *Cost Behaviour and Price Policy* (New York, 1943), chap. v.

[75] W. Leontief, *The Structure of the American Economy*, 1919–1929 (Cambridge, Mass., 1941).

[76] In Hayek, ed., *Collectivist Economic Planning*, pp. 112ff.

[77] R. Dunayevskaya, "A New Revision of Marxian Economics," *American Economic Review*, September 1944. In this article Miss Dunayevskaya comments on the much-discussed Soviet article "Some Problems in the Teaching of Political Economy," *Pod Znamenem Marksizma* (*Under the Banner of Marxism*), no. 7–8, July-August 1943. A translation of this

ism. On the question of what theory of value does apply, Sweezy has taken in turn two different positions. At one time, he argued that orthodox economics holds under socialism: "Marxian economics is essentially the economics of capitalism, while 'capitalist' economics is in a very real sense the economics of socialism."[78] More recently, he seems to have taken the position that orthodox economics does not apply either; he now advances in its place the "principle of planning."[79] The nature of this principle is not explained. Presumably the Board is to work out the logic of choice on its own.

Dobb[80] is also difficult to classify. On the one hand, he makes free use of orthodox value theory in the analysis of socialist resource allocation. On the other, he seems to be unwilling to accept the necessary implication that rent and interest must appear as accounting categories in socialist calculation.[81] By a well-known and very awkward adjustment for differences in the organic composition of capital, Dobb formulates optimum conditions in terms of the labor theory.[82] It is difficult to avoid the conclusion that in Dobb's analysis the labor theory is not so much an analytic tool as excess baggage.

According to a recent Soviet article already cited,[83] the labor theory of value continues to operate under socialism. As the article explains, this represents a change in position from the view formerly held in the USSR, according to which the labor theory referred only to capitalism. In judging the portent of this doctri-

---

article appears in the *American Economic Review*, September 1944. See also the comments on the article by C. Landauer, "From Marx to Menger," *American Economic Review*, June 1944; P. A. Baran, "New Trends in Russian Economic Thinking?" *American Economic Review*, December 1944; O. Lange, "Marxian Economics in the Soviet Union," *American Economic Review*, March 1945; R. Dunayevskaya, "A Rejoinder," *American Economic Review*, September 1945.

[78] P. M. Sweezy, "Economics and the Crisis of Capitalism," *Economic Forum*, Spring 1935, p. 79.

[79] P. M. Sweezy, *The Theory of Capitalist Development* (New York, 1942), pp. 52–54.

[80] See above, n. 67.

[81] See especially *Political Economy and Capitalism*, pp. 308–309, 326ff.

[82] *Ibid.*

[83] See above, n. 77.

nal change, however, account must be taken of the fact that here, as in so many spheres of the Soviet system, there seems to be a wide gap between theory and practice. The existence of such a gap is acknowledged in the article; it is explained that "the prices of commodities are set with certain deviations from their values, corresponding to the particular objectives of the Soviet state, and the quantity of commodities of various kinds which can be sold under the existing scale of production and the needs of society."

THE DEBATE

To come finally to Mises, there are two questions to ask: What does he say and what does he mean?

On the first question we must let Mises speak for himself:

And as soon as one gives up the conception of a freely established monetary price for goods of a higher order, rational production becomes completely impossible. Every step that takes us away from private ownership of the means of production also takes us away from rational economics . . .

The administration [of the socialist state] may know exactly what goods are most urgently needed. But in so doing, it has only found what is, in fact, but one of the two necessary prerequisites for economic calculation. In the nature of the case, however, it must dispense with the other—the valuation of the means of production . . .

Where there is no free market there is no pricing mechanism; without a pricing mechanism, there is no economic calculation . . . Exchange relations between production goods can only be established on the basis of private ownership of the means of production.[84]

As to what Mises means, there appear to be two views. According to that which seems to have gained the wider currency, Mises' contention is that without private ownership of, or (what comes to the same thing for Mises) a free market for, the means of production, the rational evaluation of these goods for the purposes of calculating costs is ruled out conceptually. With it goes any rational economic calculation. To put the matter somewhat

[84] Mises, in Hayek, ed., *Collectivist Economic Planning*, pp. 104–111. Essentially the same argument is repeated in Mises, *Socialism* (London, 1936).

more sharply than is customary, let us imagine a Board of Supermen, with unlimited logical faculties, with a complete scale of values for the different consumers' goods and present and future consumption, and detailed knowledge of production techniques. Even such a Board would be unable to evaluate rationally the means of production. In the absence of a free market for these goods, decisions on resource allocation in Mises' view necessarily would be on a haphazard basis.

Interpreted in this way, the argument is easily disposed of. Lange[85] and Schumpeter,[86] who favor this interpretation of Mises, point out correctly that the theory is refuted by the work of Pareto and Barone. As the analysis of these writers shows, once tastes and techniques are given, the values of the means of production can be determined unambiguously by imputation without the intervention of a market process. The Board of Supermen could decide readily how to allocate resources so as to assure the optimum welfare. It would simply have to solve the equations of Pareto and Barone.

According to the other interpretation of Mises, which has the authority of Hayek,[87] the contention is not that rational calculation is logically inconceivable under socialism but that there is no practicable way of realizing it. Imputation is theoretically possible; but, once private ownership of the means of production has been liquidated, it cannot be accomplished in practice.

Hayek's own thinking,[88] and that of Robbins,[89] seems to be along these lines. Lange, who interprets the views of Hayek and Robbins as being in reality a retreat from the original position of Mises, considers that his own analysis refutes their argument: "As we have seen, there is not the slightest reason why a trial and error procedure, similar to that in a competitive market, could not work in a socialist economy to determine the accounting prices of capital goods and of the productive resources in public owner-

[85] *On the Economic Theory of Socialism*, pp. 51ff.
[86] *Capitalism, Socialism, and Democracy*, chap. xvi.
[87] *Economica*, May 1940, pp. 126–127.
[88] "The Present State of the Debate," chap. v, in Hayek, ed., *Collectivist Economic Planning;* "Socialist Calculation: The Competitive Solution," *Economica*, May 1840; "The Use of Knowledge in Society," *American Economic Review*, September 1945.
[89] *The Great Depression*, p. 151.

ship."[90] Hayek apparently is not entirely convinced: "Whether the solution offered will appear particularly practicable, even to socialists, may perhaps be doubted."[91]

Which of these two interpretations of Mises is correct, I leave to the reader to decide. The issue between Hayek and Robbins on the one hand and Lange on the other, however, calls for further consideration.

Operationally, how is it possible to tell whether any given planning scheme is "practicable" or not? Here again, it seems necessary to deal with two different views.

According to one, expressed most clearly by Schumpeter,[92] the question is not how well or ill socialism can function, but whether a planning scheme can be devised such that it can work at all. If there is no "practicable" basis for rational calculation, the economy presumably would break down. The symptoms would be waste on a vast scale and even chaos.

If this is the test of practicability, there hardly can be any room for debate: of course, socialism can work. On this, Lange certainly is convincing. If this is the sole issue, however, one wonders whether at this stage such an elaborate theoretic demonstration is in order. After all, the Soviet planned economy has been operating for thirty years. Whatever else may be said of it, it has not broken down.

According to Hayek, the test is this:

It was not the possibility of planning as such which has been questioned, but the possibility of successful planning . . . There is no reason to expect that production would stop, or that the authorities would find difficulty in using all the available resources somehow, or even that output would be permanently lower than it had been before planning started. What we should anticipate is that output, where the use of the available resources was determined by some central authority, would be lower than if the price mechanism of a market operated freely under otherwise similar circumstances."[93]

In familiar terms, the question for Hayek is: Which is more efficient, socialism or capitalism? This, of course, is the question

[90] Lange, in *On the Economic Theory of Socialism*, p. 89.
[91] *Economica*, May 1940, p. 149.
[92] *Capitalism, Socialism, and Democracy*, p. 185.
[93] *Collectivist Economic Planning*, pp. 203–204.

all participants in the debate eventually come to face anyhow. As I see it, it is now the only issue outstanding. The discussion in preceding sections, it is hoped, will provide a partial basis for judgment on this important matter. For the rest, with the following few cautions, I leave this issue, too, for the reader to decide.[94]

First, in order to reach any conclusion on comparative efficiency, it is necessary to agree on the test of efficiency, that is, on the ends according to which the optimum allocation of resources is to be defined. A comparison of the total market value of the consumers' goods produced in the rival systems, such as Schumpeter proposes,[95] already implies the acceptance of the principle of consumers' sovereignty. It is necessary to decide, too, whether the egalitarian principle of distribution is one of the ends, whether consumers are to be sovereign in respect of decisions on investment, and so on.

Second, one must distinguish between blueprints of economic systems operating in hypothetical worlds and rival economic systems in the real world. There seems to be very little point, for example, in a comparison of perfect competition in a capitalist world that never existed with socialism in Russia; or, alternatively, of the Competitive Solution in an established socialist state where there is a unanimity on ends with monopolistic and unstable capitalism in the United States. We must compare ideals with ideals or facts with facts. Participants in both sides of the debate have erred in failing to observe this elementary rule.

Finally, it is necessary to bear in mind that in the real world the question of comparative efficiency cannot be divorced altogether from questions of politics. In this connection it suffices only to allude to the matter of working-class cooperation and discipline, which Schumpeter[96] rightly emphasizes, and the question of social stratification in relation to the problem of assuring the effective use of natural talents.

[94] In addition to the studies already cited, mention must be made of the very balanced study of A. C. Pigou, *Socialism versus Capitalism* (London, 1944).

[95] *Capitalism, Socialism, and Democracy*, pp. 189-190.

[96] *Ibid.*, pp. 210ff.

10

SOCIALIST CALCULATION:

A FURTHER WORD*

The previous essay was first published seventeen years ago. As it has turned out, that was an opportune time for a survey, such as was attempted, of contributions to the theory of socialist economics. Such contributions had been numerous in the decades before the essay appeared, especially in the interwar period, but lately they have been relatively few. The essay would not have to be greatly expanded in order to take into account more recent theoretic writings.

Yet a central theme was the much debated one concerning the comparative economic efficiency of socialism and, in judging this question, one can now refer not only to abstract analyses, but to an extensive empirical experience. In the USSR, the outstanding country in question, a party committed to socialism had already seized power in 1917, but when my essay on socialist economics appeared, some fundamentals of the novel social system that resulted were still not very old. In any event, the system has now endured seventeen years more, and since the Second World War it has come to prevail also in numerous other countries. The years since World War II have also witnessed the publication in the West of a great number of serious, scholarly writings on the organization and performance of socialism both in the USSR and in other countries.

This is not the place to survey this literature, but I should at least express my opinion that, in view of the experience with

* I have benefited from thoughtful comments by Professor Alexander Erlich.

socialism to date, the critics of this system have turned out to be nearer the mark than its proponents. At any rate, if we may judge from the experience of the USSR, there are reasons to doubt that socialism is especially efficient economically.[1]

Admittedly, those responsible for the direction of economic affairs in the USSR have been able to exercise a significant control over the use of resources in the large. Among other things, they have been able to increase rapidly and maintain at high levels the share of total output going to capital formation. Chiefly on this basis, they have often been able to achieve high rates of growth, though not nearly so high as has been officially claimed.

Lately, however, growth has slowed, and even rapid growth could be especially indicative of economic efficiency only if that desideratum is seen in a novel way, with material alternatives valued in terms of "planners' preferences." With valuation in terms of the more conventional standard of "consumers' preferences," the rapid growth arguably must in some degree indicate economic waste. It must do so precisely to the degree that, in respect of the volume of savings, consumers' preferences are violated. Moreover, even in terms of such planners' preferences, economic efficiency must turn not simply on the rate of growth but on how near this rate is to what it might have been, and beyond this, on the effectiveness of resource use generally. Even to the casual observer, it must be evident that socialism in the USSR must often leave something to be desired from this standpoint, and more systematic inquiry seems only to confirm this impression. Even in the form that has lately become familiar, where reference is to the output of labor and capital together, factor productivity is not the same thing as economic efficiency, but if it is at all indicative of the latter, economic waste in the USSR probably much exceeds any recently experienced in the United States. Factor productivity in the USSR has been calculated to be far below that in the USA.[2]

But, granting the imperative of public ownership, a socialist economy might be administered in different ways. If socialism in

[1] Abram Bergson, *The Economics of Soviet Planning* (New Haven, 1964), chap. xiv.
[2] *Ibid.*, pp. 340ff.

the USSR has not been especially efficient, has this not often been due to the particular procedures employed, and hence not at all inherent in the system itself? Indeed, are not some outstanding deficiencies even now in the process of being removed? Thus a cardinal feature has been the reliance on a system of planning where decision-making is notably centralized, the prototype of the Centralist Scheme, and in sharp contrast to the Competitive Solution discussed in theory. Especially under this system, will not decision-making be facilitated as a result of the current trend toward increased use of mathematical techniques and advanced computers? What, too, of the steps reportedly now being taken to reduce centralization of decision-making in any event? Could not such steps also contribute to increased efficiency?

How alternative procedures might work under socialism is a leading theme of the theoretical writings already surveyed, and what might have been achieved in the USSR in the way of economic efficiency must be pondered in their light. But, having said so much on the Soviet experience, I must in fairness say more. If critics have been more nearly right than proponents on socialist economic efficiency, they have not always been so for the right reasons. The principal contention was that, in seeking to supplant, by a system of national planning, the market economy of the West, the architects of socialism would be undertaking an extraordinarily complex task. Essentially for this reason waste on a vast scale would be unavoidable. As Western study of the USSR has made clear,[3] the complexity of the task has been a major cause of waste there, but there have also been other causes that were not so clearly anticipated in theory.

Reared on obsolete economic doctrines, the system's directors have not always understood the requirements of economic efficiency, and necessarily waste has occurred simply on this account. This has been so even where economic efficiency is seen in terms of planners' preferences rather than consumers'. Losses due to lack of understanding have been pervasive, but an outstanding aspect has been the influence of Marx's labor theory of value. In diverse ways this has been deleterious from the stand-

---

[3] In *The Economics of Soviet Planning*, while surveying the Soviet economic system, I also have sought to include pertinent bibliographical references.

point of either kind of preferences. Waste has occurred, too, because in choosing among alternative working arrangements, the system's directors almost inevitably have not been concerned solely with economic efficiency. They have also had to consider that the nature of the procedure employed might matter ideologically and politically, and that this might be so even apart from material consequences however these are valued. (One result is that the obsolete labor theory of value has only enjoyed the greater status.) In deciding on working arrangements, it would be surprising if the system's directors should not have been guided also by purely personal predilection, that is, by the satisfactions they derive from administering the economy through some procedures rather than others; and so far as the system's directors have been so motivated, this too must have been a cause of inefficiency. Finally, while reflecting the prevailing planners' preferences, the intense pursuit of growth has itself limited in diverse ways the possibilities of achieving economic efficiency, and hence has in effect also been a source of waste.

These few observations hardly exhaust the question of what might have been in the USSR, and still less can I pursue here the related question of future prospects. By all accounts the concern for growth in the USSR is not quite so intense as it was formerly, while understanding of and concern for economic efficiency are now on the increase. It would be surprising if the working arrangements should not, in consequence, improve economically in one way or another. But it would be surprising, too, if ideology, power and politics, and personal predilections should not continue to have a place in the choice of procedures. Then, too, if the task of determining resource use has been complex it seemingly is only becoming more so as the number of interrelated enterprises and the variety of products continually increase. With respect to choices among consumers' goods, the system's directors apparently are now becoming more attentive to consumers' preferences than they were previously. With this the task must become still more intricate.

The reader will wish to judge for himself the possible upshot of these diverse currents. Efficiency surely should rise in the course of time, but it is difficult to gauge how much.

While reference has been to the Soviet case, socialism in other countries as well has obviously had its limitations economically, but the evidence on economic efficiency in such countries still has to be systematically assessed.[4] As before, the USSR has been considered as socialist on the understanding that reference is essentially to one outstanding feature: predominantly public ownership of the means of production. Socialism elsewhere is understood similarly. Yet if socialism obtains in the USSR, admittedly it is of a special sort, and the experience with this system there, including the supplanting of consumers' by planners' preferences, necessarily must be viewed in the light of the peculiar political institutions that prevail. Thus far, however, authoritarianism seems nowhere to have been avoided when public ownership has been predominant, although the degree has varied in different countries and at different times.[5] In contending, as they often have, that socialism is inimical to freedom, therefore, critics of this system have been on even stronger ground than when they have disparaged it economically. Of course, many advocates of socialism sincerely aspire to avoid authoritarianism, while some who consider themselves socialists do not seek thoroughgoing public ownership to begin with.

On page 201, I refer to the import of the utilitarian conception of social welfare as not merely an increasing function but a sum of household utilities. This matter has now been discussed, I believe, in a more illuminating way on page 67, note 15. On page 202 I consider the question of the relation of consumers'

---

[4] For surveys and bibliographical information, see Thad Paul Alton, *Polish Postwar Economy* (New York, 1955); Jan Marczewski, *Planification et Croissance Économique des Démocraties Populaires*, I and II (Paris, 1956); Nicholas Spulber, *The Economics of Communist Eastern Europe* (New York, 1957); János Kornai, *Overcentralization in Economic Administration* (Oxford, 1959); Bela A. Belassa, *The Hungarian Experience in Economic Planning* (New Haven, 1959); John Michael Montias, *Central Planning in Poland* (New Haven, 1962); Albert Waterston, *Planning in Yugoslavia* (Baltimore, 1962); Stanislaw Wellisz, *The Economics of the Soviet Bloc* (New York, 1964); Dwight Perkins, *Market Control and Planning in Communist China*. (To be published by Harvard University Press, December 1965).

[5] Austria, however, may be an exception to the stated rule, for I understand that public ownership is very extensive there, though often of an indirect sort, while the political process certainly is not authoritarian.

sovereignty to "real" income distribution. I have tried to deal with this interesting subject more rigorously in the Addendum to Chapter 3.[6]

[6] After the appearance of "Socialist Economics," Professor D. M. Wright explained to me by letter that I had misinterpreted him on the question of cycles under socialism (see p. 225). Among other things, under the cycles he envisages he did not contend that mass unemployment need occur, though discontinuities would be inevitable. The reader, therefore, will certainly wish to consult the work of Professor Wright that was cited in order to understand his views correctly.

INDEX

243

INDEX

INDEX

RENEWALS 458-4574
DATE DUE

NOV 0 5 2008			